PÉTAIN

. . . . .

PÉTAIN

Nicholas Atkin

LONGMAN
London and New York

Addison Wesley Longman Limited
Edinburgh Gate,
Harlow, Essex CM20 2JE,
United Kingdom
and Associated Companies throughout the world

*Published in the United States of America
by Addison Wesley Longman Inc., New York*

© Addison Wesley Longman Limited 1998

First published 1998

ISBN 0 582 070376 PPR
ISBN 0 582 070368 CSD

British Library Cataloguing-in-Publication Data

A catalogue record for this book is available from the British Library

Library of Congress Cataloging-in-Publication Data

Atkin, Nicholas.
Pétain / Nicholas Atkin.
p. cm. — (Profiles in power)
Includes bibliographical references and index.
ISBN 0–582–07036–8 (case). — ISBN 0–582–07037–6 (pbk.)
1. Pétain, Philippe, 1856–1951. 2. Marshals—France—Biography.
3. France. Armée—Biography. 4. Heads of state—France—Biography.
5. France—Politics and government—20th century. I. Title.
II. Series: Profiles in power (London, England)
DC342.8.P4A9 1997
944.08′092—dc21
[b]   97–14220
                                          CIP

Set by 35 in 10½/12pt Baskerville
Produced by Longman Singapore Publishers (Pte) Ltd.
Printed in Singapore

CONTENTS

LIST OF MAPS

LIST OF ABBREVIATIONS

ACA	Assembly of Cardinals and Archbishops
ADMP	Association pour Défendre la Mémoire du Maréchal Pétain
AN	Archives Nationales
BEF	British Expeditionary Force
CDJC	Centre de Documentation Juive Contemporaine
CFLN	Comité Français de la Libération Nationale
CGT	Confédération Générale du Travail
CGQJ	Commissariat Général aux Questions Juives
CIGS	Chief of the Imperial General Staff
CSAR	Comité Secret d'Action Révolutionnaire
CSDN	Conseil Supérieur de la Défense Nationale
CSG	Conseil Supérieur de la Guerre
DGEN	Délégation Générale à l'Equipement National
DGFP	Documents on German Foreign Policy
GMR	Groupements Mobiles de Réserve
GQG	Grand Quartier Général
LVF	Légion des Volontaires Français contre le Bolchévisme
MBF	Militärbefehlshaber in Frankreich
MUR	Mouvements Unis de la Résistance
OAS	Organisation de l'Armée Secrète
OCs	Organization Committees
PCF	Parti Communiste Français
PPF	Parti Populaire Français
RNP	Rassemblement National Populaire
RPF	Rassemblement du Peuple Français
SNI	Syndicat National des Instituteurs
SOL	Service d'Ordre Légionnaire
STO	Service du Travail Obligatoire

For my father

PREFACE

At first sight, Philippe Pétain might seem a curious choice for inclusion in a series entitled 'Profiles in Power'. On the eve of the First World War, at the age of 58, the only authority he had exercised was that which a middle-ranking officer commands over his men in peacetime. Retirement already beckoned. It was the outbreak of fighting in August 1914 that propelled him into positions of importance. In 1916 he was placed in charge of Verdun, for many the most momentous battle ever fought by French soldiers; in 1917 he was named Commander-in-Chief of the French armies, and quelled the mutinies that were born out of nearly three years of unforgiving trench warfare; and in 1918 he received his marshal's baton. None the less, to that date the offices he had enjoyed were largely in the military domain. The same was true of the 1920s when he occupied a seat on the many committees that comprised the High Command; in 1925 he even returned to active service, directing colonial troops in the Rif. Political office came late in the day: in February 1934 he served as Minister of War in the brief-lived Doumergue cabinet. Thereafter, a number of newspapers campaigned for a Pétain government, yet the marshal himself discouraged their efforts, and wisely kept a distance from the extreme right-wing leagues that sought to overthrow the Third Republic. Unwilling to play the part of a Boulanger, he preferred semi-retirement, resurfacing in March 1939 to take up the minor post of ambassador to Spain.

Given the pattern of this career, it is tempting for the historian interested in power to begin any study of Pétain on 17 June 1940 when the 'Victor of Verdun' announced on the radio that he was taking charge of government and had offered the nation the 'gift of his person'.[1] His 'sacrifice' was received with enormous public gratitude, and the following month the National Assembly voted itself out of existence, endowing Pétain, the newly crowned *chef de l'état français*, with full powers. Not since Napoleon I had a French ruler been granted such authority,[2] although in practice the marshal's influence was severely curtailed by a number of factors: the German presence; the division of France into several zones; inter-ministerial rivalries; and the wider developments of the war. By 1942, the year in which the Germans occupied all of France, he had become little more than a figurehead. Yet he had not lost his appetite for wheeler-dealing, and retained an enormous popularity in the countryside, an appeal that was vital for the survival of the Vichy regime.

There exists a further temptation for beginning this study in summer 1940: the legacy of the Nazi occupation of France. This episode has left an indelible imprint on the French national consciousness, an imprint which is perhaps deeper than that of the Revolution of 1789. Indeed, the experience was so traumatic that it has only been in the last two decades that the French public has begun to reconcile itself to what actually happened. There remains particular shame and embarrassment over the fate of the Jews, and it is telling that much of the recent literature on the Occupation has concentrated on racial persecution. In the words of one historian, this process of coming to terms with the Vichy years has constituted a 'syndrome', an evocative term that conjures up the image of an illness.[3] Only when the disease has been fully diagnosed and a cure devised will the health of the nation's history be restored.[4]

There are, then, compelling arguments for focusing this profile in power on Pétain's time at Vichy, and it will not go unnoticed that five of the nine chapters presented here deal with the post-1939 period. By and large it is only hagiographers that dwell on his early years, especially his life as an unknown soldier, perhaps with the intention of distracting attention from the role he played during the Occupation.[5] Yet Pétain's pre-Vichy career should not be excluded altogther. Because of his great age and varied posts, his experiences on the fringes of power constitute a prism through which it is possible to view several of the phenomena that have shaped the development of modern France: the political outlook and involvement of the French army; the strategy and tactics pursued by the

High Command in two world wars; the evolution of Franco-German relations; the political intrigues of the Third Republic; and the ideological make-up and influence of the French right. As one biographer has observed, in explaining Pétain the historian is involved in explaining much that happened around him.[6]

An analysis of his pre-1940 career also provides clues to his actions during the Occupation, and the opening three chapters of this book keep a close eye on how he later behaved at Vichy. Bismarck, in boastful mood, once remarked of another ill-fated French politician, Napoleon III, that the emperor was a sphinx but a sphinx without a riddle. A similar observation could be made about Pétain. Although never as paradoxical a figure as Napoleon III, outwardly his career does appear a puzzling one: the great patriot and Germanophobe of 1918, the architect of victory, who in 1940 readily conceded an armistice and instigated a policy of collaboration with Nazi Germany; the apolitical soldier of the 1920s and 1930s, reputedly the most Republican and compassionate of the High Command, who in 1940 embarked on a reactionary National Revolution which openly persecuted Jews and other minorities. On closer scrutiny, however, it may be seen that there was little contradictory about his behaviour at Vichy. Examination of his political philosophy and dealings before 1940 demonstrate that it would have been astonishing if he had acted in any other way.[7]

Finally, to ignore his pre-Vichy career is to ignore the origins of his power as a symbol. Throughout the Occupation, his authority rested less on the legislative powers granted to him by the National Assembly than on the cult of marshalship. This adoration did not merely spring from the shock of defeat in 1940. Its roots may be traced back to the upheavals of the First World War.[8] When in 1918 he received his marshal's baton, he became inextricably linked with the French victory. Thus, through the office of marshal, he was invested with super-human qualities, qualities that he never possessed, and was entrusted with jobs that lay beyond his capacities. Pétain himself never acknowledged this. While he feigned to despise fame, he developed an enormous vanity and came to accept much of the propaganda that was written about him. Forever confident of his own abilities, he considered that he alone held the key to his nation's success. During the Occupation, he acted on this premise, believing himself to be France's saviour, even

though the harsh realities of wartime soon laid bare his inadequacies.[9] Given this self-belief, it is small wonder that in 1945
he refused to acknowledge the right of the Provisional Government to put him on trial. In the event, the hastily convened
court, afraid to probe too far lest it should reopen the wounds
of the Occupation, failed to uncover the 'real' Pétain. If anything, the shoddy way in which he was treated during the proceedings and the heartless manner in which he was then left
to die in exile, only served the interests of his hagiographers.

Inevitably, every biography of Pétain will be, in some measure, a reworking of his trial. The present study cannot claim to
be very different. Yet, by providing a conspectus of all of his
life, and not just an account of his time at Vichy, it has hope-
fully explained why an obscure middle-ranking officer went on
to become a marshal of France and later his country's leader.
What follows is the tale of an extremely ordinary man who was
woefully ill-equipped to deal with the responsibilities and choices
that accompanied his mythic status.

. . .

I have incurred several debts in writing this book, not all of
which I can acknowledge here. I should, however, like to thank
Keith Robbins for inviting me to contribute to the 'Profiles in
Power' series, and for his comments and advice on the text.
Andrew MacLennan has been a sympathetic and understanding publisher. Rod Kedward saw an early plan of the book and
has been a source of encouragement throughout. Richard Vinen
looked at the early chapters, forcing me to reconsider several
of my assumptions about Pétain. Michael Biddiss and Julian
Jackson read the full manuscript and made many useful suggestions. Thanks also extend to members of the French History Seminar at the Institute of Historical Research who listened
to a paper based on one of the chapters included here. None
of the above bear responsibility for any of the book's remaining shortcomings. Above all, I must thank my wife Claire and
daughter Charlotte for their love, patience and support.

. . .

NOTES AND REFERENCES

1. Such is the approach adopted by Marc Ferro in one of the best biographies of the marshal: M. Ferro, *Pétain* (Paris: Fayard, 1987). Later
sections of this book do, however, integrate Pétain's pre-1940 career.

2. P. Thody, *French Caesarism from Napoleon I to Charles de Gaulle* (London: Macmillan, 1989), p. 75.
3. H. Rousso, *Le syndrome de Vichy, 1944*... (Paris: Seuil, 1987).
4. K. Munholland, 'Wartime France: Remembering Vichy', in *French Historical Studies*, 18 (3) (1994), p. 803.
5. Most obviously L.-D. Girard, *Mazinghem ou la vie secrète de Philippe Pétain, 1856–1951* (Paris: privately published, 1971).
6. R. Griffiths, *Marshal Pétain* (London: Constable, 1970), p. xii. Also see G. Pedroncini, *Pétain. Le soldat et la gloire, 1856–1918* (Paris: Perrin, 1989), p. 9.
7. Griffiths, *Pétain*, p. xi and p. 339.
8. See especially P. Servent, *Le mythe Pétain. Verdun ou les tranchées de la mémoire* (Paris: Editions Payot, 1992).
9. Griffiths, *Pétain*, p. xi.

Chapter 1

THE OFFICER, 1856–1914

Given that Pétain exercised little power before 1914, it remains tempting to pass over his days as an unknown soldier. This would be a mistake. It should not be forgotten that, on the eve of the First World War, he was 58 years of age and already possessed a well-defined character which, in many respects, remained unchanged for the rest of his life. Thus an examination of this personality, and the forces that shaped it, is essential in any overall appreciation of his career.[1]

. . .

Henri Philippe Bénomi Omer Pétain was born on 24 April 1856 at the village of Cauchy-à-la-Tour in the Pas-de-Calais, a department in northern France. Given his vocation as a soldier and future role at Vichy, it was appropriate that his birthplace should have been in an area accustomed to battle and enemy occupation. It was here that the English had set up camp during the Hundred Years War. At the beginning of the eighteenth century, this part of France had again been besieged by the English, this time by the Duke of Marlborough. Then in 1870, 1914 and 1940 came the three German invasions.[2] Yet apart from a great uncle who had served under Napoleon I and an uncle who had fought for Napoleon III, Pétain's family had few military connections. It was instead of solid peasant stock, able to trace its ancestry back to the seventeenth century.

This rural background left an indelible impression on the young Pétain, helping to shape his personality. Like many peasants from the Artois, he possessed a prudent and phlegmatic temperament peppered with a caustic sense of humour. Undoubtedly, these qualities enabled him to remain calm at moments of crisis, yet they also fostered a pessimism which clouded his vision in both 1918 and 1940. His attachment to the soil also instilled in him a taste for simple things, an abstemiousness that was hardened by years of military service. Even when he knew fame, he retained a humble lifestyle and spurned ostentation. Most importantly, his peasant upbringing engendered a dislike for the 'society born of the Industrial Revolution'.[3] In the 1850s Cauchy comprised approximately 400 inhabitants whose lives were regulated by the surrounding countryside. Yet already the Nord-Pas-de-Calais was experiencing the early stirrings of industrialization;[4] it was here that Emile Zola set his novel *Germinal* which recounted the brutal conditions of a new workforce condemned to toil in the mines. Later in his career, when he bothered to do any reading at all, Pétain preferred the classical drama of Corneille and the romantic tales of Sir Walter Scott, and considered that it was the values of an unspoiled peasantry which had made France great. During the Occupation, Vichy propaganda never tired of reminding its audience that the marshal was of farming stock; the moral recovery of the nation, it was argued, could only be achieved through a return to the primitive values of the earth.[5]

None the less, it would be a mistake to overplay Pétain's personal attachment either to the land or to his birthplace. It is significant that when in 1918 he thought again of retirement, he chose not to return to the rain-swept plains of northern France, his original intention in 1914. Instead, he preferred the sunnier climes of the south and purchased a country house, *L'Ermitage*, at Villeneuve-Loubet in the department of Alpes-Maritimes, an area he had known as a junior officer. It is also worth noting that his distaste for industrialization did not mean he was incapable of understanding its dynamics. During the First World War he quickly saw how success in a conflict of attrition depended on the smooth running of a highly developed economy. Clearly, the military had done much to broaden his horizons. So too had several of his relatives.

Although Pétain frequently alluded to his rural origins, he had not been raised in an inward-looking peasant family. His father, Omer-Venant, had once lived in Paris where he had worked for Daguerre, an early pioneer of photography. Omer would probably have remained in the capital had it not been for the 1848 revolution which forced a return to the family farm. In 1851 he married Clotilde Legrand and together they had five children, including Philippe. Little is known about Pétain's mother except that she died when he was 18 months old and that she too had connections outside of Cauchy. These proved important. After Clotilde's death, Omer remarried and had three further children with his new wife, Marie-Reine Vincent, who displayed little affection towards the offspring of the previous marriage.[6] Pétain was thus entrusted to the care of relatives, notably his maternal grandmother, Françoise Crossart, who regaled her charge with blood-curdling stories of the excesses of the French Revolution. Two priests also had a hand in his upbringing, the origins perhaps of a later liking for clerical company. The first, abbé Jean-Baptiste Legrand, was Clotilde's brother. The second, abbé Philippe Marcel Lefebvre, Clotilde's great uncle, had once served as an administrator in Napoleonic Italy and enchanted Pétain with his campaign anecdotes.

Indebted to the goodwill of such relatives, Pétain never relinquished a belief that the family was the most effective of social units. It became a key element in his political philosophy and that of the Vichy regime. Yet he himself was hardly the epitome a good family man. An incorrigible philanderer, he did not marry until he was 64 years of age and never had children of his own. It was probably the army rather than a dislike of his step-mother that accounts for the contradictions between his political thought and his private behaviour. Life as a career soldier was dull, enlivened by occasional flutters at the roulette wheel and constant womanizing. His handsome features, notably his piercing blue eyes and blond hair, won over several women; and he himself retained a healthy appetite for sexual pleasures. At the very end of his life, a senile Pétain remarked to his jailor, Joseph Simon: 'le con et la gueule, il n'y a que ça de vrai!'[7] The marshal further claimed to Simon that he had made love in 1942 at the age of 86![8] Whatever the truth behind this boasting, it is clear that as a young man he had actively sought a wife, only to discover that a meagre salary and poor prospects made him an unattractive prospect. Eventually, age also counted against him. In 1901 he proposed to Eugénie Hardon, whom he had known since her childhood, yet her parents vetoed the wedding on the grounds that he was 45 years old and she 21. She married instead a painter, Pierre de Hérain, whom she divorced shortly before 1914. That gave Pétain his chance, and in 1920 he wed Eugénie in a civil service.

Because he was marrying a divorcée, a nuptial mass was out of the question; yet when in 1929 his wife's first marriage was annulled, Pétain did not seek a religious ceremony. This was eventually performed by the Church in 1941 without the marshal present.

After adolescence, Pétain appears to have lost his personal faith, seemingly another casualty of his life as a professional soldier. He stopped attending mass and once quipped that an organ concert on the radio was enough for his spiritual needs.[9] None the less, he retained a deep respect for the Church which had played a significant role in his childhood. Thanks to the influence of abbé Legrand and a small scholarship bequeathed by abbé Lefebvre, Pétain was able to attend the Catholic boarding college of Saint-Bertin in the nearby town of Saint Omer. Had Pétain been born 20 years later, he might have been a beneficiary (as was Pierre Laval, his leading minister under the Occupation) of the wide-ranging educational changes initiated by the Third Republic. Anxious to combat the political threat posed by clericalism, during the 1880s the new regime steadily undermined the grip which the Church had hitherto exercised over primary education. In future, the state elementary school was to be free, compulsory, and neutral in religious affairs. Not having witnessed these reforms first-hand, Pétain nurtured a mistrust of the *école publique* and was especially suspicious of its teachers, who he believed were motivated by left-wing and anti-patriotic sentiments. By contrast, he possessed a soft spot for Catholic education which he felt had been unfairly victimized by the 'godless Republic'. According to Jérôme Carcopino, one of Vichy's many ministers of education, the marshal sought to crush Catholic schools beneath the weight of his favours.[10]

It was, however, the army which commanded Pétain's greatest loyalty and played the most important part in his development. The reason why he joined up remains a matter for speculation. As noted, some biographers have suggested that he was captivated by the campaign stories of abbé Lefebvre. Another possibility is that, while at school in Saint-Omer, he was enthralled by the uniforms of cavalry officers stationed at a nearby recruiting depot. Others argue that, following the French defeat at the hands of Prussia in 1870, he was motivated by a spirit of revenge. After the war, military drill was introduced at Saint-Bertin and Pétain himself became an instructor. In a speech of 1936, he informed army volunteers from Alsace and Lorraine that he had joined up to recover the lost provinces.[11] In truth, his reasoning was less romantic. He recognized that when he finished his education he would not be welcome at the family farm. Thus he needed to find another career. The priesthood was one option, engineering another. Neither offered the same kind of financial stability as the army. Accordingly, in 1875 he enrolled at the Dominican college of Albert-le-Grand in Arcueil with the intention of preparing for the military academy of Saint-Cyr. The following year he was admitted to this famous institution, listed 403 out of 412. His life as a soldier had begun.

. . .

Even by peacetime standards, Pétain's pre-war career was an undistinguished one.[12] On leaving Saint-Cyr, he spent five years as a *sous lieutenant* in the 24th Battalion of Chasseurs at Villefranche-sur-mur (1878–83) and then another five as lieutenant in the 3rd Battalion of Chasseurs at Besançon (1883–8). Next, he proceeded to the prestigious École de Guerre (1888–1900) where he attended lectures delivered by some of the most distinguished military theorists in France. Now a captain, he was assigned to the 15th Corps at Marseilles (1890–2) before being put in charge of the 29th Battalion of Chasseurs at Vincennes (1892–3). This brought him close to the nub of military affairs and, within a year, he was in the capital attached to the staff of General Saussier, military commander of Paris.[13] This posting lasted for much of the decade (1893–9) and under Saussier's successors, Zurlinden and Brugère, he became an *officier d'ordonnance*.

To achieve further promotion, Pétain was required to take another command;[14] so he joined the 8th Battalion of Chasseurs based near Amiens (1899–1900) reaching the rank of major. Noted as a skilful rifle instructor, he then taught at the École Normale de Tir at Châlons, yet only stayed a few months (1901). His unorthodox views on fire-power contradicted those of the director, Colonel Vonderscherr, and Pétain requested a transfer. After a spell with the 5th Infantry Regiment in Paris (1901), he returned to the École de Guerre as lecturer in infantry tactics (1903–11). Here, his dry sense of humour and terseness of speech earned him the nickname, among students, of 'Précis-le-sec'.[15] His superiors were more agitated by his unconventional military thinking, and he found himself temporarily posted to the 104th Infantry Regiment (1903) and the 118th Infantry Regiment (1907). By 1911, however, he was a full colonel and left Paris to lead the 33rd Infantry Regiment at Arras (1911–14); on the eve of war, he moved to the 4th Infantry Brigade, expecting this to be his last posting before retirement.

Why was his rise through the ranks so slow? In fairness to Pétain, it should first be remembered that promotion was difficult in peacetime. Contrary to what sometimes is believed, the officer corps was not dominated by an aristocratic elite eager to monopolize every post. Instead it comprised an eclectic mix, including former NCOs and sons of gendarmes, minor civil servants and better-off peasants.[16] All looked to the army for financial security with the result that competition for jobs was fierce. It should be further noted that peacetime allowed officers little opportunity to excel in action. One way to shine was through colonial campaigns, yet Pétain expressed no desire to leave metropolitan France and did not fight overseas until the Rif war of 1925 when the French and Spanish Protectorates in Morocco were threatened by an uprising of the Berber tribes led by Abd el-Krim.

Pétain's initial lack of interest in colonial ventures has led to suggestions that he lacked ambition, something he had aplenty after 1914. Apparently in 1903 he was offered the directorship of the rifle school at Châlons, yet considered himself too junior for such responsibility. It has also been speculated that he refused the position as he knew it would have to be approved by General Percin, *chef de cabinet* of General André, the minister of war known to be compiling information on officers' religious opinions in the so-called *Affaire des fiches*.[17] This explanation seems unlikely. It is clear, however, that his cold and increasingly outspoken manner alienated superiors. Several biographers recall an incident in 1913 when Pétain was on manoeuvres. After the officer-in-charge had issued orders to the assembled troops, Pétain added, 'I am sure that General Le Gallet has intended, in order to strike your minds more forcibly, to present a synthesis of all the faults which a modern army should no longer commit.'[18] This comment points to perhaps the most important factor holding back Pétain's prospects: his unorthodox military opinions. These will be discussed later, but it has already been noted how these views got him into trouble with the authorities at both the Châlons rifle school and the École de Guerre.

Pétain resented his slow promotion. As a marshal he reflected, 'I was an old lieutenant, an old captain; I've been old in all my ranks.'[19] None the less, before 1914 he was rarely tempted to seek a career elsewhere. One of those few occasions came in 1888. Anxious to marry the daughter of a rich engineer, he thought of entering her father's firm. Having consulted the abbé Legrand, Pétain decided to forgo the wedding and apparently swore an oath, similar to that he had made at Saint-Cyr, declaring an intention to remain faithful to his 'mystical fiancée', the army.[20] He later claimed that this private pledge was the 'first gift of his person' to France, a moment when he renounced 'everything else'.[21] Given his many love affairs, this remark should not be taken too seriously. Of more importance to Pétain was the security provided by military service. The army had become his life. Having taken him out of the closed environment of Cauchy, it had profoundly influenced his world view, notably his political attitudes.

Much has been written about the politics of the French army during the Third Republic's pre-1914 phase. Older histories suggest that this was a period of civil–military conflict. They point to an aristocratic, Jesuit-educated officer corps out of step with a Republic committed to the revolutionary idea of a nation-in-arms. This view needs modifying on two grounds. Not only is it questionable whether the officer class was monopolized by sons of the nobility, it is also arguable whether the army was ideologically opposed to the Republic. During the nineteenth century it had served several regimes and cared little about who sat in the Elysée or Tuileries so long as government remained firm.[22] The Republic quickly demonstrated its strength, displaying a determination to crush the Commune and re-establish France's reputation overseas. Accordingly, by the early 1880s a majority of officers had rallied to the regime, and were not seriously tempted to support the Bonapartist pretensions of General Boulanger.

It should not be believed, however, that such officers had become fervent Republicans. Many harboured suspicions about the regime in particular and politicians in general. They were especially hostile to any attempt on the part of civilians to interfere in military matters. During the 1880s, the moderate 'Opportunists' in charge of government wisely refrained from encroaching on the army's independence. In the following decade civil–military relations were rocked by the Dreyfus

Affair, a scandal surrounding the Jewish General Staff officer falsely accused of selling secrets to the Germans. In the political fall-out, Radical deputies, self-conscious guardians of France's revolutionary tradition, came to dominate parliament. Frightened of a miltary take-over, they endeavoured to reshape the political outlook of officers. This policy led to the *Affaire des fiches* when it was discovered that André was determining promotions on the basis of information supplied by masonic lodges. Momentarily, the army's loyalty to the Republic was in question; yet, once the affair died down, the military quickly readopted its position of neutrality towards the state.

Pétain himself played no direct role in either the Dreyfus Affair or the *Affaire des fiches*; none the less, his non-involvement is telling of the ways in which the army had shaped his political outlook. Contrary to the claims of his supporters,[23] he always believed in Dreyfus' guilt. In part, this certainty derived from the fact that the accused was Jewish. Pétain displayed an unthinking racism typical of his generation and background; as will be seen, during the Occupation his ill-thought-out prejudices made possible the persecution and murder of thousands of Jews. His conviction that Dreyfus was guilty also sprang from a sense of military discipline which dictated that the rights of an individual should be subordinated to the collective interests of the whole. Once it had been decided to prosecute Dreyfus, it was imperative that the decision of the tribunal be upheld otherwise the nation's discipline and confidence in the army would be undermined. Thus Pétain was scornful of those politicians who sought to make capital out of the case; it was not their place to criticize the military. Even so, this anger did not lead him to join any of the extreme right-wing movements, such as the Action Française, which were emerging in the early 1900s. Although he no doubt read their newspapers in the staff-room and shared their values, he considered it inappropriate for military men to engage in politics. A soldier, he maintained, should stand above politics. Ironically, this attitude meant that after 1914 he himself was oblivious to the fact that he was often meddling in civilian affairs. It also meant that he was a loyal, albeit unenthusiastic, supporter of the Third Republic. This was to prove important during the 1930s when he shunned the unconstitutional road to power.

Although Pétain was reticent about pronouncing on political issues, he was outspoken in his military opinions. Here he had little hesitation in contradicting his army superiors who placed their faith in the offensive. After the defeat of 1870, the French gradually abandoned defensive tactics, and in 1911 General Joffre, Commander-in-Chief, adopted the infamous Plan 17 which championed the principle of *l'attaque à l'outrance*. This almost laid as much stress on the morale of troops as it did on material. Armed with a heady patriotism and bayonets fixed, infantrymen would march towards enemy positions; the enemy, in turn, would be so bewildered and morally over-whelmed that it would flee in terror. The most enthusiastic supporter of such tactics was Colonel de Grandmaison, head of the Troisième Bureau (Operations) of the General Staff, who declared that in an attack only two things were necessary: 'to know where the enemy is and to decide what to do. What the enemy intends to do is of no consequence.'[24] Such mis-guided nonsense ensured the slaughter of thousands of French soldiers during the first two years of the war.[25]

Despite what is sometimes believed, Pétain was not totally opposed to the offensive.[26] It was, after all, the necessary con-dition for victory. Yet an attack was to be adopted with caution and should always be accompanied by superior fire-power. Fire-power was axiomatic to his tactics, and was the most original aspect of his thought. He had first recognized its importance at the École de Tir of Châlons. According to conventional doc-trine, the introduction of bolt-loading magazine rifles meant that there was no longer a need for accurate marksmanship; instead, troops were trained to shoot as a group and aim in a wide trajectory. Pétain disagreed and placed greater onus on individual accuracy. In his lectures at the École de Guerre, based on a wide-ranging survey of nineteenth-century conflicts, he took these theories a step further. With the introduction of heavy artillery and machine guns, it was vital for infantry to seek as much protection as possible; otherwise a commander would expose his men to pointless risks. To underscore this danger he coined the simple phrase, 'le feu tue'. Conscious of the destructive capabilities of modern weaponry, Pétain looked increasingly to the defensive. Not only would this strategy pro-vide the necessary shelter from enemy shells, it would also enhance the fire-power of one's own troops. It was essential, therefore, that artillery and infantry coordinated their efforts. Such cooperation would ensure that enemy positions were worn down, making an attack possible – even then, that assault should be accompanied by artillery bombardment. In another of his famous adages he observed, 'An offensive is gunfire leading an advance. A defensive is gunfire stopping an advance. The gun wins ground, the infantry occupies it.'[27]

The experience of the First World War vindicated several of Pétain's theories. Fire-power was to prove critical in a conflict of attrition. None the less, his powers of prophecy should not be exaggerated. He had not envisaged the static nature of the fighting to come. Nor had he recognized the value of barbed wire as a line of defence.[28] It was however to his credit that he remained throughout the war the most flexible of France's military thinkers. It was not until the interwar years that his ideas ossified. By that stage his beliefs had become the ortho-doxy exerting a powerful influence over his country's military strategy.

Pétain never expected to wield such influence. In 1914 he believed his career was ending. Although he retained his caus-ticity, there is no sign that he was frustrated with the army. His tremendous ambition appears to have been nurtured during the war ahead. None the less, in 1914 it is already possible to identify the characteristics of the man who was to head the Vichy regime. Already we may see the stirrings of a philosophy which laid stress on values which Pétain had known at Cauchy and in the army: the soil; the family; the church; and the nation. Already we may see a contempt for politicians and all those forces – industrialization, urbanization, secularization – which he felt were undermining the fabric of France. Above all, we see a very ordinary man who, apart from his military opinions, held a canon of simple beliefs common to many of his genera-tion and upbringing. Such a man was not suited to exercise power; he was certainly not suited to governing a country. Yet, with the outbreak of war in 1914, power beckoned.

· · ·

NOTES AND REFERENCES

1. A good introduction to Pétain's early life is provided in H.R. Lottman, *Pétain* (Paris: Seuil, 1984), pp. 13–54.
2. Ibid., p. 14.
3. R. Griffiths, *Marshal Pétain* (London: Constable, 1970), p. 160.
4. In 1919 Cauchy, by then inhabited by several miners, elected a left-wing council which refused to contribute to a monument in honour of Marshal Joffre, preferring instead to display a portrait

of the socialist leader Jean Jaurès in the town hall. See P. Alméras, *Un français nommé Pétain* (Paris: Robert Laffont, 1995), p. 18.

5. G. Miller, *Les pousse-au-jouir du maréchal Pétain* (Paris: Seuil, 1975), pp. 129–33.

6. B. Serrigny, *Trente ans avec Pétain* (Paris: Plon, 1959), p. 222.

7. Pétain quoted in Griffiths, *Pétain*, p. 91.

8. J. Simon, *Pétain, mon prisonnier. Présentation, notes et commentaires de Pierre Bourget* (Paris: Plon, 1978), p. 141.

9. J. Duquesne, *Les catholiques français sous l'occupation* (Paris: Grasset, 1966), p. 18.

10. J. Carcopino, *Souvenirs de sept ans, 1937–1944* (Paris: Flammarion, 1953), p. 318.

11. J. Isorni, *Philippe Pétain*, vol. 1 (Paris: La Table Ronde, 1972), p. 48.

12. Pétain's early military career is mapped out in G. Pedroncini, *Pétain. Le soldat et la gloire, 1856–1918* (Paris: Perrin, 1989), pp. 23–40.

13. Griffiths, *Pétain*, p. xvi.

14. E. Laure, *Pétain* (Paris: Berger-Levrault, 1942), p. 9.

15. Ibid., p. 16.

16. D. Porch, *The March to the Marne. The French Army, 1871–1914* (Cambridge: Cambridge University Press, 1981), p. 17.

17. S. Ryan, *Pétain the Soldier* (New York: A.S. Barnes and Co., 1965), p. 23.

18. Pétain quoted in R. Tournoux, *Pétain and de Gaulle* (London: Heinemann, 1966), p. 23.

19. Pétain quoted in ibid., p. 21.

20. L.-D. Girard, *Mazinghem ou la vie secrète de Philippe Pétain, 1856–1951* (Paris: privately published, 1971), pp. 119–22. Also see P. Pellissier, *Philippe Pétain* (Paris: Hachette, 1980), p. 30.

21. Lottman, *Pétain*, p. 34.

22. D.B. Ralston, *The Army of the Republic. The Place of the Military in the Political Evolution of France, 1871–1914* (Cambridge, Mass.: MIT Press, 1967), pp. 2–3.

23. Notably Girard, *Mazinghem*, p. 150, who claims that, by virtue of his position on the staff of the military governor of Paris during the 1890s, Pétain was privy to confidential information testifying to Dreyfus' innocence.

24. Grandmaison quoted in A. Horne, *The French Army and Politics, 1870–1970* (New York: Peter Bedrick Books, 1984), p. 32.

25. Ibid., p. 32. See too A. Horne, *The Price of Glory. Verdun 1916* (London: Macmillan, 1962) and Porch, *March to the Marne*, p. 213.

26. Ryan, *Pétain*, p. 25.

27. Pétain quoted in Tournoux, *Pétain and de Gaulle*, p. 23.

28. Griffiths, *Pétain*, p. xix.

Chapter 2

THE GENERAL, 1914–18

In 1914 Pétain was preparing for retirement. Always the practical man, he bought a small pair of shears with which he planned to tend his garden.[1] Such dreams of domesticity were shattered by the outbreak of a war which relaunched his career, thrusting him into positions of military, political and diplomatic importance. In 1918 he received the supreme accolade when he was made a marshal. With power came enormous popular acclaim. Throughout the country his portrait adorned crockery, cigarette cards and magazine covers. Although this idolatry did not reach as yet the proportions of 1940, it is clear that the seeds of a cult of Pétainism were sown during the First World War. How did the unknown officer of 1914 come to exercise such authority, and how did power affect his world-view?

. . .

In autumn 1914 it initially appeared that the battle for western Europe would be the war of movement both sides had anticipated fighting.[2] Assuming a conflict on two fronts, the Germans had devised the Schlieffen Plan. In order to deliver a quick knockout blow against France, this envisaged an attack through Belgium and the Netherlands so as to cross the French frontier where fortifications were weakest.[3] French troops would subsequently be enveloped and Paris isolated. The fact that this strategy violated Belgian neutrality, and was thus likely to bring Britain into the fray, was of little concern. Britain, it was argued, was a naval power; its limited land forces would be ineffectual in a short war. The Germans calculated that it would take no more than six weeks to achieve victory in the west, allowing them time to counter Russian mobilization in the east.

12

The broad contours of the Schlieffen Plan had been known to the French since 1905, yet this information had not led to a significant overhaul of Plan 17. Speed remained vital to Joffre's plans. Without waiting for the British, the right flank of his armies was to march into Lorraine; the left was to meet the oncoming Germans in Belgium. What the Belgians themselves did remained a matter of speculation.[4] In the event, they had no choice but to defend their homeland from the German advance. This moved at pace and quickly repelled the French assaults into Belgium and Lorraine. Momentarily, in early September, a German victory seemed certain as the Kaiser's troops moved within sight of Paris. Its nerve shaken, the French government retreated to Bordeaux, just as it had done in 1870 and just as it would do in 1940. Then came a 'miracle'. On 6 September Joffre successfully counter-attacked on the Marne. This initiative transformed the war in the west. The 'battle of the frontiers' ended and the 'race for the sea' began as both sides tried to outflank one another. There was, however, little room for manoeuvre and by November a static front of trenches stretched from the Belgian coastline to the Swiss frontier. Not even Pétain had foreseen this deadlock; yet during the opening months of the war many of his theories about the use of fire-power and the defensive had been vindicated.

It will be recalled that at the start of the fighting, Pétain was attached to the 4th Infantry Brigade at Saint Omer. On 13 August this brigade entered Belgium as part of the left flank of Plan 17. It was soon pushed back into France and on 28 August engaged in a rearguard action at the Battle of the Guise. The day before Pétain had been made a brigadier-general and on 1 September took charge of the 6th Infantry Division at Fismes. The Battle of the Marne followed, and the newly promoted commander helped drive the Germans back to the Aisne canal where they held their lines. As the war reached a stalemate, Pétain received a fresh posting and greater responsibilities. Appointed an officer of the Légion d'honneur on 16 October, four days later he was in charge of one of his former regiments, the 33rd Army Corps, part of General Maud'huy's 10th Army. His task was the defence of Arras, a vital communications centre.[5]

In part, Pétain owed his rapid elevation to the fact that he was still alive. In the opening fortnight of the conflict, France lost 300,000 men either dead, wounded or missing. Among this number were 4,778 officers, one-tenth of the total officer strength.[6] Joffre also found that he had to dismiss a large number of officers for incompetence. By contrast, Pétain kept his head under fire. In the retreat from Belgium, he displayed formidable organizational talents. These skills were also evident in his command of Arras. Here he had opportunity to put his pre-war theories to the test mobilizing artillery in support of heavily entrenched positions. It was not long, however, before he was involved in a series of offensives. Throughout 1915 the French High Command was preoccupied with the *percée*, the one big push which would pierce enemy lines and restore a war of movement.

After an abortive offensive in February 1915, Joffre planned a more ambitious Franco-British operation in the Artois region. Launched on 9 May, this drew on troops from the 10th Army which, of course, included the 33rd Army Corps. Pétain's meticulous preparation ensured that his men were the only ones to enjoy any real success, reaching the Vimy ridge on the first day of the fighting. However, they lacked the artillery to consolidate their positions and were forced to withdraw. Pétain launched further assaults but to no avail. At the close of the battle on 10 June, the Allies had advanced 4 kilometres. For this ground, the French lost over 100,000 men, the British some 60,000 and the Germans approximately 75,000.[7] Undaunted, Joffre devised a further campaign with the British striking in Artois and the French in Champagne. Once again, Pétain fought in this battle. On 10 May he had been made a commander of the Légion d'honneur and on 21 June took over the 2nd Army which in September spearheaded the Champagne offensive. This time his troops made little headway; ironically, their principal achievement was the capture of a cemetery. Occasionally, Pétain has been criticized for his use of prolonged bombardment prior to the assault, thus ruining the element of surprise. Yet it appears that – as with previous offensives – details of Joffre's strategy were known to the enemy beforehand. The resulting casualties were heavy. Together, the French and British suffered 242,000 fatalities; they had advanced 3 kilometres.

The failure of the 1915 offensives convinced Pétain that the war had become one of attrition. He was not alone in this belief. Both the British and French High Commands had arrived at a similar conclusion. Yet Pétain's concept of attrition was different to that of his superiors. They remained wedded to the idea of the *percée*. If that failed, all was not lost. Victory would eventually be secured because allied reserves of manpower were greater than those of the enemy. Pétain was contemptuous of such cynical thinking. He appreciated that barbed wire and machine guns made a decisive breakthrough unlikely. In this situation, an offensive was only possible after enemy defences had been whittled down by a series of limited attacks supported by heavy bombardment. Thus it was vital for the French to build up their stores of heavy artillery. To his dismay, production of large quantities of heavy cannon began only in summer 1915, too late to salvage the offensives of that year.

Concern for the superiority of artillery fire and the conservation of manpower quickly established Pétain as one of the most humanitarian generals. His *Journal de route*, a diary he kept until 22 October 1914, indicates his preoccupations.[8] Not only does it provide descriptions of the many pretty women he met on his way into Belgium, it also displays an awareness of the morale of his troops. Conscious of the appalling conditions in which his men had to fight, Pétain took steps to improve material conditions, ensuring proper leave and sufficient rations. He also visited the front line, something few senior officers were prepared to do. On occasion, when mixing in the trenches, he purposely wore a great overcoat which hid his rank. He then took a childlike pleasure in startling his new-found companions by announcing he was General Pétain.[9] Such displays were frowned upon by other officers; at least he led his men from the front and not from the safety of the Grand Quartier Général (GQG), the French military headquarters. Accordingly, his soldiers acknowledged him as a genuine leader. His cold manner retained this respect, as did his reputation as a stern disciplinarian. Already he possessed the qualities necessary for quelling the mutinies in 1917.

Behind this cold reserve, Pétain was also nurturing a vanity which had not been so evident in 1914. Never one to suffer fools gladly, his rapid rise through the ranks and early tactical successes gave him a sense of superiority over fellow officers. Fayolle, a future marshal, was one of the first to notice this. On 3 April 1915, he remarked on Pétain's disappointment at not being appointed commander of the 10th Army as replacement for Maud'huy.[10] The post had gone instead to d'Urbal, whom

Pétain dismissed as a 'fool'. Clearly Pétain was hungry for more power. The wait would not be long.

. . .

On 21 February 1916 General Passaga, stationed at Lac Noir in the Vosges, noted in his diary, 'Through the earthen floor of my shelter I can detect the incessant rumble of drums, punctuated by the pounding of big basses.'[11] What he had heard was the beginning of the Battle of Verdun, situated nearly 100 miles away. During the first day of battle, the Germans fired over one million shells, creating, in Pétain's words, 'a zone of death'.[12] Over the next ten months, 259 French battalions out of a total of 330 were drawn into the fighting. Apart from four colonial divisions, no foreign troops were involved. By contrast, only 109 batalions were at the Somme which was, in any case, a Franco-British affair. Small wonder, then, that many French men and women came to see Verdun as the supreme test of their nation. Defeat would have been a severe body-blow for morale.

This was understood by Erich von Falkenhayn, the new German Commander-in-Chief, the brains behind the Verdun offensive. In a lengthy memorandum of December 1915, he argued that the eastern front no longer offered the best chance of victory. Although Russia was weakened, its armies were not at breaking-point. By contrast, in the west France was near to collapse. Only Britain remained rich in men and resources. How, then, to defeat Britain? An invasion was impracticable and a colonial war offered no certainty of success. Unrestricted submarine warfare was another possibility, but would not produce immediate results. Given these problems, Falkenhayn concluded that the best way to overcome Britain was to knock out its closest – and weakest – ally, France. To accomplish this, a breakthrough was not necessary; instead, Germany needed to select a target which the French would feel compelled to defend to the last. In this way, their forces would be 'bled white'. It was a terrifying concept of attrition which underlined Falkenhayn's ruthless nature. It was also a misguided strategy. If France held firm, Germany too would be exhausted. Here Falkenhayn's idea of attrition differed from that of Pétain's. While both men rejected the *percée* – the option still favoured by Joffre – Pétain would never have countenanced an operation which endangered so many lives. Nor would he have possessed the ruthlessness to have seen it through.

Having adopted his strategy, Falkenhayn chose a killing ground. He settled on the series of underground fortresses defending Verdun, a quiet garrison town overlooking the Meuse. Although this rain-swept section of the western front was of little tactical importance, it was of enormous symbolic value. For the Germans, it was here in 843 that the heirs of Charlemagne had given birth to the German nation.[13] For the French, it was site of repeated resistance – 1792 and 1870 – to Prussian might. In 1914 it had provided the pivot for Joffre's manoeuvre which won the Battle of the Marne. As Pétain himself acknowledged, Verdun was the 'boulevard moral' of France.[14] Clearly, then, this was a target the French would be determined to defend, yet in 1915 Verdun's defences had been neglected. Not only were its fortressess regarded as out of keeping with the attacking spirit, they also contained valuable cannon needed for the Artois and Champagne offensives. Only in January 1916 did GQG, aware of a possible attack in the region, begin to replace these guns. By that stage, it was almost too late. With amazing secrecy, the Germans had assembled a massive quantity of artillery ready for their attack. And in the *Stollen*, dank underground shelters dug by the infantry, waited the attackers: 72 battalions of crack assault troops.

On 21 February, the barrage began. Initially French positions held firm, but by 24 February it seemed Verdun was about to fall.[15] Worried at this prospect, de Castelnau, the Chief-of-Staff and second-in-command, urged Joffre to send reinforcements in the shape of Pétain's 2nd Army. Several authors have since claimed that Pétain was selected for his expertise in defensive tactics. It is more likely he was chosen simply because his troops were in reserve at Noailles. Controversy also surrounds the brief given to Pétain. Originally, he was to take charge of only one bank of the Meuse. Yet when de Castelnau arrived at Verdun in the evening of 24 February he was so alarmed at what he saw that he placed Pétain in command of both banks with orders not to surrender any further ground. This appointment was not referred to Joffre. Apparently, earlier that evening de Castelnau had woken the 'Victor of the Marne' to seek permission to travel to the front. Angered at being disturbed, Joffre supposedly exclaimed, 'Let him do what he wants.' Once at Verdun, de Castelnau had no wish to rouse his superior a second time. Whatever the truth of this story, which may well have been fabricated by Joffre's many detractors,[16] it seems unlikely that the Commander-in-Chief would have entrusted Pétain with such powers. He no longer believed Verdun was vital to France's defences, and had even drawn up contingency plans for a withdrawal.

Further controversy surrounds Pétain's whereabouts on the night he was placed in charge of Verdun. When the telegram of his appointment reached Noailles late in the evening of 24 February, he could not be located. Serrigny, his aide-de-camp, had a good idea where to find him and immediately drove to Paris.[17] Arriving at 3 a.m., he headed for the Hôtel Terminus directly opposite the Gare du Nord. After an argument with the concierge, he entered the hotel and made for a bedroom door outside which he discovered his commander's boots nestling alongside a pair of lady's slippers. Perhaps with greater reason than Joffre, Pétain was unhappy at being woken but refused to be flummoxed by events. He arranged for a room for Serrigny, and waited until morning before travelling to Joffre's headquarters at Chantilly. Given Pétain's constant womanizing, this story rings true. It is now known that his night-time companion was his future wife, Eugénie.[18]

Arriving at Chantilly on the morning of 25 February, Pétain was briefed on the desperate state of the battle and soon fell despondent. His gloom grew en route to Verdun when he learned that the fort of Douaumont, a key element in the town's defences, had fallen. It has since been speculated that a tactical withdrawal would have been the best strategy at this stage. If the French had retreated behind the left bank of the Meuse, they would have lured their attackers into the open countryside around Châlons-sur-Marne where machine guns and light cannons would have decimated German forces.[19] Pétain himself is thought to have favoured this move, yet his orders were to hold Verdun, and in the evening of 25 February he took charge of the battle.

His first task was to establish his headquarters at Souilly away from the panic-stricken atmosphere of Dugny where operations had been previously conducted. The general was fortunate that panic did not resurface. On arriving at Verdun he fell ill with pneumonia, the result of his gruelling journey to the battlefield. For the next five days, he issued orders from his sick-bed. Amazingly, his condition was kept a secret lest it should damage the morale of his troops. Once he was on the mend, Pétain's next task was organizing supply. Because Verdun lay in a salient, the enemy had been able to surround the town and sever the main arteries with the rest of France. A narrow-gauge railway line and a second-class highway running some 50 miles to Bar-le-Duc remained the sole links with the outside world. As a long-term measure, Pétain ordered the laying of new railway track. In the short term, he rebuilt the road to Bar-le-Duc. Under the guidance of a remarkable engineer, Major Richard, gangs of workmen repaired the road's surface. Only motor vehicles were allowed on the road itself; troops marched by its side. The route held and became part of Verdun's mythology. Maurice Barrès, the nationalist writer, christened it 'la voie sacrée'. Undoubtedly, it was an invaluable lifeline. For each week of the battle, some 50,000 tons of supply and 3,500 trucks travelled down this conveyor-belt.

The steady stream of men and materials enabled Pétain to concentrate on other aspects of the battle. True to his pre-war beliefs, he ensured that French fire-power worked in liaison with the infantry. In addition, he improved conditions for his troops. He deplored the German system of only replacing casualties. Instead, he constantly rotated men in the front line, ensuring that they were rested away from the fighting. This system of rotation, coupled with the heavy losses of the battle, placed enormous strain on French reserves. Joffre frequently complained that Pétain's requirements were preventing France from launching the Somme offensive. Bitter arguments ensued, yet Pétain held his ground, reminding his superior that his orders were to defend Verdun.

Confronted by revitalized French defences, German attacks on Verdun faltered. In March, offensives on Mort Homme and Côte 304, two strategically important hills on the left bank, were repelled. Not usually one to be cheery, Pétain was quick to celebrate the recent victories. General order number 94 of 10 April announced, 'Courage, on les aura'. A stickler for good grammar, Pétain initially disliked this colloquial phrase which was coined by Serrigny, yet acknowledged that it would boost morale.[20] Pétain was far more agitated by the decision of his superiors who, on 19 April, placed him in charge of Army Group Centre. For once, he was not happy at his elevation, and suspected that Joffre had instigated the move. Although Pétain remained in overall charge of Verdun, he was now based at Bar-le-Duc. The new head of the 2nd Army was General Nivelle, a former cavalryman and unreconstructed Grandmaisonite.

It was not long before Nivelle and his subordinate, General Mangin, known affectionately by his men as 'le boucher', were planning offensives. Pétain magnanimously accepted responsibility for these wasteful attacks, but found it difficult to contain his anxieties. In early June Fort Vaux, another of Verdun's key defences, was lost. On 23 June the Germans launched a vicious new weapon, phosgene gas. That day a worried Pétain informed de Castelnau that the right bank of Verdun might have to be abandoned.

Two factors saved the situation. First, Falkenhayn was running out of troops and munitions; at long last, both sides were being 'bled white'. Second, on 1 July the Allies launched their long-awaited offensive on the Somme, thus relieving pressure on Verdun. Mounting German losses along the western front eventually cost Falkenhayn his job. In August he was replaced by Hindenburg, who halted further assaults on Verdun. This gave Pétain his opportunity. Keeping a tight rein on Nivelle and Mangin, he launched a series of counter-offensives, each supported by heavy artillery. In October, Douaumont was recaptured; by December the battle of Verdun was won.

Ever since, historians have questioned whether Pétain was truly the 'Victor of Verdun'. It has been frequently pointed out that if he had been granted all of his requests for men, the whole of the French army would have been pulled into the battle, just as Falkenhayn wanted. There is some truth in this charge. Pétain's skill lay more in the application of tactics than in the formulation of strategy. Yet it needs to be remembered that Joffre's careful rationing of the troops available for Verdun only meant that there were more available to be slaughtered at the Somme.[21] A further criticism pertains to Pétain's pessimism, particularly the incident on 23 June when he telephoned de Castelnau to declare that he was on the point of relinquishing the right bank. This gloominess was undoubtedly a weakness as it undermined his overall view of the battle, but it was only fleeting and did not translate into defeatism. His tendency to fear the worst was to be far more of a problem in March 1918 and June 1940.

The most serious charge levelled at Pétain is that he was overly commmitted to the defensive; it was instead the offensives of Nivelle and Mangin in November and December that won the day. Again, there is an element of truth in this claim, yet it should be recalled that Pétain's orders were to defend Verdun.

Left to his own devices he would probably have conducted a strategic withdrawal. Once instructed to hold the forts, his tactics paid off, halting the German advance. As the fighting dragged on, he recognized the importance of the battle to public morale and became even more determined to guard his positions. Ultimately, he knew when to switch tactics. Never entirely a man of the defensive, he waited his moment and, by restraining Nivelle and Mangin, ensured that French counter-attacks had a chance of success.[22]

Given his husbanding of resources, appreciation of public opinion and tactical timing, there is much to be said in favour of Pétain being the 'Victor of Verdun'. Yet in view of the casualties – 337,000 German dead and 469,000 French – it is questionable whether anybody emerged a winner out of this indecisive battle. Admittedly, Verdun had stretched the French army to the limit, devolving the main burden of the western front upon Britain; yet Germany, too, was exhausted, unable to exploit France's predicament. It is significant that the Kaiser's first peace proposals were drawn up immediately after the battle. If anything, Verdun was a triumph for the French infantryman, the *poilu*.[23] He had to fight against overwhelming odds and in appalling conditions. Small wonder Verdun has been interpreted as a victory for the French race.

Pétain was aware of the debt he owed to his soldiers and later requested that he should be buried in the *ossuaire* at Douaumont, a wish that has yet to be granted. Always the humanitarian, he had been sickened by the loss of life at Verdun. In his account of the battle, he recalled how he watched young men marching to the front: 'I loved the confident glance with which they saluted me but the discouragement with which they returned . . . Their eyes stared into space as if transfixed by a vision of terror.'[24] This compassion sharpened his criticisms of his superiors. Joffre was a frequent target; so too the British. Like many French officers of his generation, Pétain harboured a mild anglophobia. Yet, as the struggle for Verdun continued, he became impatient at Haig for failing to launch the Somme offensive. Thereafter he remained intensely suspicious of British intentions, a suspicion that would resurface in 1918 and 1940.

Pétain reserved most of his vitriol for politicians. It will be recalled that he had inherited a soldier's mistrust of civil authority. In 1914 he was quick to blame French reverses on parliament. In truth, Joffre's triumph at the Marne meant that the day-to-day running of the war had largely been the province of the military. Yet after the failure of the 1915 offensives both parliament and cabinet were anxious to curb the powers of the High Command, and several deputies made their way to the front. Pétain detested these visitors. Poincaré, the President of the Republic, was held up for particular ridicule. Although Poincaré was a fervent patriot and a moderate Republican, Pétain viewed him as a meddler whose trips to the front put soldiers' lives at risk. At Verdun, in March 1916, the general was astounded when the President advised against surrendering the right bank lest this should precipitate a parliamentary crisis. Pétain was further shocked to find the President struggling for something to say when addressing officers in the line. Although Pétain himself was a man of few words, he was never short of some choice remarks. The following month he informed Poincaré that he cared little for the constitution;[25] he even indicated a preference for dictatorship. The next year, he grumbled that France was neither commanded nor governed.[26] Pétain's apologists shrug off these comments and point out that none of the French generals liked parliamentary inspections. This is true. It is also clear that in 1916 Pétain was not planning a *coup d'état*. None the less, there is no disguising his growing contempt of parliamentary democracy. Nor is there any hiding his propensity for politicking. Although he despised politicians, he learned how to manipulate the visits of deputies, using these occasions to voice criticisms of GQG. Already he was learning the lessons of intrigue that would serve him well in later life.

For the time being, these new-found skills did not secure extra power. With the failure of the Somme offensive, criticism of Joffre became uncontainable and in December 1916 he was relieved of his duties as Commander-in-Chief. Although he received a marshalship and was made a technical adviser to the government, he no longer played any part in the formulation of French strategy. These changes raised the question of a successor. De Castelnau was the obvious choice. Yet his clerical opinions and right-wing leanings were too strong for many deputies. After de Castelnau, Pétain seemed the most likely candidate. Yet he too was passed over. Why was this? Some historians suggest that, like de Castelnau, Pétain was discriminated against because of his religious beliefs. Given that Pétain had largely lost the faith of his childhood, this seems implausible. It is more likely his sharp tongue had alienated both Poincaré and GQG. He also appeared too wedded to the defensive. The idea of the *percée* had not died with Joffre's dismissal. Thus attention focused on Nivelle. In his counter-attacks of October 1916 he appeared to have discovered the secret of the successful attack. Few appreciated that his tactics had been masterminded by Pétain. Momentarily, Nivelle had outshone his superior, and was rewarded with the mantle of Commander-in-Chief.

Pétain resented being passed over for the supreme position. His pique was intensified by the enormous popular acclaim which accompanied his successes in 1916. Outwardly he shunned publicity. He was no Joffre burying himself away for hours to read his fan-mail. Even so, he delighted in his new-found fame. According to Fayolle, he was mesmerized by his triumph at Verdun and thought of himself as a 'great man'.[27] Conscious of his own worth, Pétain was soon undermining Nivelle's plans for a fresh offensive. In the event, this was the disaster which many had feared. As morale sagged, Pétain took over as Commander-in-Chief with Foch as his Chief-of-Staff. At last, he had the power he craved.

. . .

In January 1917 neither the Allies nor the Central Powers appeared close to victory. In this situation, both sides reluctantly contemplated the possibility of a negotiated peace; yet they still hankered after a military solution. With the failure of the Verdun offensive, Germany decided to adopt the other suggestion outlined in Falkenhayn's memorandum: unrestricted submarine warfare. It was calculated that this policy would exhaust Britain and conserve Germany's dwindling infantry reserves. The drawback was that it might drag the United States of America into the war. Yet it was understood that Washington was already aiding the Allies; in the short term, American troops were unlikely to have an impact on the war. Meeting at Rome in January 1917, the Allies were also mulling over their options. Despite the experiences of the Somme and Verdun offensives, they believed that a breakthrough was still feasible, and so began to plan simultaneous offensives on all fronts.

French preparations were eagerly drawn up by Nivelle. Building on a scheme bequeathed by Joffre at the close of 1916, the new Commander-in-Chief envisaged a large-scale offensive which would bring success within 48 hours. While the British launched a diversionary raid on Arras, French troops would attack along a front stretching from Reims to Soissons, a line that largely coincided with the Chemin des Dames highway. The tactics to be deployed were those of the Verdun offensives.[28] After large-scale bombardment, there would be a rapid infantry assault. Proctected by a constant barrage, the attackers would prise open enemy defences. The French would then be in open country, at liberty to cut off German positions.

Nivelle's plan never stood much chance of success. First, the enemy knew his intentions and soon acquired a copy of the plan. Second, the Germans had adopted well-protected defences along the so-called Hindenberg Line. To attack such fortified positions was always going to be a hazardous venture. Third, the French possessed insufficient artillery and ammunition to see their offensive through. Fourth, Nivelles's tactics were misplaced. He failed to appreciate that the methods employed at Verdun – limited objectives, surprise and superior fire-power – were all absent from his proposed operation.[29]

Oblivious to these problems, Nivelle set out to win support for his plan. To begin with, he had to convince the British. Haig, the Commander-in-Chief, remained sceptical; Lloyd George, the Prime Minister, was impressed, swayed by the charm and the excellent spoken English of the French general. Next, Nivelle had to elicit the support of his own politicians, who, with Joffre gone, were anxious to clip the wings of the High Command. In the event, he had little trouble winning over the octogenarian Alexandre Ribot, who became Prime Minister in March 1917. Paul Painlevé, the new Minister of War, was a different proposition. A Republican Socialist deputy from the Seine, Painlevé had deep misgivings about any further offensives. Not only was he troubled by the erection of the Hindenberg Line, he was also worried about the timing of the operation. Conscious that the USA was close to intervening in the conflict, he wondered whether it made more sense to withhold an attack until the Allies possessed overwhelming superiority in manpower. Furthermore, American assistance might remedy the problems created by the Russian Revolution of February 1917. Although the Provisional Government remained in the war, there was always a danger that it might pull out at any moment, thus allowing the Germans to transfer large quantities of men to the western front.

In addition to the British and the politicians, Nivelle had to win over his own generals. On 5 April Ribot received a letter purportedly from General Messimy, a former Minister of War, warning against the proposed offensive. In all probability, the real author of the document was General Micheler, in charge of French troops at the Somme. Nivelle knew, however, that he faced a more formidable critic in the shape of Pétain. The 'Victor of Verdun' was so dismissive of the coming operation that the press began to speculate about divisions within the High Command. This unwanted publicity prompted Pétain to write to his superior on 17 March reassuring him that he was not behind these stories. He neglected to mention that he was in alliance with Painlevé. As in the past, Pétain's contempt for parliamentarians did not mean he was above politicking himself.

On 1 April Pétain met privately with Painlevé and made known his objections to the offensive. The next day the Minister of War organized a dinner attended by a select number of politicians and soldiers, including Pétain but not Nivelle. When Ribot arrived, he quickly understood he had been invited to a conference as various guests spoke out against the coming operation.[30] A shrewd observer of men, the Prime Minister was impressed by Pétain but noted that he had too critical a mind and did not inspire confidence. Afterwards, the dinner created a fuss. Aware of his duties as a soldier, Pétain informed Nivelle that it had taken place,[31] but did not indicate what had been discussed. Nivelle could guess and was furious. Unabashed, on 3 April Pétain dined with Poincaré and again criticized his Commander-in-Chief.

Three days later Pétain was in a more reticent mood. Troubled by the disagreements within the High Command, the President organized an extraordinary war council at Compiègne, the new home of GQG. After Nivelle had outlined his plans, the generals were asked to comment. None showed much enthusiasm, but none spoke out against the operation. When it came to Pétain, he displayed embarrassment and muttered a few brief reservations.[32] If it had ever been the politicians' aim to force Nivelle to moderate his plans, the meeting had been a failure. The parliamentarians ought to have known that a sense of military discipline would always prevent soldiers from openly voicing criticism of their Commander-in-Chief when in his presence.[33] Nivelle recognized this and, sensing he did not have the full backing of his generals, offered to stand down. This created alarm among the politicians, who feared that his resignation, only a few days before a crucial operation, would undermine morale. In the event, Poincaré persuaded him to remain on the understanding that he would only use a prudent number of troops in the forthcoming battle.

Against an inauspicious backdrop of political wrangling and bad weather, the Chemin des Dames offensive was launched on 16 April. Despite initial gains, the French soon ran into difficulties and within days the battle was beginning to resemble the Somme. Alarmed at the deadlock, on 24 April Painlevé called for an end to the attacks and Nivelle's replacement by the 'Victor of Verdun'. The cabinet was not so sure. It was felt the assaults had not been granted sufficient time to succeed. Moreover, Pétain did not arouse enthusiasm. Too many ministers had been stung by his sarcasm, and suspicions lingered about his political views. Forced to rethink his tactics, Painlevé then suggested that Pétain be made second-in-command with the title Chief of the General Staff.[34] Pétain, however, was reluctant to go along with this scheme as he knew this post would mean close contact with Nivelle. On 29 April, a compromise was reached whereby Pétain would indeed be appointed Chief of the General Staff, but be stationed at the Ministry of War in Paris, away from Compiègne. Whether this solution would have worked remains questionable. As it was, the outbreak of mutinies among French troops made Nivelle's position untenable. On 15 May Pétain became Commander-in-Chief with Foch as Chief of the General Staff. A resentful Nivelle was posted to North Africa. He did not return to France until after 1918 and died not long after in 1924. He wrote no memoirs to justify an offensive which cost the lives of 150,000 Frenchmen.[35]

With Pétain's appointment, the April offensive was brought to a halt. It was agreed that there would be no further attacks until the USA, which had entered the war in April, could assist. Such attacks would, in any case, have to wait until the French army recovered its discipline.

. . . .

Since 1914 the morale of the *poilu* had remained remarkably healthy. Admittedly, the order of mobilization had not been greeted with tremendous enthusiasm, yet most conscripts went willingly to the front. This was not necessarily because they relished the prospect of revenge for 1870; rather they believed that France had been needlessly provoked by Germany and considered that national soil should be defended against the invader. A highly developed sense of nationhood sustained their commitment, as did strict military discipline. In 1914 summary courts martial had been created with extensive powers. To the dismay of the High Command, in 1916 the authority of these courts was reduced and defendants' rights were extended. Meanwhile, senior officers resorted to their own means to keep discipline. Even Pétain employed draconian methods. In January 1915 he was confronted with 40 men, all from the same unit, who had self-inflicted wounds. As an example to others, he wanted to shoot 25 of these. Eventually he had the offenders bound and thrown into no-man's land where they remained overnight.[36]

Such displays of indiscipline were nothing compared to the mutinies which began on 17 April 1917. The disturbances reached a climax in June. Thereafter they were less frequent, but it was not until January 1918 that the problem was contained. Even then, isolated protests dragged on into the summer. The mutinies themselves took different forms. Most were a refusal to go to the front rather than a refusal to defend the line. A typical example is that of the 20th Infantry Regiment. On 29 April it was ordered to head a fresh offensive. Having already participated in the attack of 17 April, it was angry that other regiments were being kept in reserve. Accordingly, on the day the 20th was due to be embussed for the front, 300 men failed to turn up for duty. Occasionally, the mutinies were marked by violence and drunkenness. Usually, they were well-disciplined affairs. Several units emulated the Russian Soviets, electing delegates to voice their grievances. There was even talk of marching to Paris, a scheme which was quickly foiled by the military authorities.

Because of the long duration of the mutinies and the varied range of protests, it has been difficult to calculate the number of men involved. Some historians have suggested 100,000. A more realistic figure would be between 35 and 40,000. Altogether there were 250 cases of mutiny affecting 65 infantry divisions and 3 colonial divisions. In other words, nearly two-thirds of the French army had been troubled to some extent.[37]

How may the mutinies be accounted for? Needless to say the generals had their own diagnosis. Alarmed by events in Russia, they were convinced that the army's discipline had been eroded by left-wing agitators in the employ of Germany. The conviction that a revolutionary movement was afoot was strengthened by strikes on the home front and the decision of the French Socialist party to enter into talks with its German counterpart at the International Socialist Congress at Stockholm. Unquestionably some mutineers were swayed by pacifist and communist propaganda, yet it would be a mistake to believe the alarmist conclusions of GQG. The mutinies may be best characterized as strikes on the part of soldiers disillusioned with the appalling conditions in which they had to fight and angered at the strategy of their superiors. Thus the protests were not a renunciation of the war itself; rather they were a rejection of the way in which it was being conducted. This conclusion is borne out by the timing and geography of the mutinies. A majority of these broke out among infantry regiments based between Soissons and Aubérive, the sector of the April–May offensive.

Pétain's analysis of the protests displays both his strengths and weaknesses. On the one hand, his training as a professional soldier ensured that he shared the prejudices of GQG. In his reports to Painlevé and in his own account of the events of 1917, written in 1925,[38] he had little hesitation in blaming contamination from the interior. Particular scorn was directed at politicians who had criticized the strategy of the High Command. This was ironical given that Pétain had fuelled the deputies' attacks on Nivelle. Yet, as before, he regarded himself as being above politics. Now that he was Commander-in-Chief, he felt an added responsibility to defend the High Command even though he was alive to its failings. On the other hand, Pétain's sense of compassion led him to recognize that the fundamental causes of the mutinies were military in origin. The irregularity of leave, inadequate billeting, poor food, the easy availability of alcohol and the relentless demands of an offensive strategy had all contributed to a slackening of discipline.

Given his empathy for the lot of the *poilu*, there is little doubt that Pétain was the right man to quell the mutinies. Admittedly he interfered in political affairs, calling for tighter press censorship and the revocation of the passports of those socialists wishing to travel to Stockholm. For the most part, however, he concentrated on military matters. Here his initial task was to reassert discipline. He soon persuaded Painlevé to restore the courts martial. On 11 June, Pétain, as Commander-in-Chief, was empowered to grant mercy in capital cases, a right which had previously belonged to the President. Considerable controvery surrounds the number of men executed. Sometimes a figure as high as 3,000 has been suggested. One reason for this inflated total is the fact that those receiving clemency were often transferred to other regiments, thus creating the impression that they had been killed.[39] In sum, there were 554 death sentences of which only 49 were carried out.[40] Although several troops were demoted or court-martialled, overall it was a moderate purge.

It was also one mixed with compassion. In an effort to restore morale, officers were instructed to treat their men with greater respect. Pétain himself frequently visited the front. Mixing *bonhomie* with an aloofness fitting for his rank, he distributed gifts of tobacco and awarded medals for bravery and good conduct. These were the methods he had employed earlier in the war, and they consolidated his reputation as a humane general. In addition, he implemented a wide range of practical measures designed to improve conditions: leave was organized on a rational basis; rest billets were refurbished and situated away from the front; food and rations were improved. Finally, Pétain reassured his troops that in the months ahead France would adopt a defensive posture and await the arrival of the Americans. In truth, he had decided on this strategy before becoming Commander-in-Chief; even so, such a commitment helped assuage fears at the front.

Not everyone was reassured. Many on the left equated his crushing of the protests with the suppression of the working class. One such critic was Laval, then Socialist deputy for Aubervilliers in northern Paris. Later in 1945, at the time of the *épuration*, Communists called for strict justice for collaborators in retaliation for Pétain's handling of the mutineers of 1917. It is hard to believe, however, that Pétain deliberately set out to punish the working class. Although the mutinies instilled in him an exaggerated fear of Bolshevism, this charge ignores the fact that most of the protesters originated from the countryside, not from the towns.[41] Pétain's real objective in stamping out indiscipline was to re-establish his army as an efficient fighting-machine and, by the end of June, was already succeeding in his task. Had the disturbances not been so skilfully dealt with, they might well have fostered greater discontent on the home front leading to the disintegration of the French state. Thus, along with his defence of Verdun, Pétain had again saved France. After the war, he always claimed that the containment of the mutinies was his greatest achievement.

. . .

Until 1917 Pétain had had a 'good war'. His mettle had been tested on a number of occasions and rarely faltered. Now that he was Commander-in-Chief, he had to confront a series of fresh problems. In addition to ending the April offensive and containing the mutinies, he had to contend with the husbanding of resources, the formulation of new tactics, and the pursuit of a winning strategy. How did he respond to these challenges?

After the mutinies, his immediate objective was the conservation of manpower. The 'class of 1917' had been called up as early as 29 December 1915. Verdun and the Nivelle offensive had exacerbated the situation, forcing GQG to reduce the number of divisions. It had been hoped that the British army would relieve the growing pressures on the western front, yet towards the close of 1917 Haig became preoccupied with mustering troops for a fresh offensive in Flanders. Nor could France rely on assistance from the USA. It was understood that American troops would not arrive in any great numbers until 1918.

Pétain's answer to the manpower shortage was a change in tactics. Directive no. 1 of 19 May 1917 announced, 'The balance of the opposing forces on the north and north-eastern front does not permit us for the moment to envisage a breakthrough followed by strategic exploitation. It is therefore necessary to wear out the enemy with the minimum of losses.'[42] In future, there would be no wasteful offensives; instead the enemy would be ground down by a series of surprise attacks conducted on a limited scale and accompanied by heavy artillery fire. As soon as the Germans regrouped, the assaults would be aborted to save lives. New tactics required new training. Directive no. 2 thus instituted the regular rotation of troops in the line, the method employed at Verdun. Those being rested would be instructed in how to fight alongside artillery.

Pétain was enough of a realist to understand that the Germans would not stand idly by and allow themselves to be pummelled by limited offensives. He was acutely aware that, until the arrival of American troops, the enemy possessed numerical superiority and would soon be in a position to transfer resources from the eastern front in readiness for an offensive in 1918. Accordingly, it was vital to reorganize French defences. Through his Directive no. 3 of 4 July and Directive no. 4 of 20 December, the second of which followed the Bolshevik defection from the war, he articulated a policy of 'defence in depth'. This advocated that the main battle should be fought in secondary positions. The front trenches only needed to be lightly manned so as to cushion the suprise of any attack. The main defence would be conducted by the secondary lines which would be in a state of full readiness. To support the defenders, Pétain again advocated the use of artillery but also championed the use of new weapons such as aeroplanes and tanks which were at a developmental stage. Unhappy with the clumsy Schneider tanks, he placed great hopes in the lighter Renault models and requested their production in large numbers. In so doing, he has been heralded as a prophet of tank warfare.[43] This claim is exaggerated. Unlike Liddell Hart, Guderian and de Gaulle, he failed to appreciate the full offensive capacity of mobile armour; he always thought of deploying tanks in a supportive role to infantry, the part they played in the First World War. Pétain was, however, one of the first generals to recognize the industrialization of conflict. Success in battle depended on an efficient economy able to produce a steady supply of material. As already observed, he never possessed a closed peasant mentality. At the close of 1918, in one of his rare flights of fancy, he contemplated using his experience as a general to become a captain of industry running a large newspaper.[44]

New tactics paid early dividends. Limited attacks of the type Pétain envisaged were conducted at Verdun in August and La Malmaison on the Chemin des Dames ridge in October. These victories went some way in restoring morale on the home front and reducing pressure on British positions in Flanders. None the less, they were not the sort of wasting assaults Haig had wished for. Nor did they please the partisans of the offensive who still stalked the corridors of GQG. Complaints also emanated from political quarters. In November 1917 France had a new Prime Minister: the veteran Dreyfusard and staunch Republican, Georges Clemenceau. In future, government was conducted in a different way to that to which the High Command had become accustomed. Although never a dictator, 'the tiger' exerted enormous personal power and quickly asserted his ascendancy over parliament. Anxious to wage war 'in every respect', he extended his authority over the military. Intolerant of the defensive tactics pursued by Pétain, he was more impressed by the aggressive spirit displayed by Foch. Aware of the Prime Minister's displeasure, on 13 December Pétain volunteered his resignation. Scenting an opportunity to underscore his ascendancy over the generals, Clemenceau rejected this offer.

Clemenceau's reservations about his Commander-in-Chief raise a wider question of whether Pétain ever developed a strategy by which to defeat Germany. Some historians think not. They believe that he was essentially a defensive tactician with little grasp of the broader picture. It is claimed that his policy in 1917 may be summed up in his own phrase, 'I am waiting for the Americans and tanks.' Given the parlous health of the French army, this was in many respects a sensible policy. Yet, in fairness to Pétain, it should be acknowledged that he was conducting more than a waiting game. Overall, he had two long-term strategic objectives. The first was to guarantee that his army remained the dominant force among the Allies, a task made easier by his tactical changes. The second was to ensure that France played a key role in the defeat of the Central Powers so as to secure a favourable peace. Thanks to his anglophobia, he was fearful that the British, with American connivance, would conclude a settlement with Germany that ignored French interests. His fears were heightened in the second half of 1917 when Haig repeatedly refused to take charge of a greater proportion of the western front. This obstinacy largely stemmed from the need to husband troops for the forthcoming Flanders offensive, yet Pétain continued to harbour suspicions about British intentions.

To counteract the possibility of a separate 'Anglo-Saxon' peace, Pétain devised his so-called 'strategy of guarantees'.[45] This sought to gain territory which could later be employed as a bargaining counter in any future negotiations. He had his eyes on Alsace, which – along with Lorraine – did not figure in British war aims until January 1918. Alsace was considered more of a prize than the northern battlegrounds as it contained valuable economic assets. The offensive itself would not be launched until late 1918 by which time the French army would have recovered from the difficulties of 1917. This policy marked a turning point for the High Command. In the past, it had rejected a policy of guarantees, setting its sights on total victory. Although this new strategy did not rule out this possibility, it acknowledged that a decisive outcome to the war was increasingly unlikely.

Pétain did, therefore, possess a broader strategy, albeit one based on a cynical reading of British intentions. Historians are on stronger ground when they criticize his generalship in the final months of the war. Occasionally apprehensive, frequently vain and increasingly prone to pessimism, in 1918 he appeared uncertain about how best to proceed. As before, his skills lay as a tactician, not as a strategist.

The limits of his strategic sense are clearly seen in his opposition to a unified command structure. Previously, the allies had doubted the worth of a *generalissimo*. In October 1917 – with the Russians on the verge of leaving the war and the Italians suffering a heavy defeat at Caporetto – there was an obvious need for greater cooperation. At the Rapallo conference, held the following month, it was decided to establish a supreme war council, assisted by a military council under the chairmanship of Foch. However, the scope of these bodies remained vague. Clearly national susceptibilities were an important obstacle to progress. So too were personalities. If there was to be a *generalissimo* there was no doubt in Pétain's mind who this ought to be. Clemenceau had other ideas and preferred Foch instead. The ambitious Chief-of-Staff was also keen on this job, and at the beginning of 1918 began to plot to remove Pétain in much the same way as Pétain had conspired against Nivelle. Aware of this manoeuvring, the Commander-in-Chief soon discovered an ally in thwarting Foch's ambition: Haig. Despite their differences, the British general liked Pétain's businesslike manner. Such briefness of speech was, he believed, rare in a Frenchman. No doubt Haig's reasoning was also based on the realization that if there was to be a sole allied commander it would not be him. Like Clemenceau, Lloyd George was eager to assert control over his military.

In casting doubts on the wisdom of a unified command, Pétain and Haig inadvertently weakened the allied position. In February 1918 Foch proposed the creation of an inter-allied reserve of some 30 divisions under his control. Although this would have allowed him a powerful voice in the formulation of strategy, it would also have provided a much-needed bulwark against any fresh German offensive. Fearful that a unified command was being introduced through the back door, Haig and Pétain turned down this proposal. They merely agreed that the British and French armies should assist one another if the need arose.

The failure to establish greater cooperation and the absence of a general reserve created serious problems. On 21 March 1918 the German armies, bolstered by troops from the eastern front, launched a fresh offensive. The main thrust of the attack was directed at British positions between Arras and Saint Quentin, close to where the British and French sectors met. Aware that this area was under-manned and conscious of the conflicting interests of the Allies, the German intention was to 'push the two sides of the door apart'. Once the attackers had broken through, it was anticipated that the British would retreat northwards to cover the Channel ports and the French to the south-west to protect Paris. To ensure success, the Germans were counting on new offensive tactics. After initial bombardment, stormtroopers were to head the assault, bypassing en route any heavily defended positions. These would be mopped up by battle units afterwards.[46]

Although the Allies had been anticipating an offensive, it still caught them by surprise. By 23 March the southern flank of the British lines was already crumbling. More serious was the lack of understanding between Haig and Pétain. When the two men met that day, they agreed on the necessity of their armies remaining in contact. When they assembled the following evening, cooperation appeared to break down. To resolve the crisis, a high-level meeting was held at Doullens on 26 March. Here Pétain appeared on edge and drew an extremely pessimistic picture of the allied position. Hope came from Foch, who burst out, 'We must fight where we are! We must not give an inch of ground!' This was the language the British delegates had come to hear and it was agreed that the Chief-of-Staff should become the 'coordinator' of the allied armies. It was not long before he was appointed *generalissimo*. On 14 April he became 'Commander-in-Chief of the Allied Armies in France'. In future, the heads of the French, British and American armies would be concerned primarily with tactics; strategy was the province of Foch. Although each commander had the right to appeal to his government if he disagreed with a decision, Pétain was aware that Clemenceau was more likely to listen to Foch. Later this arrangement created tension when

Pétain's tactics were those more suited to the state of battle. In March 1918 Foch was the right man for the moment. By the end of the month, his careful use of reserves had already halted the enemy advance.

It is during the March events that Pétain's generalship is most open to criticism.[47] His pessimism was especially troubling. Whereas in the past his doleful nature had stemmed from his dry sense of humour and sense of realism, in 1918 he appeared to reveal a real pessimism: a tendency to fear the worst. This had been briefly glimpsed at Verdun; hereafter, it became a more central feature of his personality, prefiguring the defeatism of 1940. This despondency, along with his anger at the British, also appears to have undermined his sense of calm. Whether he was a 'commander in a funk', as Haig later claimed,[48] remains dubious, yet it is clear that Pétain had momentarily lost a sense of proportion. This had serious implications for his strategy. Already at fault for not having agreed to a unified command and for not having sufficient troops in reserve, he now seemed unwilling to assist his ally. At the meeting with the British on 26 March, Pétain argued that the main thrust of the German offensive was still to come. To fend off this attack, he was thus dispatching his troops southwestwards to defend the capital. When Haig retorted that this move would separate the allied forces and place the whole of the western front in jeopardy, Pétain replied that his government had ordered him to defend Paris. Despite the efforts of sympathetic biographers to cloud the matter,[49] it is now known that the cabinet never issued such a command. Instead Pétain was acting on his own intiative. Here his behaviour ominously foreshadows that of 1940. Mistrustful of the British and impatient of the politicians, he was prepared to place the national interest before that of the allied cause.

Because of the shortcomings displayed by Pétain in March, Foch has frequently been portrayed as the architect of the final victory over Germany. It has even been suggested, notably by members of the Resistance, that Pétain was a hindrance to that victory, all too ready to concede an armistice just as he had done with Hitler. Such views need modifying. Tactically, he remained an astute soldier and soon overcame the anxieties he had betrayed at Doullens. In May and June the Germans launched further campaigns, bringing them within reach of Paris. Wherever Foch's instructions for holding every bit of ground were heeded, French losses were heavy. Wherever Pétain's policy of 'defence-in-depth' was deployed, the attacks were withstood. Bitter recriminations followed. In June the Commander-in-Chief invoked his right to complain to his government about Foch's mistakes. In July Pétain's tactics of elastic defence again proved their worth, fending off another German attack. Strategically, however, Pétain remained overly cautious. In July he delayed the French counter-offensive. Foch was furious and the assault went ahead. Thereafter, the *generalissimo*'s aggressive spirit prevailed. Although Pétain's Directive no. 5 of 12 July laid down prudent guidelines for forthcoming operations, their timing largely depended on his superior. On 26 September Foch launched a triple offensive employing French, British and American troops. For once, cooperation among the Allies was excellent; yet progress was slow. Whether these strikes, supported by the plentiful supply of American soldiers, would have won the war in 1918 remains unclear. In the event, political and diplomatic concerns brought the Germans to the negotiating table. In October Ludendorff, aware of the vulnerability of Germany's allies, urged his government to accept President Wilson's Fourteen Points as a basis for negotiations. At the start of the following month Bulgaria, Turkey and Austria-Hungary all agreed to an armistice. On 11 November Germany followed suit.

Ironically, it was at this late stage that Pétain chose to be daring. Still fearful of Anglo-Saxon intentions, he wanted nothing less than a complete victory over Germany. Thus in October he modified his 'strategy of guarantees' and proposed a grand offensive directed at Alsace. From there, French and American troops would march into the Rhineland. Foch, however, was unwilling to deploy such a scheme and argued that an armistice was just as valuable as a victory. Pétain disagreed. Although he acknowledged that large numbers would be killed in any fresh offensive, their lives would not be sacrificed in vain. Instead, they would have secured a victory worthy of the one-and-a-half million French soldiers who had already died in the war. It was in their memory that Pétain openly wept when he heard that an armistice was to be agreed. This hard-line position towards Germany has subsequently been used to defend his role in 1940. It is suggested that if he had had his way in 1918, there would have been no renaissance of German power. While there is something in this argument, it ignores the complicated factors that led the French to the armistice table at Rethondes in June 1940.

.   .   .

It was Napoleon who remarked that every French soldier carries in his cartridge-pouch the baton of a marshal. In 1914 Pétain was no mere infantryman; yet his rise through the ranks was no less remarkable, and on 8 December 1918 Poincaré presented him with his marshal's stick. This honour was fully deserved. Although his strategic sense had often been wanting, he had displayed a tactical awareness lacking in other officers. Never entirely a man of the defensive, he had proved himself an innovative and flexible military thinker. At the same time, he had been the most compassionate of French generals, acutely aware of the needs of his troops. These many strengths had been amply demonstrated at Verdun and in his containment of the mutinies. On both occasions, he had saved his country from certain defeat. Outwardly, these achievements did not appear to have changed Pétain. Inwardly, the war had hardened many of his prejudices and personality traits. The Pétain that emerged out of the conflict harboured an intense mistrust of the British, an irrational fear of Bolshevism, a contempt for parliamentarians, a liking for politicking and a lurking pessimism. And, of course, he had developed a tremendous vanity. Behind his impassive façade, Pétain believed that he was unlike ordinary mortals.[50] The power and popularity that he enjoyed during the interwar years only hardened that conviction.

.   .   .

NOTES AND REFERENCES

1. G. Pedroncini, *Pétain. Le soldat et la gloire, 1856–1918* (Paris: Perrin, 1989), p. 39.
2. D. Stevenson, *French War Aims Against Germany, 1914–1919* (Oxford: Clarendon Press, 1982), p. 9.
3. J. Joll, *The Origins of the First World War* (London: Longman, 1984), p. 83.
4. K. Robbins, *The First World War* (Oxford: Oxford University Press, 1985), p. 30.
5. R. Griffiths, *Marshal Pétain* (London: Constable, 1970), p. 7 and Pedroncini, *Pétain. Le soldat*, p. 64.
6. A. Horne, *The Price of Glory. Verdun 1916* (London: Macmillan, 1962), p. 18.

7. J.-B. Duroselle, *La France et les français* (Paris: Editions Richelieu, 1972), p. 117.
8. This diary is discussed in Griffiths, *Pétain*, pp. 3–5.
9. R. Tournoux, *Pétain and de Gaulle* (London: Heinemann, 1966), pp. 30–1.
10. E. Fayolle, *Cahiers secrets de la grande guerre* (Paris: Plon, 1964), p. 97.
11. Passaga quoted in G. Blond, *Verdun* (London: André Deutsch, 1965), p. 38.
12. Pétain quoted in J.C. King, *Generals and Politicians. Conflict Between France's High Command, Parliament and Government, 1914–1918* (Westport, Conn.: Greenwood Press, 1951), p. 96.
13. Horne, *Price of Glory*, p. 46.
14. P. Pétain, *La bataille de Verdun* (Paris: Payot, 1929), p. 9.
15. Griffiths, *Pétain*, p. 21.
16. A. Ferry, *Les carnets secrets d'Abel Ferry, 1914–1918* (Paris: Grasset, 1957), p. 141.
17. B. Serrigny, *Trente ans avec Pétain*, (Paris: Plon, 1959), pp. 44–5.
18. H. Amouroux, *Pétain avant Vichy. La guerre et l'amour* (Paris: Fayard, 1967), pp. 139–40.
19. Horne, *Price of Glory*, p. 130.
20. Serrigny, *Trente ans*, pp. 82–3. Pétain is also credited with the other rousing battle-cry of Verdun: 'Ils ne passeront pas.' In fact, Nivelle was the originator of this phrase.
21. Horne, *Price of Glory*, p. 330.
22. Ibid., p. 308.
23. M. Ferro, *The Great War, 1914–1918* (London: Routledge & Kegan Paul, 1973), p. 77.
24. Pétain, *Verdun*, p. 79.
25. Serrigny, *Trente ans*, p. 82.
26. Griffiths, *Pétain*, p. 32.
27. Fayolle, *Cahiers secrets*, p. 197.
28. Griffiths, *Pétain*, p. 35.
29. Ibid., p. 36.
30. P. Painlevé, *Comment j'ai nommé Foch et Pétain. La politique de guerre de 1917. Le commandement unique interallié* (Paris: Librairie Félix Alcan, 1932), pp. 48–50 and A. Ribot, *Journal d'Alexandre Ribot et correspondances inédites, 1914–1922* (Paris: Plon, 1936), p. 76.
31. Griffiths, *Pétain*, p. 37.
32. Painlevé, *Comment j'ai nommé Foch et Pétain*, pp. 38–54.
33. Griffiths, *Pétain*, p. 38.
34. Ibid., p. 40.
35. A. Clayton, 'Robert Nivelle and the French Spring Offensive of 1917', in B. Bond (ed.), *Fallen Stars. Eleven Studies of Twentieth-Century Military Disasters* (London: Brassey's, 1991), p. 63.
36. Fayolle, *Cahiers secrets*, p. 79.

37. Ferro, *The Great War*, p. 183. For a full breakdown of the numbers of mutineers, see G. Pedroncini, *Les mutineries de 1917* (Paris: Presses Universitaires de France, 1967), pp. 53–100.
38. Contained in E. Spears, *Two Men who Saved France* (London: Eyre & Spottiswoode, 1955).
39. Ferro, *The Great War*, pp. 183–4. For a full breakdown on sentencing, see Pedroncini, *Les mutineries*, pp. 181–278.
40. G. Pedroncini, 'L'armée française et la grande guerre', in *Histoire militaire de la France*, vol. 3 (Paris: Presses Universitaires de France, 1992), p. 184.
41. Pedroncini, *Les mutineries*, p. 204.
42. Pétain quoted in Griffiths, *Pétain*, p. 49.
43. G. Pedroncini, *Pétain. Général en chef, 1917–1918* (Paris: Presses Universitaires de France, 1974), p. 189. See too Pedroncini, 'L'armée française', p. 177.
44. J. de Pierrefeu, *GQG. Secteur 1. Edition définitive revue et augmentée*, vol. 1 (Paris: Les Editions G. Crès et Cie, 1922), p. 221.
45. P. Bernard and H. Dubief, *The Decline of the Third Republic, 1914–1918* (Cambridge: Cambridge University Press, 1985), p. 66–7.
46. Griffiths, *Pétain*, p. 64.
47. See the discussion in ibid., pp. 72–5.
48. D. Haig, *The Private Papers of Douglas Haig, 1914–1919* (London: Eyre & Spottiswoode, 1952), p. 298.
49. G. Blond, *Pétain* (Paris: Presses de la Cité, 1965) pp. 120–5. See too Griffiths, *Pétain*, p. 73.
50. Griffiths, *Pétain*, p. 88.

Chapter 3

THE MARSHAL, 1919–39

In 1920 Pétain again toyed with the idea of retirement. Now married, he settled at *L'Ermitage*, the country house that he had bought in the south of France. There he enjoyed playing, perhaps too self-consciously, the role of the simple peasant, rearing chickens and cultivating his own wine. He remained, however, hungry for power and was usually to be found in Paris. Between 1920 and 1931 he sat on all the key military committees; in 1925 he returned to active service when he fought in the Rif; in 1931 he was elected to the Académie Française; and in 1934 he briefly served as Minister of War. Thereafter a number of newspapers spoke of him as a future head of government. Although he distanced himself from these campaigns, his appetite for office had not diminished, and in March 1939 he accepted the ambassadorship to Spain.

Why was Pétain entrusted with such power? One reason is that government came to regard him as the most trustworthy member of the High Command. Given his incautious remarks to Poincaré and others, this confidence might seem strange. Yet, unlike Foch, Pétain kept his tongue during the armistice talks and subsequent peace negotiations, and refrained from criticizing Clemenceau. Unlike de Castelnau, Pétain was not a militant Catholic. Unlike Franchet d'Esperey, Pétain did not associate with the extreme right. Accordingly, even the left came to view the 'Victor of Verdun' as a 'Republican general'. While deploring his appointment to the ambassadorship to Spain, Léon Blum described him as, 'The most noble, the most humane of our military commanders'.[1] The silent Pétain did little to puncture these illusions, rarely commenting on political affairs. Inwardly, however, the old soldier retained his contempt for parliamentary democracy.

A more important reason why Pétain was granted power is to be found in the aura surrounding marshalship. At no other point in French history has this rank carried such weight. Before 1914, the post had imperial and royalist connotations; the last holders of it had been Bazaine and MacMahon, neither of them a good Republican.[2] In 1916 the position was revived, but only as a method of removing Joffre. After 1945, the office was tarnished by the activities of its most recent holder and was overshadowed by the prestige surrounding a two-star general.[3] In 1918, marshalship was associated with the glory of victory. The holders – Foch, Pétain, Lyautey, Franchet d'Esperey, Fayolle and Joffre – were all associated with that triumph. Unaware of the sharp rivalries which existed among these men, the public looked on each general as worthy of praise.[4] It was, however, Pétain who received the greatest acclaim. His name remained firmly linked with Verdun, the most powerful symbol of French courage during the war. The fact that in 1934 he and Franchet d'Esperey were the only marshals left alive merely intensified Pétain's standing as a great patriot.

Given the authority of marshalship in interwar France, it is already becoming clear why the French turned to Pétain in 1940. It may also be seen that the office of marshal was more important than the man himself. Consequently, Pétain was entrusted with jobs which lay outside his experience. Confident in his own abilities, this did not trouble him. Yet before long his shortcomings were exposed. Even in the military sphere, where his expertise was greatest, his skills were found wanting.

. . .

Between the two world wars, Pétain played a key role in the formulation of French military policy. On balance, however, his influence was greatest in the 1920s. Commander-in-Chief until demobilization in January 1920, for the next 11 years he served as vice-president of the Conseil Supérieur de la Guerre (CSG). Comprising the élite of the High Command, this prestigious body advised the Minister of War on issues relating to army organization, troop instruction and deployment of new weaponry.[5] Apart from the Minister, it was Pétain who carried the most weight. As vice-president he was the senior military figure on the council and Commander-in-Chief designate of French forces in time of war. In time of peace, control of the army was entrusted to the Chief of the General Staff, who also sat on the CSG. This division of authority did not mean a diminution of Pétain's powers. Anything but. During the 1920s the Chiefs of the General Staff – Buat (1920–3) and Debeney (1923–30) – were the marshal's former subordinates and were happy to comply with his wishes. It was prudent to do so. From 1922 to 1931, Pétain was Inspector-General of the Army. This post entitled him to veto decisions of the Chief of the General Staff and gave him an advisory role on the Conseil Supérieur de la Défense Nationale (CSDN), a political body concerned with a wide range of military matters.

In 1931 Pétain again thought of retirement and resigned his many posts. Yet that same year he accepted the minor office of Inspector-General of Aerial Defence of the Territory. Many observers were puzzled that a marshal of France was prepared to take on such a lowly position. This was testimony that, at the age of 75, Pétain could not relinquish the reins of power. Frustrated in his new job, he was soon working to extend his authority. Power was restored unexpectedly in February 1934 when he became Minister of War in the Doumergue government. Although this cabinet collapsed six months later, Pétain's brief ministerial career enabled him to recover something of the influence he had wielded in the 1920s. From 1934 to 1940 he sat on both the CSG and the CSDN, and attended meetings of the newly created Haut-Comité Militaire, charged with the coordination of national defence.

Not surprisingly, Pétain employed his authority to advance a predominantly defensive strategy. This was outlined in the elaborately named *Instruction provisoire sur la conduite des grandes unités* (Provisional Instruction on the Utilisation of Larger Units) of 1921. Despite its title, this document was far from temporary and remained official army doctrine until 1935 when General Gamelin, appointed *generalissimo* that year, conducted an overhaul of French military policy. Written by General Debeney, the crisp and simple style of the *Instruction* bears the hallmark of Pétain's editorship and provides a faithful exposition of the marshal's opinions. Drawing on the experiences of the First World War, it underscored the dangers of trying to pierce a continuous front.[6] The development of machine guns and barbed wire made such a breakthrough unlikely. Thus an offensive should only be contemplated when the attackers possessed sufficient fire-power. Even then, the assault needed to be restricted in its objectives. To support such limited operations, Pétain did ascribe a role to new weapons but, as will be seen, failed to grasp their full potential. The main fighting would be conducted by the infantry, supported by artillery.

Given the experiences of the First World War, these ideas carried a lot of weight in the early 1920s. Implicit in the *Instruction* was the recognition that in the early months of a war with Germany, France would be at a disadvantage in terms of troop numbers and industrial capacity. Accordingly, in the west the French needed to adopt a defensive posture and not risk a full-scale offensive. Meanwhile, their allies in central and eastern Europe – the fledgling democracies created by the Versailles settlement – would engage the enemy in a two-front war. Squeezed on both sides, Germany would be forced into a long conflict in which its economy would be undermined by blockade and outmatched in production. Only when the enemy was completely exhausted would France risk an out-and-out offensive.[7]

By the early 1930s such thinking was desperately in need of an overhaul. Not only had developments in weapon technology called into question the passivity of the tactics to be employed, doubts were also expressed over whether such a strategy would enable France to assist its eastern allies should they be attacked directly by Germany. It might be thought that Pétain was the ideal candidate to conduct that review. Before 1918 he had been a flexible military thinker, critical of the instransigence of his superiors. During the interwar years he appeared to have forgotten Napoleon's maxim that tactics change every ten years. Why was he so obstinate in his views?

Naturally enough, Pétain's supporters deny this charge. They have scoured each one of his post-1918 speeches for signs of his adaptability. The very ingenuity of their attempts belies the desperate nature of their quest.[8] Even a cursory analysis of Pétain's writings strengthens the impression of a man no longer receptive to new ideas. In 1939 he provided the preface for General Chauvineau's book, *Une invasion est-elle encore possible?* Recalling the losses of 1914–18, the marshal repeated his warnings about a war of movement.[9] Here lies the real reason why he had become so inflexible: the terrible experiences of the First World War. Anxious to avoid the casualties that characterized that conflict, he drew on the past to provide policy for the future; and, given his vanity, it is no surprise that he looked to his achievements, especially the victory at Verdun. Like the bones of those unfortunate soldiers buried for ever in the rubble of the underground fortress of Douaumont, the lessons of his own triumphs had become encrusted deep in his mind where they lay undisturbed by advances in modern warfare.

How did such such thinking affect France's preparation for war? The most obvious way was the erection of the Maginot Line, a system of fortification along the Franco-German frontier. Ever since the days of the barbarians, France's eastern frontier had been vulnerable to attack. With the development of the railway, the Germans had shown in 1870 and 1914 that they could reach France's industrial heartlands within weeks.[10] Thus in 1918 there was general agreement on the need for some kind of permanent defensive system. Its exact form remained uncertain until Pétain pointed the way forward. At Verdun he had been impressed by the defensive capacities of underground positions. Now he championed the construction of more sophisticated forts. Accordingly, the CSG pondered the lessons of Verdun as it discussed the merits of Pétain's ideas. For much of the 1920s these arguments remained academic as there was no money available for such an expensive venture. It was only in 1930 that the National Assembly voted the necessary credits and the Maginot Line, named after the then Minister of War, was begun. Strictly speaking the wall was not a continuous front, as Pétain had originally wanted, but a series of fortified regions which permitted the tactical deployment of troops.

Today, the rusting towers of this once-great line of fortifications have become a potent symbol of the flawed thinking of the French High Command before 1940. Undoubtedly the huge expense of these concrete defences consumed precious monies needed for new equipment. Yet the criticisms levelled at the Maginot Line have not been always justified. Certainly Pétain should not be made the scapegoat for all of its failings. His decision not to extend the fortifications along the Belgian frontier – notably along the Ardennes, which he once described as 'impenetrable' – has been especially questioned. For some historians, this was the mortal defect of the Line. If there was to be a defensive wall, why not make it complete?[11] After all, in 1940 Belgium was the German invasion route. In Pétain's defence, it should be noted that he was not the only person to oppose the Line's extension. Nearly everyone agreed on this. This consensus was due to a series of factors: the financial costs involved; the unsuitability of the watery Belgian terrain for such earth-works; and, most importantly, the Franco-Belgian alliance.[12] To have fortified the Belgian frontier would have created the impression that France was ready to sacrifice its ally. It should also be noted that Pétain did not intend the Belgian frontier to be left unmanned. While he considered that the Ardennes was an unlikely battleground, he still believed that it needed adequate defences.

In many ways, then, there is much to be said in support of the much-maligned Maginot Line. Its objectives were perfectly sensible. Unless the Germans entered Belgium, they had to confront an enormous physical barrier which safeguarded French troops and territory. This hindrance also constituted a shield behind which France could mobilize in its own time. The real problem lay not with the Line itself but with the defensive and passive mentality it encouraged.[13] Protected by concrete and steel fortresses, the French army felt little need to experiment with up-to-date weaponry. Thus Pétain's defensive philosophy had not only buttressed France's eastern frontier; it had also erected an obstacle in the way of adopting new machinery, particularly tanks and aircraft.

To be fair to Pétain, few military thinkers of the early 1920s recognized the future importance of tanks. During the First World War, these lumbering giants had not been effective fighting-machines. The French had deployed the lightly armoured Renault F.T. model. Exceptionally slow, this proved incapable of surmounting concrete obstacles. Its main use had been in support of infantry. This, then, was the role which Pétain ascribed to tanks in his *Instruction* of 1921. Elsewhere, different views were beginning to emerge. The British officer Captain Liddell Hart was one of the first tacticians to suggest that offensives should be led by dense concentrations of highly mobile and heavily armoured tanks. Once such tanks had broken through the weakest sections of enemy lines, they would create further holes by attacking the rear of the enemy's defences. In France, General Estienne, Director of Tank Studies from 1921 to 1926, was thinking along similar lines. Yet it was not until the publication of Colonel de Gaulle's *Vers l'armée de métier* (Towards a Professional Army) in 1934 that the debate over tank warfare came to a head in France. He advocated the creation of a professional army of some 100,000 men and 3,000 tanks organized in motorized divisions.[14] In truth, the author only partly understood the full attacking capabilities of motorized armour, but his views were no less remarkable for this.

With his eyes fixed firmly on the past, Pétain was unimpressed by such ideas. Certainly he was not taken with the theories of de Gaulle. Here his opposition was based as much on personal grounds as it was on tactical considerations. This marks a curious turnaround of events. Initially, the colonel had been a *protégé* of Pétain; he had served under him in 1912 and at Verdun. In the 1920s, the young officer was appointed to the marshal's general staff. Maybe Pétain recognized something of his old rebellious self in de Gaulle. In the 1930s, however, they were to quarrel over a literary matter. For a long time Pétain had been planning a book on the French soldier through the ages. As was his custom, staff writers were employed to produce the work and de Gaulle undertook a number of chapters. To everyone's surprise, he then requested that his contribution should be acknowledged, although Pétain would still be credited as the main author. The marshal was furious; none of his staff writers had made such a demand in the past.[15] So the book was abandoned and confined to a drawer. It resurfaced in 1936 when de Gaulle was commissioned to publish a study provisionally entitled, *L'homme sous les armes* (Men Under Arms). Unable to find time to compose anything new, he redrafted the chapters he had originally done for Pétain. Furious that a piece of staff work was about to appear in de Gaulle's name, Pétain initially forbade publication, but relented on the condition that it included a dedication, written by himself, alluding to his own part in writing the book. A dedication did indeed appear, yet one drafted by de Gaulle.[16] The ensuing argument marked the end of their friendship and prefigured the hatred that would characterize their relations during the Second World War.

None the less, Pétain alone was not responsible for obstructing the implementation of de Gaulle's views. The colonel's arrogant manner and outspoken opinions had ruffled the conservative feathers of other senior officers. He had also aroused political suspicions. Although he had a champion in the centrist politician Paul Reynaud, several deputies expressed reservations about the right-wing sympathies of the officer class and feared that a professional army might be a threat to internal liberties. Aware of the sensibilities of the politicians and the backward-looking position of the CSG, it was Gamelin who prepared the way for the wide-scale adoption of mobile armour. By 1939 France possessed large quantities of good-quality tanks, in particular the highly acclaimed Char B. The problem was that, for the most part, these machines were scattered among infantry divisions and not concentrated in dense units.

A similar process of muddled thinking affected the development of French air-power. Here, Pétain displayed more of an open mind than he had done in respect to tanks.[17] After all, in the First World War he had taken flying lessons, and in 1925 flew to the Rif in an open cockpit, suffering terrible sunburn to his nose as a result![18] Tactically, however, he continued to regard aeroplanes as an appendage to the infantry, and remained impervious to developments in aircraft design. Thus he opposed moves for the creation of an independent airforce. Eventually, in 1928, political pressure led to a Ministry of Air. Pétain had reservations about this new department of state but drew reassurance from the fact that, for operational purposes, aircraft remained under the control of the army and navy. It was not long, however, before the Ministry of Air declared a wish to organize its fighters and bombers into an independent unit. As General-Inspector of Aerial Defence of the Territories (1931–3), Pétain did his best to obstruct this development. In his view, the airforce should remain a subsidiary arm of the French forces under the strict supervision of the newly created Ministry of Defence. In the event, an autonomous airforce was established in 1933. This was ably supported by Pierre Cot, Minister of Air in 1933 and 1936. He set ambitious production targets for new planes and, during the Popular Front, oversaw the nationalization of the air industry. None the less, in 1939 there was no disguising the fact that the French airforce was inferior to its German counterpart and was missing a coherent tactical doctrine. Clearly Pétain cannot be blamed for all of these deficiencies. Others too, notably de Gaulle, failed to see the role which aircraft would play in the future. None the less, throughout the interwar years, Pétain had deployed his considerable skills as a politicker to obstruct the development of an independent air arm capable of undertaking offensive action.

In view of the marshal's unwillingness, indeed inability, to grasp the changes in modern warfare, it is little surprise that he placed most emphasis on the infantry and armaments. Here, he struggled to make his influence felt. During the 1920s, public pressure and budgetary requirements ensured that the period of national service was steadily reduced. In 1918 it stood at three years; in 1921 it was cut to two years; in 1923 it was limited to 18 months; in 1928 it fell to one year. Pétain, who valued conscription as a means of inculcating traditional French values among the young, was aghast and, in an influential article of 1 March 1935 for the right-wing journal *La Revue des Deux Mondes*, warned against further curtailments.[19] His intervention succeeded in sparking a national debate which led later that year to the restoration of a two-year period of service. Pétain also spoke out against cuts in arms spending although, ironically, he himself had contributed to this problem by initiating the Maginot Line, which devoured monies needed elsehere. It is also ironic that when he became Minister of War in 1934 he invoked the principle of collective cabinet responsibility and refused to increase arms expenditure. Eventually, in 1936, France did undertake a massive rearmament programme but this was largely due to the German remilitarization of the Rhineland and owed little to Pétain's forebodings.

Any discussion of Pétain's contribution to military policy during the interwar years must reach some overall assessment of his contribution to French readinesss for war in 1940. Often he is made the scapegoat for all that was wrong-headed with strategic and tactical thinking during this period. He should not shoulder the blame alone. The majority of the High Command supported his defensive philosophy. When in 1931 Weygand became vice-president of the CSG he did not question the ideas of his predecessor. None the less, it is Pétain who bears much of the responsibility for French shortcomings. After all, it was he who wielded the greatest influence over policy. In so doing, he remained obsessed with the lessons of his own achievements and seemingly oblivious to developments in tanks and planes. Consequently, he prepared France for a war it had already fought. In 1935 Gamelin attempted to repair this damage. His efforts came too late in the day and failed to break sufficiently wih the past. For Pétain they went too far. In 1940 he would have no hesitation in blaming others for his own mistakes.

. . . .

During the interwar years, Pétain not only shaped military policy; he also took on an active command when fighting in the Rif War of 1925–6. Before then, he had displayed contempt towards colonial ventures and had not sought to advance his career by serving overseas. Now he was only too eager to travel to North Africa even though this involved usurping the authority of Marshal Lyautey, the veteran colonial soldier who occupied the political and military post of Resident-General of Morocco. For some observers, Pétain's involvement was an indication of the lengths to which he was prepared to go in order to exercise power. De Gaulle, for example, charted his senile ambition from that date.[20] The Rif was significant for Pétain in two other respects, reaffirming his military beliefs and hardening his political prejudices.

The long-term origins of the Rif are located in the imperialistic struggle for control in Africa.[21] By the 1890s, colonial competition had brought the European powers to Morocco. Here, in 1912, France outmanoeuvred its rivals by forcing the Sultan to accept a French protectorate over his lands. Acknowledging that Madrid had interests in the region, France consented to a Spanish sub-protectorate in the northern part of the country. Intent on conquering this area rather than colonizing it, Spanish troops advanced deeper into the hinterland, brutally suppressing the indigenous population. By 1920 they had reached the foothills of the Rif mountains, home of the fiercely independent Berber tribes led by Abd el-Krim, a former journalist and brilliant guerrilla leader. Open warfare ensued and in 1921 the tribesmen routed the Spanish at Anual. This was one of the worst defeats a European army has suffered at the hands of Muslims. Some argue that it precipitated the fall of the Spanish monarchy and hastened the arrival of Primo de Rivera's dictatorship. Whatever the case, this was a new type of colonial rebellion. Neither a localized revolt nor a 'holy war', it was a battle for independence from imperial rule.[22]

Paris was troubled by these developments. If Abd el-Krim's influence was allowed to spread, it might well damage French suzerainty in Morocco and perhaps in Algeria and Tunis as well. The fears of the Colonial Office were heightened in 1921 when the Spanish retreated to the coastal towns, leaving the border between the Franco-Spanish protectorates in an exposed position. How, then, to respond? Preferring to avoid force, Lyautey tried to conciliate the rebels by offering them greater autonomy in their own affairs. Abd el-Krim was unimpressed. He desired nothing less than an independent Rif Republic. Paris was also unhappy with Lyautey's methods. It wanted an all-out victory over the tribesmen. To this end, in July 1925 the cabinet opened negotiations with Madrid over possible joint action and sent Pétain to Africa on a fact-finding mission.

Given that Pétain's position as vice-president of the CSG made him ultimately responsible for troops in the field, this trip to Morocco was entirely reasonable. Lyautey himself welcomed the presence of the 'Victor of Verdun' as he believed it would bolster morale and guarantee extra reinforcements. The Resident-General had not bargained on his visitor's arrogance and skills as a politician. Dismissive of Lyautey's tactics, Pétain called for a Franco-Spanish operation to annihilate rebel forces and began negotiations with Primo de Rivera. Once back in Paris, he advocated the same methods and worked behind the scenes to undermine confidence in his fellow marshal.

Pétain has subsequently been blamed for Lyautey's eventual dismissal. This is not entirely fair. Lyautey may well himself have been looking for an opportunity to stand down, although not in the manner that eventually came to pass.[23] It should also be noted that politicians in Paris, tired of the Resident-General's dogged independence and aristocratic views, were anxious to replace this veteran colonial soldier. Pétain merely hurried their intentions along. On 4 August the cabinet approved Pétain's plans for Franco-Spanish cooperation and placed him in charge of military operations in Morocco. In mid-August the French press ran a story, clearly from official sources, suggesting that the Resident-General would soon be quitting his post on health grounds. This was news to Lyautey. On 3 September Pétain was given sole command of French troops in Morocco; he was no longer answerable to the Resident-General. Feeling betrayed, Lyautey resigned the following month.

Pétain was now free to implement his schemes for Franco-Spanish military action. Drawing on tried and trusted techniques, French troops launched a series of limited offensives supported by heavy artillery. Tanks and planes were used, but only in support of infantry. These tactics saved French lives, but won little ground. Greater success was enjoyed by the Spanish army which, under the skilful leadership of young officers such as Colonel Franco, employed the methods of guerrilla warfare. A quick victory remained elusive, however. It was not until May 1926 that Abd el-Krim, confronted with overwhelming odds, conceded defeat and the French and Spanish partitions were restored.

Naturally enough, this victory reinforced Pétain's military ideas and bolstered his self-confidence. It also hardened his political prejudices, especially his fears about Bolshevism. He was angered that on the home front members of the French Communist party had openly sided with the Rifians.[24] Ironically, one of Abd el-Krim's staunchest supporters was Jacques Doriot, who was later to found the overtly fascist Parti Populaire Français (PPF).[25] Much to Pétain's embarrassment, during the Occupation Doriot declared himself a 'man of the marshal'. More importantly, the Rif brought Pétain into contact with a military dictatorship. He liked what he saw. In his view, Primo de Rivera had rescued his country from disorder and had restored patriotic values. The two men soon developed a respect for one another. In 1925 Primo de Rivera invited Pétain to Madrid in order to award him the Spanish Military Medal, the country's highest military honour. When in 1930 Primo de Rivera was overthrown, Pétain had no hesitation in welcoming the former dictator to Paris. In 1936 Spain was governed by another dictator and another veteran of the Rif campaign, General Franco. He too had impressed Pétain. Although the marshal had no intention of emulating his Spanish counterparts, he was clearly developing a political philosophy and ambition of his own.

. . .

It will be recalled that in 1914 Pétain already possessed a firm canon of beliefs. The First World War strengthened these. Occasionally his philosophy has been described as 'fascist'. This was not the case. He never sought inspiration from those fascist writers and politicians who were beginning to emerge in France. Nor did he look abroad. While he was impressed by Primo de Rivera's dictatorship, neither Fascist Italy nor Nazi Germany provided him with a plan of action. Indeed, it is doubtful whether Pétain ever comprehended the dynamics of Nazism, even during the Occupation itself. In his many pre-war meetings with German military figures, he seemed incapable of differentiating between committed ideologues, such as Göring, and professional soldiers, such as General Beck. They were all comrades-in-arms.[26] As to Hitler himself, Pétain remained convinced that the Führer was merely one of a long line of bellicose German leaders, a view quickly reaffirmed by the remilitarization of the Rhineland in March 1936.

Unwilling to draw inspiration from fascists at home and abroad, Pétain's political ideology remained that of a traditional French right whose opinions had been most ably represented by such writers as Barrès and Maurras at the turn of the century. This is not to say that he was an ideologue avidly digesting the views of the Action Française. Du Moulin de Labarthète, head of Pétain's *cabinet civil* at Vichy, doubted whether the old soldier had ever read more than 20 pages of Maurras.[27] Rather Pétain's sympathy for Maurrasian values stemmed from his peasant origins, his respect for Catholicism and, most importantly, his military training. Consequently, there was little original in what he had to say. His beliefs were similar to those of several military men of his generation.[28] Nor was the message very complicated. Yet, in the interwar years, his pre-eminence as a marshal ensured that it received a wide hearing. It also struck a resonant chord with many on the traditional right who believed conservative values were being subverted by modern society. Pétain, of course, was flattered by this attention, and in his speeches, articles and occasional interviews articulated a political and social doctrine that would find further expression in Vichy's National Revolution.

At the core of Pétain's thinking lay a devotion to France. His was a corporatist vision of nation which believed that the country was a living community made up of several organic parts. Of these, the institution of the family occupied a key role. As he remarked in September 1940, 'the family is the essential cell; it is the very seat of the social edifice; it is on the family that one must build; if it weakens, all is lost; when it holds firm, all can be saved.'[29] Alongside the family stood a further element which bound the nation together: the workplace. In this respect, his eyes were fixed not so much on the factory shopfloor, but on the fields of the countryside. In a speech of 1936, delivered before the war memorial at the little village of Capoulet-Junac deep in the heart of rural Ariège, Pétain evoked an idealized vision of peasant life. Although conditions were tough, the soil instilled in the *paysan* an attachment to the land.[30] Here was another component which contributed to a sense of national belonging: the love of one's native province. This sentiment, together with his view of the family, might seem strange coming from a childless *roué* who preferred Paris and the Alpes-Maritimes to his birthplace of the Pas-de-Calais. Characteristically, the marshal himself saw nothing contradictory in his behaviour.

These, then, were the uncomplicated values that Pétain held dear: the nation; the workplace; the family; the soil. Already it is possible to see the origins of Vichy's triptych of *travail, famille, patrie* (Work, Family, Fatherland). It has also been suggested that the word *ordre* could have been added to this slogan.[31] Certainly Pétain felt his vision of society was under threat. The enemy appeared in several guises: communism; individualism; intellectualism; internationalism; liberalism; materialism; pacifism; parliamentarianism; and socialism. Left to their own devices, these forces would tear the nation apart and place the external safety of France at risk. Thus Pétain came to believe that he was continuing the struggle against internal subversion he had first begun when quelling the mutinies in 1917.

Worried at the prospect of domestic discord, Pétain looked to a number of agencies to safeguard the moral health and internal discipline of the nation. First, it was incumbent on individuals to display a sense of commitment to their country. Like the *poilus* who had endured the hardships of the trenches, people needed to turn their backs on material enjoyment. This was a theme to which he would return in 1940 when, in a speech of 20 June, he claimed that since 1918 the 'spirit of pleasure' had overwhelmed the 'spirit of sacrifice'.[32] Discipline, however, had to be taught. Hence he laid great stress on schooling. In 1934, at the time of the Doumergue government, he even offered to take over the Education portfolio. At Vichy he also took a keen interest in the young. In his view, the school needed to dispense a general education which trained the body as well as the mind. Under the Third Republic, teachers had been failing in this task. By placing too much stress on a narrow intellectual formation, they had encouraged an unbridled egoism which had diluted traditional values. It was fortunate, therefore, that Catholic schools had retained a foothold in France. Although Pétain himself still had no personal need for religion, he retained a faith in Catholicism as the most effective of social cements.

Given his emphasis on order, it is no surprise that Pétain also looked to the army to maintain the morale of the country. In common with other leading soldiers, he considered that this body was the supreme repository of national values. As such, it had a social and educational role to fulfil. Writing in 1934 he proclaimed that for the conscript the military should be the last stage of education as the army itself was 'a school of tradition, honour and high moral training'.[33] Little wonder he was against any reduction in national service. Nor is it a surprise that he believed the army should be non-political, free from the ideological fissures which kept the nation apart. It was with this aim in mind that he worked in 1937 to prevent serving soldiers from receiving the vote. Yet by 'non-political' it is clear that Pétain believed conscripts should be shielded from the influence of the left.[34] His experience of the mutinies and the stinging criticisms of Doriot during the Rif war had made him all the more determined to halt communist subversion among the ranks. As will be seen, this fear led him to tolerate the existence of extreme right-wing organizations within the army: the Cagoule and the Corvignolles.

Ultimately, Pétain believed that responsibility for the upkeep of a nation's discipline rested with government. In his opinion, liberal democracy had failed France in this task. His dislike of parliamentarianism was, of course, nothing new. It had been cultivated at Saint Cyr and had ripened in the trenches. During the interwar years his distaste for political life became more intense. With Verdun firmly in mind, he considered that victory in 1918 had been bought at the expense of millions of young lives. In honour of this sacrifice, it was necessary to infuse into political life the values which the troops had displayed in the trenches. This had not happened. The deputies had reverted to type, placing self and party before country. Not even Poincaré, who returned as Prime Minister between 1926 and 1929, or the Doumergue government of 1934, in which Pétain himself had served, had been able to halt this trend.

Pétain was thus convinced that France required firm direction; yet, in championing a more authoritarian form of government, he stopped short of advocating dictatorship. Nor did he advocate the abolition of the Republic. Shortly before the defeat of 1940, he admitted in a letter to his American friend, Madame Pardee, that, 'the best form of government would be the Republic, if all men were wise'.[35] By this, the marshal had in mind the creation of a strong regime under the control of a leader who would embody the powers of the executive. Thus his concept of a Republic owed little to the democratic ideals of a revolutionary tradition; instead, it drew inspiration from the military sphere. As he informed Senator Lémery, government was like an army command: 'One leader at the head with capable ministers. When that no longer works, they are replaced. But only one leader. The powers of the chief of state and head of government must be merged.'[36]

Others, too, wanted to see an overhaul of the 'regime of parties' and thought Pétain the right man for the job. From 1934 a number of forces – the press, extra-parliamentary organizations and even some Republican politicians – urged him to take charge of government. In an uncertain world of economic depression and international instability, he seemed the best cure for the nation's ills. Significantly, many newspapers compared him to Joan of Arc, a popular figure of national unity in the 1930s. Not only had she boosted France's international standing, she had also quelled domestic discord. Such editorials calling on Pétain to serve his country made unlikely divine voices, but there is no doubt the old man was listening to what they were saying and was flattered by the comparisons being drawn. Seemingly, he had forgotten an earlier disparaging comment he had made about *la pucelle*. In 1929, when accompanying Poincaré and Doumergue to a ceremony celebrating the Maid of Orléans, he quipped that he cared little for Joan: 'the least of my *poilus* did a hundred times as much'.[37]

What, then, was the extent of Pétain's political involvement? Was he, as the prosecution alleged in 1945, the inveterate schemer always on the look-out for power? Or was he, as the defence maintained, the disinterested patriot anxious to serve his country? Neither portait is entirely accurate; yet both contain a grain of truth.

. . .

Pétain's first political post was, of course, the War portfolio in the Doumergue government of 9 February 1934. This 'cabinet of national union' was formed to fend off the sense of crisis which was then overtaking the country. Exploiting the general sense of unease created by the onset of the Great Depression, the extreme right used revelations that the Radical party had connections with a small-time crook, Serge Stavisky, to denounce the corruption of parliamentarianism. Typically the government mishandled the situation; and on 6 February members of the right-wing leagues, which had grown up in France during the late 1920s, protested on the streets of Paris. Occasionally, older histories present these demonstrations as an attempted *putsch*. This was far from the case. Most of the leagues involved – the Croix de Feu, the Solidarité Française, the Faisceau and Francisme – were veterans' organizations. Admittedly they borrowed the uniforms and insignia of Fascist Italy, but their political message remained jumbled. It was perhaps not until

1936 and the founding of Doriot's PPF that France could boast an indigenous fascism. Whatever the case, it is clear that on 6 February 1934 the leagues did not possess a blueprint for the take-over of power. It is commonly remarked that most protestors were concerned with catching the last *métro* home, not with toppling the regime.[38]

Pétain's attitude to the events of 6 February was ambivalent, leading to suggestions that he approved of the riots. The fact that several prominent Vichyites and collaborators were among the demonstrators has lent credence to these claims. Undoubtedly, the marshal felt some sympathy towards the leagues. He shared in their dislike of parliamentarianism and was struck by the fact that several of their members were former soldiers who had probably served under him at Verdun. On 13 February he made a point of visiting the injured in hospital where he spoke not only to police wounded but to rioters themselves, notably Georges Lebecq, head of the Union Nationale des Combattants. Later, in May 1936, in a rare newspaper interview primarily designed to dissuade people from voting for the Popular Front, he remarked that Colonel de la Rocque's Croix de Feu, the largest of the leagues, represented one of the healthiest elements in the country. None the less, such evidence does not mean that Pétain approved of the methods or even the policies of these organizations. While he shared some of their concerns, he retained a profound respect for civilian authority and disliked brawling in the street. Thus he took no part in the riots. The only senior military figure who had links with the protests was Lyautey, who foolishly believed that he could unite the leagues under his leadership. Even he had the good sense to be seen dining elsewhere on the evening of 6 February.

Pétain also kept a low profile in the discussions leading to the formation of the Doumergue cabinet. Although he dearly wanted office, his soldier's dislike for politics meant that he could not advertise his desire. Instead, he had to be 'called upon'. On taking up his appointment, he proudly declared, 'The President has told me that the country has need of me. I have not avoided this duty, but I have never made politics and I do not wish to do so now.'[39] To be fair, once in cabinet he stuck to military matters and refrained from wheeler-dealing. Politicking was left to the parliamentarians – Laval, Tardieu, Herriot and Flandin – who fronted the key ministries. In meetings, Pétain adopted an aloof air; his caustic interjections punctuated the animated debates, thus underscoring his contempt for political life. This dislike grew as the ministry battled for survival. In November 1934 Herriot and eight other Radical ministers resigned, worried about Doumergue's proposals for the strengthening of the executive wing of government. Pétain, a supporter of these reforms, was furious and suggested that the cabinet should remain in office with everyone doubling up their ministries. In addition to War, he volunteered to take over Education. Clearly such a solution would have been unacceptable to parliament and the cabinet duly collapsed. This left a bitter aftertaste in Pétain's mouth and reinforced his worst impressions about parliamentary practice. To emphasize his disgust, he refused a post in the ministry put together by Pierre-Etienne Flandin, Doumergue's immediate successor. In June 1935 Pétain did agree to serve in the cabinet of Fernand Bouisson, but this fell the day it presented itself to the Chamber. If any was needed, this was further proof of the follies of parliamentarianism, leaving Pétain with an ill-defined desire for stronger leadership.[40] Could he provide that direction? Certainly, the press was encouraging him to think along these lines.

The first intimation of a press campaign aiming to make Pétain head of government came on 20 November 1934 when the populist newspaper, *Le Petit Journal,* announced that it was going to poll its readers on the most suitable French dictator.[41] Forty candidates and their horoscopes were discussed. Pétain was considered on 2 December. In his favour, it was pointed out that he was the 'Victor of Verdun' and the most humane of the High Command. On the negative side, it was argued that soldiers do not necessarily make good leaders in peacetime. Age and a lack of ministerial experience were also seen as drawbacks. None the less, when the results were announced on 11 January 1935 Pétain came first with 38,561 votes; Laval second with 31,403; Doumergue third with 23,868; and Marianne, the symbol of the Republic, fourth with 20,102. As has been remarked, the fact that three members of Doumergue's government had trounced the representatives of the extreme right was an indication that what the readership really wanted was stability, not dictatorship. Above all, the referendum reflected the negative attitudes of the 1930s: a disenchantment with the 'game of politics', a fear of war, and a sense of economic insecurity.[42]

A more serious campaign was launched shortly afterwards by Gustave Hervé in his newspaper, *La Victoire*. A curious and somewhat marginal figure, Hervé had started life on the left before championing an authoritarian Republic. In 1935 his paper, *La Victoire*, commemorated the February riots by advocating such a regime. It further suggested that Pétain and Weygand should put up for election on a platform of constitutional revision. Aware that Weygand was likely to arouse opposition on the left, the general's name was quickly dropped. Instead, Hervé coined the headline, 'C'est Pétain qu'il nous faut'. Thereafter, in the build-up to the elections of May 1936, the editor ran a series of articles on the marshal, later published in book form.[43] Although a revised edition of this volume appeared in 1937, the ideas remained the same: France was tired of parliamentarianism, but not of a Republic. What was required was a firm regime headed by a figure who would stand above factional interest. Pétain was that man; and, in an attempt to underscore the marshal's authority, Hervé took care to describe the imposing physical stature of the 'Victor of Verdun', a technique that would later be copied by Vichy propagandists.

Gradually Hervé's campaign gathered momentum. Between 1934 and 1936 a handful of right-wing newspapers – among them, *La Voix de Combattant*, *Le National*, *Le Jour*, *Action Française* and *L'Ami du Peuple* – all declared their support for a Pétain government. In March 1936 Germany's remilitarization of the Rhineland prompted *Le Figaro*, the voice of respectable conservatism, to run an article urging the French people to rally round Pétain. Hervé was delighted at this response but, true to his socialist origins, was keen to enlist left-wing backing. Given that the omens in 1936 were for a Popular Front victory, this was always unlikely to be forthcoming. The only left-wing paper to support Pétain was *Vu*, and then in very different circumstances to those which Hervé had envisaged. In November 1935 it devoted an article to the growth of the right-wing leagues.[44] Here Cot, the future Minister of Air in the Blum government, spoke of how these forces might launch a *coup d'état*. In the event of such a crisis, Cot looked to Pétain to save the Republic. That a committed democrat could advance such an argument is vivid testimony to the strength of Pétain as a symbol of national unity and helps explain why in July 1940 many Republicans, even on the left, were prepared to grant him absolute powers.

Ultimately, Hervé's campaign failed to enlist the support of mainstream newspapers. It even caused some merriment among youthful and disrespectful members of the extreme right, who mocked Pétain's great age.[45] Nor did Hervé win the wholehearted approval of the marshal himself. Although the soldier knew several of the journalists concerned, he took care not to give public backing to their efforts and even issued a mild rebuke to his old friend the senator Henry Lémery who, in March 1938, wrote an article for *L'Indépendant* calling for a Pétain government.[46] It has since been speculated that he kept his distance because he knew that Hervé, Lémery and others had no chance of success. It is more likely that he wished to be seen as being above politics. There is little doubt, however, that he was flattered by all this newspaper attention. The articles confirmed his belief that he was unlike ordinary men and fuelled his political ambition.

How, then, to satisfy that ambition? At his trial in 1945, it was alleged that he was tempted by the undemocratic path to power. Much was made of his links with the Corvignolles and the Cagoule. These clandestine organizations were founded in 1936 when the Popular Front clamped down on the activities of right-wing leagues. In 1945 it did not go unnoticed that the Corvignolles had been headed by Major Georges Loustanau-Lacau, who had served Pétain at the Ministry of War in 1934 before joining his general staff the following year. It was also revealed that backing had come from Franchet d'Esperey and Captain Bonhomme, another of Pétain's entourage. Frightened by the rise of the Blum government, the Corvignolles' intention was to monitor left-wing subversion within the army. This, too, was the job of the more sinister Cagoule, the name given to the Comité Secret d'Action Révolutionnaire (CSAR), headed by Eugène Deloncle, a former naval officer. Together, these paramilitary bodies agreed to pool information, but reached no understanding beyond this. Loustanau-Lacau was especially troubled by the violence of the Cagoule, which sought to execute a military *putsch*. To this end, in 1937 it exploded a number of bombs in Paris. These escapades led to its suppresssion and an official enquiry. Although Pétain was not investigated, he was implicated in that he had known of the Cagoule's existence. The following year the Corvignolles were discovered and Loustanau-Lacau was forced to resign his post on Pétain's staff.

No evidence was uncovered, however, in either 1938 or 1945 to show that the marshal approved of the activities or the methods of the paramilitaries. Rather his toleration of them points to his unwillingness to inform on colleagues and a belief that the army should be free of politics, that is free from communist influence. It is significant, for example, that in 1937 he was imprudent enough to give Loustanau-Lacau a document on the methods the Communists might use to seize power in France, aware that this paper would then be circulated among the Corvignolles. Yet Pétain went no further than this, and abhorred the violence of the Cagoule. As in 1934, his respect for the legality of the Republic remained firm and, unlike Franchet d'Esperey, he did not support the idea of a *coup d'état.*

Unattracted by the unconstitutional path to power, Pétain was more tempted by the offers being made by democratic politicians. After the Popular Front victory of 1936, a number of right-wing deputies urged him to stand for either the premiership or the presidency. The most notable of such suitors was Laval. It will be recalled that during the First World War, this one-time socialist had been a fierce critic of Pétain's handling of the mutinies. In the 1920s, however, Laval moved towards the right, and in 1927 was elected Senator for the Seine. Between January 1931 and January 1936, he held a series of ministerial offices, including that of Prime Minister. Of these posts, it was Foreign Affairs which influenced him most.[47] Dealings with Germany and Italy hardened his pacifist leanings, and convinced him of the need for Franco-German *rapprochement.* Without this, he feared that Europe would always be at war. His encounters with the Italian and German dictatorships also led him to believe that France required a more authoritarian government if it was to meet the challenge of fascism. This belief was hardened by the election of the Popular Front. Cast out into the political wilderness, Laval looked for a means to recover his influence and urged the creation of a national government similar to that fronted by Doumergue. At its head, he contemplated the man he had once criticized: Pétain. Only the marshal could restore French prestige abroad and quell discontent on the home front. No doubt Laval further believed that he would be able to manipulate the octogenarian.

Although Pétain remembered that Laval had once been one of his fiercest critics, he retained a respect for this consummate parliamentarian. The two men had worked together in the Doumergue government and shared in their dislike of the Popular Front. There was even a family connection, albeit a remote one. General de Chambrun, a close associate of the marshal's, was the father of Laval's son-in-law. Even so, Pétain was suspicious of Laval. He never forgot that the Auvergnat was a career politician and arch-schemer. Pétain, himself well practised in politicking, had no desire to be manipulated, and was wary of any plan emanating from Laval. Already, we may see the origins of the mutual mistrust which would characterize their relationship during the Occupation. We may also see why they were unable to forge a lasting partnership before 1940.

Given Laval's methods of working, it is extremely difficult to keep abreast of his many schemes to promote a Pétain government. In April 1937 he mentioned to one of Franco's agents that he, along with de la Rocque and Doriot, was in the process of putting together a cabinet fronted by the marshal. No hard evidence has subsequently been produced to support this claim.[48] In April 1938, after the Anschluss crisis, Laval further hinted that he was assembling a Pétain government, but declared his efforts were being thwarted by the President, Albert Lebrun, and by the marshal himself, who retained 'a will of his own'.[49] Once again, the lack of supporting evidence suggests that Laval was making exaggerated claims.

Laval's actions at the beginning of 1939 are also shrouded in mystery. In the wake of the German take-over of Czechoslovakia, politicians all over the political spectrum urged Pétain to stand in the forthcoming presidential elections. Curiously, Laval preferred to give his support to Bouisson, a former head of the Chamber of Deputies. Why was this? It might have been that Laval was smarting from Pétain's rejection of his plans in April 1938. It might also have been because Laval expected Bouisson to give him the premiership.[50] A more fabulous theory was suggested at Pétain's trial. According to the testimony of a certain Mlle Petit, secretary to Mirko Giobbe, editor of *L'Italie Nouvelle* and purportedly an Italian spy, Laval was secretly planning to establish a dictatorship in France with a 'high-ranking military personage' at its head.[51] Naturally enough, it has been speculated that Pétain was that person, yet no evidence has been discovered to link the marshal with such a scheme and it remains doubtful whether this plot ever existed.

There may be a further explanation why Laval did not back Pétain for the presidency. It was well known that the marshal was unenthusiastic about standing for this office. As a soldier, he had no desire to put himself forward for election; he certainly had no wish to be actively involved in the sordid world of the hustings. He was also dismissive of the post itself, which possessed little more than ceremonial powers. In his eyes, it was only suitable for 'defeated marshals', a disparaging remark about Marshal MacMahon, the first of the Third Republic's presidents.[52] Clearly, then, Pétain remained interested in power. This was why on 2 March 1939 he took up the ambassadorship to Spain. For de Gaulle, the marshal's acceptance of this minor office was further evidence of senile ambition.

Based intially at San Sebastian, Pétain busied himself looking after the interests of French volunteers in nationalist concentration camps. He also sweetened Franco-Spanish relations which had been soured by the Civil War. Occasionally Spanish neutrality in 1940 has been attributed to the marshal's efforts. This is an exaggerated claim: Spain's position owed more to Franco's uncertainty than to Pétain's diplomacy. Indeed, there is no disguising the fact that the ambassadorship was a minor post, denying Pétain any real power.

Elsewhere, more signicant events were beginning to take place. The same month that Pétain became ambassador to Spain, German troops invaded Czechoslovakia. A fervent *munichois*, Pétain believed that Chamberlain had shown much courage in attempting to negotiate with Hitler,[53] and drew some comfort from the fact that the French government was not prepared to go to war in defence of Prague. Even so, he was not impervious to the German threat, and was angered by the behaviour of Nazi agents who had remained in Spain after the Civil War. He was also aghast at the conclusion of the Nazi-Soviet pact in August 1939. That Hitler could ally himself with the evil Stalin was further proof, if any was needed, of German duplicity and ambition.

With the outbreak of war in September, a marginalized Pétain was anxious to leave Spain for Paris, and was sorely tempted to accept an offer to become part of a national government. In the event, he rejected this invitation as it would have meant serving under Daladier, whom Pétain perversely blamed for the creation of the Popular Front. Reluctantly he remained in Spain, dispatching the ever-faithful Loustanau-Lacau to Paris to find out what Laval thought about the situation. The one-time head of the Corvignolles reported back on 22 September.[54] Angered at the way in which Daladier had led France into war and frustated by the anti-Italian policy of the Quai d'Orsay, Laval claimed there was an urgent need for a Pétain government comprising a small war cabinet of technicians and parliamentarians. Because of his success in Spain, the marshal would need to take over Foreign Affairs as well as the premiership. Laval himself claimed the Interior, yet it was clear that he anticipated playing the dominant role in foreign policy, pursuing his long-term goal of a Franco-Italian understanding. Indeed, the Auvergnat was again attempting to manipulate Pétain. On 27 October, Laval discussed his proposals with Elie J. Bois, editor of *Le Petit Parisien*. When the journalist replied that the marshal was physically and mentally decrepit, Laval replied, 'That doesn't matter. What will be asked of him? To be a mantlepiece, a statue on a pedestal!'[55]

Pétain had no intention of being used in such a way: he was flattered by Laval's assessment of his own abilities and began to assume a more active political role. At the close of October he tried to get himself recalled to Paris, where he could attend meetings of the CSG and keep up to date with political news. Perhaps aware of what he intended, Daladier refused this request. Meanwhile, the marshal contented himself with drawing up lists of potential cabinets, a clear sign that he envisaged taking over the reins of government should the moment arise. On those lists figured the names of both Lémery and Laval. Lémery even paid a secret visit to Madrid accompanied by Raphäel Alibert, a royalist and former Cagoulard, who was later to play a key role in the founding of the Vichy regime. Once again, they discussed possible cabinets. Unfortunately for the marshal, the Daladier government remained firm, forcing the old soldier to rethink his plans. In January 1940, he informed a colleague that his physical strength was not up to bearing the burden of political office; he wished instead to serve his country in a military capacity. To this end, he travelled to Paris to evaluate the state of battle. Much has been made of this brief visit. It has even been suggested that he met with Laval in order to plan the next stage in their campaign to seize power, yet all evidence suggests that the marshal restricted his interest to military matters.[56]

By spring 1940, Pétain's inclusion in cabinet appeared only a matter of time. In March, Laval launched a blistering attack on the government's handling of the war, precipitating Daladier's resignation. Reynaud, the former Minister of Finance, took charge of the cabinet, retaining Daladier at Foreign Affairs. Aware of the need to bolster his public standing, on 1 May the new Prime Minister offered Pétain a portfolio. Once more, the offer was turned down, leading to suggestions, in 1945, that the marshal was privy to German military plans, and knew that by the end of May France would be overrun. After all, he had recently been photographed shaking hands with the German ambassador to Spain, the first of the famous handshakes. Such collusion never existed. It is more likely that Pétain's refusal of a cabinet post derived from his irrational loathing of Daladier and his distaste for 'the regime of parties'. It was probably these dislikes which, in mid-May, prevented him from becoming involved in a Daladier–Laval plot to overturn Reynaud. In any case, by this stage, the marshal knew that he had little need of Laval. Pétain did feel, however, that his country had need of him, and on 18 May, eight days after the Germans had begun their offensive in the Low Countries, he accepted Reynaud's offer to become Deputy Prime Minister.

In view of this manoeuvring, it is not surprising that in both 1940 and 1945 many people believed in the existence of a Pétain–Laval plot to overturn the Third Republic.[57] No such conspiracy existed. The marshal had too much respect for legality to become involved in a *coup d'état*. None the less, he was not the apolitical soldier he claimed to be. Driven by an enormous ambition, constantly refuelled by the public adulation of marshalship, he believed he could still steer his country to recovery. Yet he had no desire to stand for President and did not want to become a part of the parliamentary game of politics. Instead, he had to be called upon. Even when the calls became deafening, he waited until the last moment, convincing himself that it was his country calling him, not just the Prime Minister. Such a mixture of vanity and patriotism had earlier led him to join the Doumergue government. In 1940, he would discover that Guderian's Panzers posed far more of a threat to France than did the political upheavals of 1934.

NOTES AND REFERENCES

1. Blum quoted in *Le Populaire*, 3 March 1939.
2. R. Griffiths, *Marshal Pétain* (London: Constable, 1970), pp. 97–8 and P. Servent, *Le mythe Pétain. Verdun ou les tranchées de la mémoire* (Paris: Editions Payot, 1992), p. 201.
3. Griffiths, *Pétain*, p. 98.
4. Ibid., p. 97 and Servent, *Le mythe Pétain*, p. 201.
5. J.M. Hughes, *To the Maginot Line. The Politics of French Military Preparation in the 1920s* (Cambridge, Mass.: Harvard University Press, 1971), p. 103.
6. Discussed in Griffiths, *Pétain*, pp. 130–2 and J.A. Gunsburg, *Divided and Conquered. The French High Command and the Defeat of the West, 1940* (Westport, Conn.: Greenwood, 1979), pp. 9–10.
7. P.M.H. Bell, *The Origins of the Second World War in Europe* (London: Longman, 1985), p. 167.
8. J. Nobécourt, *Une histoire politique de l'armée*, vol. 1 (Paris: Seuil, 1967), p. 191. See too G. Pedroncini, *Pétain. La victoire perdue, novembre 1918–juin 1940* (Paris: Perrin, 1995), pp. 21–67.
9. Griffiths, *Pétain*, p. 132.
10. A. Horne, *To Lose a Battle. France 1940* (London: Macmillan, 1969), p. 24.
11. Griffiths, *Pétain*, p. 134.
12. R. Frankenstein, *Le prix du réarmement français, 1935–1939* (Paris: Publications de la Sorbonne, 1982), p. 47.
13. Bell, *Origins*, p. 168.
14. C. de Gaulle, *Vers l'armée de métier* (Paris: Berger-Levrault, 1934).
15. Griffiths, *Pétain*, p. 347.
16. Plon published De Gaulle's book in 1938 under the title *La France et son armée*.
17. Griffiths, *Pétain*, pp. 142–3.
18. P. Alméras, *Un français nommé Pétain* (Paris: Robert Laffont, 1995), p. 102.
19. P. Pétain, 'La sécurité de la France au cours des années creuses', in *La Revue des Deux Mondes*, March 1935.
20. R. Tournoux, *Pétain and de Gaulle* (London: Heinemann, 1996), p. 90.
21. D.S. Woolman, *Rebels in the Rif. Abd el-Krim and the Rif Rebellion* (Stanford, Calif.: Stanford University Press, 1968), pp. 1–17.
22. Griffiths, *Pétain*, p. 108.
23. P. Bourget, 'La rivalité Pétain–Lyautey de 1925 au Maroc: un nouvel éclairage', in *Guerres Mondiales et Conflits Contemporains*, 181 (1996), pp. 125–33.
24. D. Slavin, 'The French Left and the Rif War, 1924–25: Racism and the Limits of Internationalism', *Journal of Contemporary History*, 26 (1) 1991, p. 6.

25. J.-P. Brunet, *Doriot* (Paris: Balland, 1986), pp. 53–70.

26. Griffiths, *Pétain*, pp. 165–8.

27. H. du Moulin de Labarthète, *Le temps des illusions. Souvenirs, juillet 1940–avril 1942* (Geneva: Le Cheval Ailé, 1946), p. 98.

28. Griffiths, *Pétain*, p. 158.

29. Pétain quoted in R. Jeanneret, *Maréchal Pétain. Pour chaque jour de l'année. Maximes et principes. Extraits des messages au peuple français.* (Tours: Maison Mame, 1942), p. 26.

30. Pétain quoted in G. Miller, *Les pousse-au-jouir du maréchal Pétain* (Paris: Seuil, 1975), p. 130.

31. Griffiths, *Pétain*, p. 161.

32. Speech of 20 June 1940 contained in J.-C. Barbas (ed.), *Philippe Pétain. Discours aux français, 17 juin 1940–20 août 1944* (Paris: Albin Michel, 1989), pp. 58–60.

33. Pétain quoted in W.D. Halls, *The Youth of Vichy France* (Oxford: Clarendon Press, 1981), p. 9.

34. Griffiths, *Pétain*, p. 164.

35. Letter of 23 March 1940 in M.A. Pardee, *Le maréchal que j'ai connu* (Paris: Editions André Bonne, 1952), p. 59.

36. Pétain quoted in Tournoux, *Pétain and de Gaulle*, p. 84.

37. J. Zay, *Souvenirs et solitude* (Paris: René Juillard, 1945), p. 272. See too N. Atkin, *Church and Schools in Vichy France, 1940–1944* (New York: Garland, 1991), p. 79.

38. M. Beloff, 'The Sixth of February', in J. Joll (ed.), *The Decline of the Third Republic*, St Antony's Papers no. 5 (London: Chatto & Windus, 1959), pp. 9–35.

39. Pétain quoted in Griffiths, *Pétain*, p. 191.

40. Ibid., p. 211.

41. Ibid., pp. 173–4.

42. Ibid.

43. G. Hervé, *C'est Pétain qu'il nous faut* (Paris: Editions de la Victoire, 1935).

44. Griffiths, *Pétain*, pp. 180–2.

45. For such an irreverent view of Pétain, see especially L.-F. Céline, *L'école des cadavres* (Paris: Denöel, 1938), pp. 84–96.

46. Griffiths, *Pétain*, p. 187.

47. N. Atkin, 'Laval, Pierre 1883–1945', in D. Bell, D. Johnson and P. Morris (eds), *A Biographical Guide to Modern French Political Leaders since 1870* (Hemel Hempstead: Harvester Wheatsheaf, 1990), pp. 239–42.

48. G. Warner, *Pierre Laval and the Eclipse of France* (London: Eyre & Spottiswoode, 1968), p. 135.

49. Ibid., p. 136.

50. Ibid., p. 139.

51. Ibid.

52. J. Carcopino, *Souvenirs de sept ans, 1937–1944* (Paris: Flammarion, 1953), p. 162.

53. Letter of Pétain, 16 September 1938, in Pardee, *Le maréchal*, pp. 24–5.
54. Letter of Loustanau-Lacau, 22 September 1939, in H. Noguères, *Le veritable procès du maréchal Pétain* (Paris: Fayard, 1955), pp. 631–4.
55. E.J. Bois, *Truth on the Tragedy of France* (London: Hodder & Stoughton, 1940), p. 141.
56. Griffiths, *Pétain*, p. 206.
57. Anon, *Pétain-Laval. The Conspiracy* (London: 1942).

Chapter 4

THE SAVIOUR, 1939–40

Shortly before Pétain's death, Franco recalled that in May 1940 he had warned the marshal not to leave Madrid for Paris lest he was blamed for a defeat which was the work of others. Deeply moved, Pétain allegedly replied, 'My country is calling me and I owe myself to her. Perhaps this will be the last service I can render her.'[1] Whatever the truth of this anecdote, there is no doubt the old soldier was proud that he had been called upon to serve his nation once more. In performing this service, he had no plan to overturn the Republic. Nor did he seek to lead the allied armies to disaster; his genuine patriotism would have prevented that. It was only when German armour swept across France's eastern frontier that his natural pessimism resurfaced and he relinquished hope of further resistance. Yet even in the slough of despair, he retained a faith in his own abilities; he alone could rescue France from disaster. What, then, were the circumstances that led him to become *chef de l'état français*? To answer this question, it is necessary to follow the tortuous path to power which led the French government from Paris to Bordeaux, and from there, after a brief stop-over in Clermont Ferrand, to Vichy.

. . .

The defeat of France in June 1940 was so unexpected and comprehensive that it has generated several contradictory explanations. In the mood of introspection that followed the débâcle, many observers sought an internal explanation for collapse, pointing to a moral malaise that had sapped the nation's vitality. Pétain himself subscribed to such an interpretation, and in his speech of 20 June 1940 complained that since 1918 a 'spirit of pleasure' had overtaken a 'spirit of sacrifice'.

68

Although different people identified different causes of this 'decadence', Vichy ministers were quick to pin blame on the republican system of government. Accordingly, in 1941, prominent political and military men of the old regime – among them Blum, Daladier, Gamelin and Reynaud – were placed on trial at Riom, charged with having failed their country. Although the defendants skilfully deployed the proceedings to indict their accusers, the image of the Third Republic as a decadent and enfeebled regime has persisted.

No doubt Pétain genuinely believed that his countrymen had relinquished a 'spirit of sacrifice', and was not merely attempting to divert attention from his own role in the débâcle. Yet few historians today accept that defeat was due to a moral malaise. It is difficult to find evidence to show that France was any more corrupt in 1940 than in 1914. That said, historians do acknowledge that at the onset of the Second World War public morale was not as strong as it had been at the start of the First. This time there would be no 'Union Sacrée' to rally the nation. If decadence was not to blame, what were the causes of this unpreparedness?

First, there was the legacy of the First World War. The terrible casualties of that conflict had filled the French with an understandable repugnance for war. Such feelings were especially strong among the peasantry, which had borne the brunt of the losses. The principal political advocates of pacifism were the Socialists, yet support also came from the extreme right and a number of prominent deputies, notably Bonnet, Flandin and Laval.[2] Second, the political quarrels of the Popular Front era had left France a divided nation. Whereas the *bourgeoisie* had been frightened by the Blum experiment, the working class was disappointed that the Daladier government had reversed many of the gains won in 1936. Third, in the build-up to war, French political parties of all persuasions appeared unable to provide clear leadership. Even the Communists, unflinching in their opposition to fascism, faltered at the last moment. Following the Nazi-Soviet Pact of August 1939, the Parti Communiste Français (PCF) reluctantly followed the Moscow line and denounced the conflict as an 'imperialist struggle'. The government, in turn, proscribed the party and arrested 40 of its deputies. It did not go unnoticed that Daladier displayed more energy in persecuting the left than he did in convincing public opinion of the need for war. It was not until July 1939 that his government established a Department of Information in charge of propaganda. At its head was the diplomat and writer Jean Giraudoux. Lacking the vulgarity and drive of a Goebbels, he subjected his audiences to academic discussions on the relative artistic merits of France and Germany.[3] The damage of such broadcasts was compounded by a fourth factor undermining morale: the so-called *drôle de guerre* (phoney war) which lasted from September 1939 to May 1940. During this period, combat was confined to eastern Europe, giving little sense that 'la patrie est en danger'. In any case, there was confidence that the Maginot Line would repel any invader. Small wonder the French people were taken aback by the speed of the defeat.

It was, then, a weary and introspective French nation that faced Hitler in 1939–40. Yet it would be a mistake to believe that the defeat may be attributed solely to the shortcomings of morale. Although a dislike of war was commonplace, defeatism was largely confined to the pro-*munichois* section of the Socialist party and pro-Nazi supporters on the far right.[4] Moreover, since Munich, there had been a toughening of resolve. Groups of war veterans, former pacifist schoolteachers, socialists of the Blum school and representatives of big business all understood that at some point France would have to stand up to Hitler.[5] Admittedly the declaration of war was not greeted with enthusiasm; nor was it met with opposition. As in 1914, a mood of resigned acceptance prevailed. Analysis of the French army's postal censorship arrangements has further shown that this attitude withstood the ups and downs of the *drôle de guerre*.[6] Had France survived the initial onslaught of German armour in May 1940, it is conceivable that a spirit of *jusqu'au boutisme* would have held the nation together just as it did in 1914–18.

The failure of the French to repeat the 'miracle of the Marne' has underscored the fact that the causes of defeat were military in origin. Here again there is controversy. Some historians have emphasized the unpreparedness of the French army, but, on paper, French forces were more than a match for their German counterparts.[7] Whereas the Nazis had 114 divisions ready for the campaign, the French had 94, which were supplemented by 10 British, 22 Belgian and 9 Dutch. As to tanks, there is general agreement that the Allies possessed superiority in numbers, fire-power and defensive armour. It was the airforce which gave most cause for concern. The Germans had between 2,700 and 3,600 aircraft of which 1,300 to 1,500 were bombers, 1,000 to 1,200 were fighters and 340 were Stuka bombers. In contrast, France could only muster between 800 and 1,200 machines of which few were bombers. Admittedly these were supplemented by British aircraft, yet London was anxious to keep the bulk of these planes at home in case of a German invasion of England. Britain's reluctance to commit planes to the Battle of France later became a source of heated arguments between Churchill and Reynaud.

Whether this shortage of aircraft ultimately cost the Allies the campaign in 1940 remains debatable. Today there is growing certainty that the real problem for France was not one of military hardware but of strategy.[8] It will be recalled that until 1935 the High Command had championed a predominantly defensive policy which owed much to Pétain's thinking. In the event of war with Germany, French troops would march into Belgium where, together with Belgian forces, they would establish easily defensible positions along the many rivers and canals.[9] The two armies would thus form a continuous line of defence with the Maginot Line. Meanwhile, Germany would be engaged in battle with France's eastern allies, and would be economically drained just as in 1914–18. Much, however, had changed since that earlier conflict. Not only had new weapons called into question the passivity of the tactics to be employed, doubts were expressed over whether this strategy would enable France to assist her eastern allies should they be attacked directly by Germany. So it proved. Instead of constituting a permanent front, in 1939 Poland quickly crumbled. There were also problems with France's western allies. In March 1936 Belgium announced its neutrality, thus posing the High Command with some uncomfortable choices about how best to defend northern France.[10]

This task was confronted by General Maurice Gamelin. A former protégé of Joffre, in 1931 he took over as Chief of General Staff; in 1935 he was appointed vice-president of the CSG; in 1938 he became *generalissimo* of the French forces when he was made Chief of National Defence. Much scorn has since been poured on this introverted general, who has been dubbed 'the man who lost the Battle of France'. This is a harsh assessment. It should be remembered that Gamelin had been bequeathed an unfortunate legacy by his predecessors, notably Pétain. It should also be noted that Gamelin was an intelligent

71

soldier who, like de Gaulle, was well aware of his country's vulnerability. It was unfortunate that his attempts to build a highly mobilized army were thwarted, first, by the restrictions of a peactime economy and, then, by the muddled command structure of the French army. Even after his appointment as *generalissimo*, he discovered that his remit was not to control but merely to coordinate the policies of the French air, maritime and colonial forces, each of which jealously guarded its independence.[11] Ironically, Gamelin may well have compounded the incoherence of this system. Aware that he was unable to direct overall war strategy and exercise specific command of armies in the field, on 6 January 1940 he effected a reorganization of the High Command. Direct control of the armies in north-eastern France was placed in the hands of General Georges. The Second Bureau (Intelligence) was stationed at Vincennes with Gamelin, the Third Bureau (Operations) at La Ferté with Georges, and the Fourth Bureau (Transport and Supply) at Montry with General Doumenc. The overlapping responsibilities of these offices had created confusion in peacetime; after the German invasion, chaos reigned supreme.[12]

It is, however, as a strategist and not a tactical coordinator that Gamelin may be most severely criticized. Following the declaration of Belgian neutrality, he plumped for a policy of forward defence.[13] Although he acknowledged that this strategy could not be implemented unless Belgium requested assistance or was invaded by Germany, he pressed ahead and devised two alternative proposals. The first (Plan E) envisaged an advance of the allied left-flank along the Escaut (or Scheldt) river which ran from Antwerp to Ghent. The general understood, however, that this manoeuvre would only afford protection to a small portion of Belgian territory and left Brussels undefended. Accordingly, in November 1939 he plumped for a second option (Plan D) known as the Dyle Plan. This involved moving allied forces along a line from Louvain to Namur, part of which coincided with the River Dyle. This operation had the advantage of covering Brussels and gave the Allies a better chance of linking up with the Belgian army. Still Gamelin was not satisfied: Plan D made no provision for helping the Dutch should they be attacked. Thus in March 1940 he adopted a variant of the Dyle Plan whereby a whole army would rush through Belgium to link up with the Dutch in the north, a proposal that was quickly endorsed by the British. Indeed, it should never be forgotten that ultimately the débâcle of 1940 was as much an allied defeat as it was a French one.[14]

On paper, the Dyle Plan had much to commend it. By establishing a common front from north-east Belgium to the southeast Netherlands, each one of the Allies would recognize that its security depended on holding firm. This front would also consititute a springboard for future offensives against Germany's industrial heartland of the Ruhr. The Plan's fatal weakness was that it misjudged Hitler's invasion route. When on 10 May 1940 the Germans launched their offensive in the west, Gamelin despatched the crack French Seventh Army under General Giraud to Holland and committed the whole of the British Expeditionary Force (BEF) to Belgium. To the Allies' amazement, the main brunt of the German attack came instead through the Ardennes. This heavily wooded and hilly terrain had previously been considered 'untankable', hence the criticisms directed at Pétain for his now infamous remark in 1934 that the Ardennes were 'impenetrable'. Yet, as noted in Chapter 3, this comment has been taken out of context. It was made at the time of Belgian neutrality as justification for not extending the Maginot Line. It never meant that Pétain intended the Ardennes to be left undefended.

In any case, by 1940, responsibility for this sector lay not with Pétain but with Gamelin, and the preparations which he had put in place were clearly inadequate. This region was protected by inexperienced reservists under General Huntziger. Contrary to what is sometimes claimed, these troops fought bravely but were let down by allied tactics. With the bulk of French armour concentrated in Belgium and Holland, German tanks found little difficulty in breaching French lines. As in Poland, the methods of Blitzkrieg – in particular, the use of Stuka dive-bombers and low-flying aircraft – did much to destroy the morale of ground troops. In contrast, the Allies could only draw on a limited number of pilots, who had not been trained in the tactical support of land forces. Matters were compounded by the semi-autonomy of the French airforce which made it difficult for army commanders to request air cover at the right moment. Already France's incoherent chain of command was becoming apparent.

The decisive breakthrough came on 14 May when the Germans crossed the Meuse at Sedan. This opened the way for the division of allied forces. While the Panzers of Hoth and Kleist sped towards the coast with the intention of isolating allied troops in Belgium, Guderian's tanks headed southwards to cut off French garrisons in the Maginot Line. It was at this moment that the full folly of committing so many allied divisions to Belgium and Holland became apparent. The following day Gamelin informed Daladier, the Minister of War, that the French army was broken and admitted there was no strategic reserve. On 17 May an uncharacteristically nervous Hitler ordered the Panzers to halt. Had they continued their relentless onslaught, victory would have been secured much earlier.[15]

A desperate military situation called for a dramatic political response. On 18 May, the day on which the Panzers advanced again, Reynaud restructured his cabinet: Georges Mandel, Clemenceau's right-hand man and a fervent anti-*munichois*, was given the Interior; Daladier, whom Reynaud distrusted, was moved to Foreign Affairs; and Reynaud himself took over at Defence, combining the post with the premiership. Reynaud recognized, however, that these changes were unlikely to boost morale and resurrect his authority in parliament. Thus, in a radio message that evening, he announced to an anxious public that Marshal Pétain – the 'Victor of Verdun' – was now at his side as Deputy Prime Minister and would remain there 'until victory'. The next day Weygand replaced Gamelin as Commander-in-Chief.

Outwardly Pétain's inclusion in cabinet appeared to have bolstered Reynaud's position. Much as the Prime Minister had hoped, the marshal's return prompted a surge of optimism not only in parliament but among the population at large. The press, desperate for good news, was especially enthusiastic.[16] Newpapers on the left echoed Cot's earlier endorsement of the marshal. On the right, Wladimir d'Ormesson announced in *Le Figaro* that the presence of Weygand and Pétain had created an impression of calm. In *L'Action Française*, Charles Maurras merely remarked, 'Finally'. Few commentators realized Pétain and Weygand had little enthusiasm for the fight. This defeatism, coupled with their contempt for civilian authority, soon placed the whole of the Allies' war effort in jeopardy.

· · ·

Although newspapers drew comfort from Pétain's appointment, there was no disguising the desperate nature of the battle. The Dutch had already surrendered on 15 May; five days later German tanks reached the Channel, thus driving a wedge between allied forces. Two options were now open to the Allies. The first was to fall back on Dunkirk and attempt a sea evacuation, an extremely hazardous venture. The second, suggested by Weygand, was to break out of the German encirclement by launching a counter-offensive in the south-west towards Bapaume and Cambrai. Although Churchill, who visted France on 22 May, was impressed by this second proposal, the British Commander, Lord Gort, and the CIGS, General Ironside, were not. In their eyes, the only means to salvage the BEF was a withdrawal to Dunkirk. Naturally enough this decision created bitter recriminations between the Allies; on 24 May Reynaud sent two telegrams to Churchill complaining about the extent of the British retreat. Such protests were to no avail, and that evening Weygand relinquished hope of a counter-offensive. Instead, he ordered the allied armies to form an arc in the north in order to cover the Dunkirk evacuations, which began on 28 May. Ominously he recognized that this manoeuvre left few divisions free to protect Paris.

Given these setbacks, it is little surprise that the French should have considered the possibility of an armistice. This debate was initiated at a War Committee meeting of 25 May.[17] Here, President Lebrun was the first to speak openly of a separate peace; yet it was Weygand who effectively broached the matter. It will be recalled that Reynaud had enlisted the services of Foch's former protégé in an attempt to boost morale. He soon rued his decision. A passionate Catholic and political reactionary, Weygand was mistrustful of parliamentarians. He temperamental nature also made him prone to defeatism. This was his mood on 25 May. Opening the meeting, he provided a gloomy assessment of the allied situation. Although he claimed he was still intending a counter-offensive, his heart was not in the fight. He concluded by contemplating the eventual defeat of France's northern armies and grumbled that his country should not have gone to war when it lacked both *matériel* and a satisfactory strategy. By touching on political affairs, Weygand had clearly overstepped his brief as Commander-in-Chief. It was at this moment that Lebrun intervened to voice the unspoken thought in the general's mind: should France seek an armistice? While recognizing that this solution might salvage the French army, the politician reminded the soldier that on 28 March 1940 France had signed an agreement with Britain not to conclude a separate peace. This point was also stressed by

Reynaud, who was furious with Weygand. In reply, the general agreed that any cessation of hostilities should be discussed with England and urged Reynaud, who had declared his willingness to visit London the next day, to raise the issue of the Franco-British Declaration in addition to requesting further military assistance. This the Prime Minister duly did. While he reassured Churchill that he was prepared to fight on, others in his entourage were not.[18] Here Reynaud was thinking not just of Weygand, but of Pétain as well.

What was the marshal's attitude to an armistice? He said little at the meeting of 25 May. His only recorded intervention was to question whether there was a complete reciprocity of obligation between France and England. He concluded by pointing out that a comparison should be made not only between the military effort of the two countries, but between the sufferings awaiting them.[19] The marshal developed these sentiments in a letter which he handed to Reynaud shortly after the conference. In this, he also spoke of the reconstruction of a new France, an indication that he was thinking ahead to the National Revolution. The Prime Minister understood this note to mean that his Deputy had already relinquished the fight; this was undoubtedly the case. Since returning to office, Pétain's pessimism of 1918 had resurfaced. Indeed, the soldier was struck by the similarities between the situation of June 1940 and that of March 1918. In both instances, Franco-British cooperation was threatened by a rapid German offensive; once again, the British were thinking only of themselves; and, as in 1918 (with Weygand unwilling to play the part of Foch), the marshal saw no way out. This was the conclusion he conveyed to his old friend General Spears, now Churchill's liaison officer, who visited Pétain on 25 May.[20] However, unlike in 1918, the marshal did not convey an impression of panic, but seemed calm and distant. No doubt this detached air was due to the fact that he was not as closely involved in the formulation of tactics as he had been in 1918; yet it also indicated his sense of superiority. He almost seemed self-satisfied that military defeat had confirmed his prognosis of the nation's ills. As Spears continued, it was as though the whole sorry affair was the work of others: the schoolteachers and politicians.

So Pétain agreed with Weygand that the fight was over. Yet, contrary to what is sometimes suggested, the two men reached their conclusions on an independent basis; there is no evidence to suggest that they were working in collusion. Their mutual distrust, a suspicion rooted in the rivalries of the First World War, would have prevented that. It was not until after the meeting of 25 May that they established an informal alliance. With Reynaud conveniently out of the country, on 26 May they discussed the situation and found they had much in common. Both believed France had gone to war inadvisedly; both were critical of Britain; both detested politicians; both were determined to salvage the French army; both were anxious to avoid civil unrest; both were keen to see a new France emerge out of the conflict; and both were dismissive of the military options remaining to France. While they agreed that the most feasible strategy was to hold a front along the Somme–Aisne line, they recognized that few divisions were available to execute this ploy. Accordingly, France might well have to secure a separate peace. This was the tenor of a note which Weygand drafted after their meeting. After receiving Pétain's blessing, the letter was presented to Reynaud on 28 or 29 May (accounts vary). Having rehearsed the huge odds which confronted the allied forces, it stated that the British should recognize that a time might come when the French would find themselves unable to continue the struggle.[21] It was small comfort to the Prime Minister that the two soldiers momentarily swallowed their defeatism and agreed to explore the possibility of a redoubt around the Brittany peninsula.

By this stage, Reynaud was not only concerned about an armistice; he also feared a Pétain government. Already a number of deputies were thinking along these lines. If France was to fall, then only a military man would possess the necessary *gravitas* to negotiate with the Germans; and, given Weygand's reactionary views, that man had to be Pétain. True to form, Laval was prominent in these claims. As early as 17 May, he had stated that there was no alternative other than a Pétain–Weygand government. Naturally enough, he envisaged a post for himself in any such cabinet, preferably Foreign Affairs, where he intended to use his influence to deter Italy from entering the war.[22]

Although Pétain was undoubtedly mulling over the prospect of leading his country, he remained characteristically cautious. In early June, he apparently informed the Spanish ambassador in Paris that a *coup d'état* would be necessary before he took power. This, however, was a 'serious matter' and as Lebrun, who was merely the 'servant of the political parties', would do nothing to help, it was therefore necessary to wait.[23] Given that Pétain was not prepared to take control illegally and was reluctant to engineer his own return to government, this story sounds plausible. Rather he was content to wait on events until he was called upon, and understood that in early June there was a strong chance of this happening. While waiting for the call, he was not averse to politicking. In cabinet, he said little, thus underscoring his dislike of the parliamentarians; in the corridors of power he was less circumspect, devoting considerable energy to a vendetta against Daladier, whom he continued to blame for the creation of the Popular Front.[24] Pétain saw nothing ironic in this behaviour. As in the past, he considered that he was not acting in a political manner; he was simply responding to politicians.[25]

In the event, a cabinet reshuffle did take place. On 5 June, Daladier was dismissed, with Reynaud adding Foreign Affairs to his other offices. A further change was the appointment of de Gaulle, whom Reynaud admired, as Under-Secretary of State for War. Otherwise, it was not a reshuffle to inspire confidence or excitement. Afterwards Reynaud justified his changes by claiming that they were designed to instil backbone into government. Recognizing that the prestige of Pétain and Weygand prevented their dismissal, he was determined to isolate them by getting rid of other defeatists.[26] This seems improbable. Not all ministers forced to resign were defeatists. Nor were all newcomers free from defeatism: Yves Bouthillier, in charge of Finance, and Jean Provoust at Information were especially keen on an armistice. In any case, several defeatists remained in place. Perhaps the real reason for the reshuffle will never be known, yet it appears that Reynaud had long been looking for a chance to drop Daladier. Pétain, too, had been keen on his dismissal, although he does not appear to have influenced Reynaud's decision. Nor did he have any say in the reshaping of government. Soon after the personnel changes, he was heard venting his dislike of de Gaulle.[27] Reynaud was amazed that, at a time of crisis, the old soldier could devote so much energy to pursuing personal quarrels.

Away from Paris, the military situation remained grim. On 27 May Belgium capitulated; on 4 June Dunkirk fell. The next day the Germans attacked Weygand's Somme–Aisne line. This held for 48 hours. Anxious to protect Paris, Weygand ordered his troops to form defences along the rivers of the Seine and

Marne. He had little confidence in this manoeuvre. Although the option of a Breton redoubt remained open, he declared that if his new defences were broken it was 'the end'. On 9 June they were already faltering. To exacerbate matters, on 10 June an opportunistic Mussolini declared war on France. On the same day, Reynaud's cabinet left Paris for Tours. Within four days it arrived at Bordeaux, the traditional seat of French governments in retreat. During this flight from Paris a series of critical meetings took place in which the question of an armistice became all-important. This issue divided the cabinet between the 'softs', those in favour of an armistice, and the 'hards', those opposed to a such a peace. Pétain played a key part in leading the 'softs' and, in so doing, eroded what was left of Reynaud's authority.

.   .   .

A foretaste of the arguments and tactics which Pétain would deploy in the days ahead was provided at the morning cabinet meeting of 9 June. As the government discussed whether to leave the capital, the marshal read out a memorandum. Unwilling to be side-tracked by the excitable discussion of politicians, he would produce a number of such pre-prepared statements in coming meetings. True to military practice, these notes were written for him by advisers. There is no doubt, however, that the views expressed were Pétain's own.

The note of 9 June spoke of the damage which the government's flight would have on morale. Genuinely concerned for the welfare of the nation, Pétain argued that to desert the French people in their hour of need was an act of betrayal. Turning to the military situation, the key task was to conclude an armistice – so long as the terms were honourable – in readiness for a peace settlement. This candidness came as a shock to some of his cabinet colleagues, but not to Reynaud, who retorted that France still had commitments to Britain, an argument Pétain breezily dismissed. Exasperated, Reynaud pointed out that no honourable armistice terms could be expected from Hitler, a point which Pétain had difficulty in grasping. As de Gaulle later remarked, Pétain's great age and inability to grasp the dynamics of Nazism meant that he viewed the struggle merely as a repetition of previous Franco-German conflicts.[28] Once the fighting had finished, it was only normal to conclude an armistice and, if necessary, crush the Commune.

Despite Pétain's intervention, the meeting of 9 June ended with the cabinet deciding to depart the following day for Tours in readiness for evacuation to Bordeaux. It was in the Loire valley that the next meeting of importance – that of the Allied Supreme War Council – was held on 11 June at the Château de Muguet near Briare. At Reynaud's request, Churchill flew over to attend. He discovered the French government in a chaotic state. With the ministries strung out in various châteaux, at Muguet there was only one telephone housed in the lavatory from where officials shouted endless orders. The meeting itself began with Weygand providing another gloomy military résumé. With no reserves left, it was essential for the British to throw in air support. According to some accounts, he concluded by mentioning an armistice, to which Reynaud snapped, 'That is a political affair.'[29] In an attempt to dispel such defeatism, Churchill reminded his hosts of the Breton redoubt and even floated the possibility of guerrilla war. He also invoked the example of Clemenceau, who, in March 1918, had stated he would fight in front of Paris, in Paris, and behind Paris. De Gaulle, who was present at the meeting, recalls it was then that Pétain spoke up. In March 1918, the marshal reminisced, it was the English who were threatened. If it had not been for his willingness to throw in extra divisions, they would have been routed. Now there were no such reserves. After the meeting concluded, Churchill learned further of Pétain's defeatism. Over dinner, Reynaud informed his British counterpart that the marshal had written a note on the need for an armistice but was 'too ashamed' to hand it over.[30] The next morning, before Churchill departed, Reynaud observed of Pétain, 'He looks particularly bouyant this morning. There must be some bad news.' As Eden recalls, 'There was.'[31]

Discussions resumed at the Château de Cangé on the evening of 12 June. Ever more outspoken in his challenge to civilian authority, Weygand made a formal request for an armistice. Exasperated, Reynaud reminded the general of his naivety: 'You take Hitler for Wilhelm I, an old gentleman who took Alsace-Lorraine from you and left it at that. But Hitler is Ghengis Khan.'[32] Even if France were occupied, Reynaud declared, the fight should continue from North Africa. For the moment, the cabinet rallied behind the Prime Minister. Only Pétain and Provoust supported Weygand's demand for a separate peace. None the less, as the general had made a formal request for an armistice, it was agreed that Churchill should be invited back to France to discuss the matter. He duly arrived at Tours on 13

June. There he met a series of politicians who conveyed different impressions. Some – Jeanneney, Herriot, Mandel, Reynaud – were determined to fight on. Others – Baudouin, Bouthillier – appeared less sure. Asked by Reynaud what Britain's position would be if France had to seek an armistice, Churchill proved evasive and suggested that both governments make an appeal for American assistance.[33] Then, contrary to what had been decided the evening before, the British Prime Minister was not invited to the French cabinet meeting. Opinions differ as to why this was so. Reynaud argues that he did not wish his ally to witness Pétain and Weygand's defeatism.[34] It is more likely that he did not want Churchill to see his own inability to control ministers.

It was at the cabinet meeting of 13 June that Pétain unfolded his note on the armistice.[35] This developed themes he had been nursing since his inclusion in government. Betraying his pessimism and mistrust of the British, he began by speaking of the desperateness of the military situation and dismissed the feasibility of further resistance. Only an armistice would salvage the French army and avoid civil disorder. It was thus necessary for the government to remain on the spot and not depart for North Africa. Abandoning the mainland would be an act of desertion and would deliver France to the enemy. Displaying the sort of compassion that he had shown for his troops in the First World War, he announced that he would remain on French soil in order to accept whatever suffering awaited the nation. Then he turned to another of his favourite themes, that of national revival. Only an armistice could guarantee the survival of 'eternal France'. Here perhaps was evidence of his political ambition, as implicit in this statement was the belief that only a soldier could produce such a renascence.

The effect of this declaration was devastating. Although it had been clear before that Pétain supported an armistice, until then it had been Weygand who had been making the running. Yet given the Commander-in-Chief's reactionary views and the fact that he was not even a cabinet member, his influence among the parliamentarians was always limited. Now it was Pétain, the most respected of France's soldiers and the most republican of the High Command, who had come out in support of a cessation of hostilities. It was difficult to resist his call, especially as he had declared that he would remain in France come what may. Accordingly, the 'softs' grew in strength, being

joined by Bouthillier and Ybarnégaray, a Croix de Feu sympathizer who had been brought into government on 10 May as
a sop to the far right. What was left of Reynaud's power now
began to evaporate. Although the cabinet meeting of 13 June
agreed to send an appeal to Roosevelt and depart for Bordeaux,
all eyes were on Pétain. He was quick to use his initiative. The
next day, he remarked that the attitude of the cabinet had been
'ignoble and cowardly'; it was time to 'be done with it'.[36] To
this end, he ordered Weygand to Bordeaux. The last moment
to make a decision, he declared prophetically, was 16 June.

Pétain's call for an armistice was boosted by the transfer of
government to Bordeaux on 14 June, the same day that the
Germans entered Paris. Soon everybody who was anybody in
French politics gravitated to the new capital. As the gossiping
grew, the pro-armistice lobby gathered strength. A key figure
in stoking up this momentum was Laval, who quickly made
contact with his old friend Adrien Marquet, a deputy and mayor
of the city. Together, they formed the so-called Bordeaux
Commune, a group of like-minded souls in favour of a Pétain
government, who were soon sending messages to the marshal.
For the moment, the soldier had no time for such schemes; his
immediate concern was the afternoon cabinet meeting of 15
June.

It was there that Reynaud proposed a new solution: following the Dutch example, the government should order the army
to lay down its arms, and then continue resistance from abroad.
Pétain appeared swayed by this argument and was delegated to
convince Weygand of its merits. The reverse happened; the
general persuaded him that it was an ignoble solution. In this
situation, with the cabinet divided on the merits of an armistice, it was Chautemps who suggested a way forward. A master
of fudge, he proposed that a neutral authority should enquire
what the terms of an armistice might be: if they were honourable, the cabinet could accept them; if they were dishonourable,
the fight would continue. Although the 'Chautemps proposal'
seemed the perfect way out, it was a dangerous conpromise.
Not only did it signify that the principle of an armistice had
been accepted, it also meant that the wishes of the 'softs', the
minority, had taken precedence over the views of the 'hards',
the majority. Aware of this, Reynaud wanted to resign but was
persuaded to stay on until the cabinet heard of Roosevelt's
response to the earlier appeal for American support.

The American reply came on the morning of 16 June. Apart from vague promises of material aid, it pointed out that only Congress could make military commitments.[37] After Reynaud had read this statement to cabinet, Pétain – like a conjurer with rabbits – pulled another letter out of his pocket to announce his resignation.[38] This move was clearly designed to intensify the pressure on Reynaud as the marshal understood full well that his resignation would bring down the Prime Minister. Anxious to defuse matters, Lebrun urged Pétain to remain until they heard the British reply to the Chautemps proposal. Two telegrams arrived, stating that Churchill would only agree to a separate peace if the French fleet was anchored in British ports safe from German clutches. (This could well have happened. Until 15 June, Admiral Darlan was opposed to an armstice; had he left for British waters, he might even have become head of the French resistance in place of de Gaulle. As it was, a sense of military discipline guaranteed his support for Pétain.) In the event, Churchill's telegrams were not communicated to cabinet. By then, they had been superseded by a telephone call from de Gaulle, currently in London, who relayed Churchill's proposal of a Franco-British union whereby the two countries would become one in order to continue the fight. This was an inspired gesture, but a flawed one. While Reynaud supported the move, his colleagues feared that under such a scheme France might become a British dominion. In the ensuing discussion, chaos reigned supreme. How the meeting ended remains unclear; what is clear is that Reynaud resigned and advised Lebrun to call for Pétain.[39]

.   .   .

Pétain's first task on assuming power was to form a cabinet. Given the deliberate way in which he had hastened Reynaud's departure, it is no surprise that he had already given the matter some thought. On meeting Lebrun late in the evening of 16 June, he was soon searching in his voluminous pockets for a list of ministers. In true Republican style, the new team consisted in part of the old. While Bouthillier kept Finances, Chautemps was made Deputy Prime Minister, and Ybarnégaray became Minister for Anciens Combattants and the Family, a new post which hinted at the direction of the government. Indeed, the cabinet was predominantly right-wing in complexion. Although it included two token socialists, Albert Rivière and André Février, they were outflanked by an influx of military men: Weygand, Minister of National Defence; Darlan, Minister of Marine; General Colson, Minister of War; and General Pujo, Minister of Air. The most notable right-winger among the new recruits was Alibert, one of the leading ideologues in Pétain's personal entourage, who was made Under-Secretary of State to the Prime Minister.

The other person whom Pétain wanted to include was Laval. Overcoming his dislike of this veteran politician, the marshal recognized that Laval's negotiating skills might well come in useful in the days ahead, and was prepared to grant him Foreign Affairs, the post he had long coveted. Here Pétain had miscalculated, underestimating the amount of mistrust Laval generated. Pressure was soon exerted by Darlan to drop Laval. Pétain complied, offering the Auvergnat the Ministry of Justice instead; Baudouin would now go to Foreign Affairs.[40] Naturally enough, Laval protested and was again promised Foreign Affairs. This time it was the turn of Weygand and Charles Roux, permanent head of the Foreign Office, to object, claiming that such an appointment would jeopardize Anglo-French relations. Once more, the marshal changed his mind and reverted to his earlier compromise: Baudouin would take charge of Foreign Affairs and Laval would go to Justice, a post which he again refused.[41] Already Pétain's first cabinet was displaying the personal rivalries and divisions which would characterize all Vichy cabinets.

The next task facing Pétain was to set in train negotiations for an armistice. Keen to get on with the task, by midnight of 16 June Baudouin had submitted, via the Spanish ambassador, a request to the Germans to cease hostilities and make known their peace plans. On 17 June at midday the marshal himself went on the radio to deliver his first message to the French people. In so doing, he betrayed his autocratic nature and contempt for democratic procedure. There was no attempt to consult cabinet beforehand; instead, he saw fit to act independently. The message itself began by testifying to his sense of pride and honour. 'Frenchmen,' he declared, 'at the call of the President of the Republic I am assuming from today the direction of the Government of France.'[42] Having praised the French army for its heroism, he demonstrated his compassion as he spoke with feeling about the plight of refugees. He then announced, 'It is with a heavy heart that I tell you today that we must cease hostilities.' Had cabinet seen the statement beforehand, this sentence would probably have been excised. Many soldiers now believed the war was over and laid down their arms. It was left to Weygand to issue an order stating that fighting must continue until an armistice had been signed. Yet the most significant part of the speech was when Pétain announced that he had given France 'the gift of his person' to relieve its suffering. This semi-religious phrase displayed the extent to which he had succumbed to the mystique surrounding his position in the interwar years. As will be seen in Chapter 5, the enthusiasm with which the population welcomed his 'gift' indicated the extent to which the French public had also been taken in by the cult of marshalship.

Although the call for a ceasefire was received with relief by a majority of French men and women, Pétain still had to contend with those politicians who were keen to carry on the fight in North Africa. This possibility was debated on 18 June. Whereas Jeanneney and Herriot (the presidents of the two Chambers) and Lebrun were keen to depart, Pétain was determined to stay.[43] As a compromise, it was agreed that the marshal, accompanied by Baudouin, Bouthillier and Weygand, would indeed remain; however, he would delegate his powers to Chautemps, who would set sail for North Africa along with Lebrun and the remainder of parliament. Whether this solution would have worked remains questionable. Pétain still believed that it was dishonourable for the government to abandon metropolitan France and was irked at the thought of losing power to Chautemps. These concerns were implicit in his broadcast of 20 June. After offering a bewildered nation an explanation for defeat ('too few children, too few arms, too few allies'), he repeated his determination to remain in France and spoke of how defeat offered atonement for past sins.[44] There was now an opportunity to build a new France. Clearly, Pétain had an agenda of his own, regardless of what cabinet wanted.

In the event, these plans for renewal were not jeopardized by the transfer of government to North Africa. Originally intended for 19 June, this was delayed by news, received that morning, of Germany's willingness to open armistice negotiations.[45] Further delay ensued as Berlin accredited the French plenipotentaries. This approval did not arrive until the morning of 20 June, whereupon Weygand persuaded Lebrun to remain in France until 6 p.m. By then others had made a more concerted attempt to sabotage the African operation. In mid-afternoon Alibert deliberately misled the President by playing down the extent of the German advance; thus departure was postponed until the following day. Alibert later claimed that he held matters up further by using Pétain's stationery to forge a note ordering members of government to stay at home until 8 o'clock the next morning.[46] Laval was also doing his bit to scupper the cabinet's intentions. On 20 June he saw Pétain. On 21 June the Bordeaux Commune visited Lebrun and put pressure on him not to go. Although the President remained defiant, his chances of setting sail from France were slim. Recognizing the extent of his support, a confident Pétain was now ready to go back on the cabinet agreement of 18 June. When told that Lebrun still seemed certain to quit Bordeaux, he allegedly replied, 'It's quite simple. I shall have him arrested.'[47] Perhaps conscious of what was afoot – after all, only four days earlier Alibert had had his arch-enemy, Mandel, arrested on trumped-up conspiracy charges – Lebrun chose to stay. Only a handful of politicians, unaware of any change of plans, boarded the *Massilia* on 21 June bound for Casablanca. That evening the French government received the German armistice terms.

In framing these proposals, Hitler's objectives were threefold. First, he was keen to prevent France from carrying on the fight from abroad, especially by bringing its fleet and empire into the war. Second, he was anxious not to draft a settlement which would inflame France's revolutionary heritage and provoke civil disorder. Third, he sought an agreement which would provide him with a breathing space in which to prepare for the forthcoming invasion of Britain. It was this need to husband men and material that dissuaded him from occupying all of French territory.

Thus the armistice terms, though harsh, were not as punitive as they might have been. No claim was laid on the French empire or navy; instead, ships were merely to return to port to be disarmed. As had been anticipated, Germany did not occupy all of France. Instead, a demarcation line dissected the country into two. The German zone comprised two-thirds of French territory including Paris and the whole of the Atlantic and Channel coastlines. Although drawn up in an arbitrary fashion, this division meant that Germany possessed the richest and most densely populated areas of France. In economic terms, the southern zone was dependent on the occupied zone

for everything other than fruit and wine.[48] The French government was disconcerted by this, but drew reassurance from the
promise that it would be allowed to administer both the occupied and non-occupied zones. The armistice even foresaw the
return of the government to Paris. Demands for reparations
and the occupation costs of the German army had been anticipated. The severity of the military clauses had not: hostilities
were to cease immediately; all French forces, with the excep-
tion of 100,000 men necessary for the maintenance of order,
were to be demobilized; and all arms, aeroplanes and fortifications were to be surrendered. Finally, it was decreed that the
armistice with Germany could not come into effect until a similar settlement was reached with Italy. This caused the French
some worry, yet the Italian terms were surprisingly modest. Not
wishing to upset the Franco-German negotiations, Mussolini
contented himself with a demilitarized zone, 50 kilometres in
width, along the Franco-Italian border.[49]

Although the armistice has attracted much criticism, it is
at least understandable why Pétain and the 'softs' sought this
option. After they had relinquished the possibility of going to
North Africa, there was little incentive to fight on. As has been
observed, the map was not encouraging; France was not Russia.[50] Nor did it appear likely that Britain would hold out for
long. Viewed in this light, an armistice was the only solution.
It was, after all, a temporary agreement that would shortly give
way to a peace treaty. Meanwhile, no more French lives would
be lost and something of the French army would be saved.
Further reassurance was drawn from the fact that France was
unique in Hitler's Europe in that it had been permitted some
measure of self-rule, and was thus able to work for national
renovation. In truth, the armistice spared France little. Reynaud
had been right in his warnings about Hitler. Within weeks of
signing the agreement, the Reich had seized Alsace-Lorraine,
and had placed the Nord-Pas-de-Calais under the direct control of the German military command at Brussels. In addition,
'reserved' and 'prohibited zones' were carved out of northern
and eastern departments. As will be seen in Chapter 6, Hitler
ultimately sought nothing less than the disappearance of France
from the map of Europe.

Unaware of Nazi intentions, on 22 June the French plenipo-
tentiaries, headed by Huntziger, travelled to Compiègne. There,
on the same spot and in the same railway carriage that Weygand

and Foch had received the German surrender in 1918, they agreed to Hitler's terms. Three days later Pétain made another call to the nation explaining the reasons why he had concluded an armistice.[51] Once again, his speech appears to have been well received by a majority of French men and women.[52] By contrast, on 18 June few had tuned in to the BBC to hear de Gaulle's appeal for French forces to join him in London.

. . .

After concluding the armistice, the next task of government was to choose a new home, as Bordeaux lay in the occupied zone. Nor were the Germans keen that Pétain should remain there. Because the town was next to the sea, it offered a constant temptation to take flight.[53] Several other options were discussed and ruled out. Paris was in the occupied zone and would afford the government little independence. In any case, it is doubtful whether Hitler would have agreed to this. In November 1940 Pétain proposed a transfer to Versailles, a move quickly blocked by the Germans, further proof that the Führer did not feel bound by the armistice. Forced to reside in the unoccupied zone, the Pétain government had few large towns to choose from. Toulouse was deemed unsuitable as it was the political power base of the Sarraut brothers; Marseilles was rejected thanks to its seedy image, position on the coast and distance from the occupied zone; Lyon was dismissed as Herriot was the mayor. Spared the ignominy of being the home of the *état français*, Lyon was to become the 'capital of the Resistance'. The other large town in the south was Clermont-Ferrand, where the government duly arrived on 29 June. Laval was especially pleased by this choice as he lived nearby at Châteldon and owned several local newspapers. Maybe for these reasons – and because the town was too cramped – on 1 July the government followed Baudouin's suggestion and decamped for the little spa-resort of Vichy in Allier. To take a British equivalent, it was as though the whole of Whitehall had upped bags and descended on Harrogate. Later Vichy propaganda made a virtue of the fact that the pulse of power was located deep in the heart of rural France. In truth, the town was selected for its ample hotels which could accommodate the various ministries.[54] Pétain himself established characteristically spartan quarters on the third floor of the Hôtel du Parc in the centre of the town.[55]

As the government trekked through provincial France, it was clear that the cabinet had been formed in exceptional circumstances. Accordingly, it was understood that it would not be able to abide by normal procedures, and it was not long before the issue of extraordinary powers was raised. The composition of the marshal's entourage did not bode well for the Republic's future. While men like Baudouin and Bouthillier were prepared to make use of the flexibility of the 1875 constitution to prorogue parliament and rule by decree,[56] others were determined on a new political system. Already on 28 June, Weygand had presented Pétain with a memorandum. This read, 'the old order of things, that is to say a political regime of masonic, capitalist and international compromise, has brought us to the present state. France wants no more of it.'[57]

Although Alibert was thinking along the same lines as Weygand, the person most insistent on change was Laval. Regretting his earlier rejection of the Justice portfolio, on 23 June he replaced Chautemps as Deputy Prime Minister. In the same manoeuvre, he even got Pétain to include Marquet as Minister of State and later as Minister of the Interior. Glad to be back in harness, on 26 June Laval remarked of the parliament which had ousted him from office in 1936, 'This Chamber vomited me up, now I'm going to vomit it up.'[58] Yet his desire for a new constitution stemmed from more than revenge. It was his belief that only a more authoritarian government could face up to the fascist powers and secure a Franco-German *entente*, an essential step in containing the threat of Bolshevism.

How did Pétain view the prospect of ending the Third Republic? His dislike of parliamentarianism was well known. He had also made it obvious that he saw the armistice and subsequent peace settlement as a prelude to a 'national renovation'. None the less, he possessed no blueprint for a new regime and remained cautious about how to proceed. As ever, he wanted to remain above politics and be seen to act in a constitutional manner. He was thus wary of Laval's intentions.

These were first discussed in Clermont-Ferrand on 30 June at a meeting of Pétain's 'inner cabinet'. Here Laval proposed that parliament be convoked as soon as possible. He would then persuade the politicians to vote Pétain the authority to issue a new constitution. Immediately there were objections. Baudouin doubted whether the deputies would 'commit suicide' and added that it was improper to change 'the constitution of a country whose capital is in enemy hands'.[59] Pétain agreed, and raised the objection of Lebrun. Forever confident, Laval claimed the President was no problem and left to seek him out. Within an hour he was back to say Lebrun had consented to a new constitution; Lebrun later claimed that he had merely noted what the Deputy Prime Minister had said. None the less Pétain, impressed by Laval's efficiency, agreed to give his minister's proposal a try, a commitment he reiterated at Vichy on 2 July.

On 4 July Laval and Alibert, an unlikely couple united only in their hatred of the Repubican regime, presented the 'inner cabinet' with the text they proposed putting to parliament. This demanded that the National Assembly surrender its powers to 'the Government of the Republic, under the signature and authority of Marshal Pétain . . . in order to promulgate . . . the new constitution of the French State'. By looking ahead to the *état français* rather than a republic, the authors had laid bare their anti-democratic credentials. It was also significant – and here Alibert's influence was manifest – that the new constitution promised to respect 'the rights of labour, the family and the fatherland'. The Vichy triptych of *travail, famille, patrie* had been born.

Although some of his cabinet colleagues had doubts about the text, Laval set about persuading fellow parliamentarians of its merits. In a series of 'briefing sessions' with deputies and senators, he used his skills of persuasion to the full and was not averse to frightening his audiences. Without a more authoritarian constitution, he argued, the country would be unable to reach a Franco-German agreement, and without such an *entente* France would be exposed to both internal and external dangers. Internally, there was a chance of a Weygand dictatorship; externally, France ran the risk of being totally occupied by the Germans or, worse still, of becoming a British dominion. In fanning the flames of anglophobia, Laval was aided by events outside of his control. On 3 June the British, unconvinced by the terms of the armistice, shelled the French fleet anchored off Mers-el-Kébir in Algeria. Some 1,300 lives were lost, as many being killed by drowning as from direct bombing.

Not everyone was persuaded by Laval's scare stories, and within days the schemer was faced with three alternative proposals on constitutional reform. The first of these was put together by a band of Senate war veterans headed by Jean Taurines. Despite Alibert's obstructions, these men managed to see Pétain on 6 July to express their anxieties about Laval's intentions. The marshal reassured them that he had no real ambitions for power. Once a peace was settled, he would retire to his home in the south. Meanwhile, he only wished to avoid the difficulties that had faced Lebrun and be free of party intrigue. He promised that he would act openly, submitting new constitutional laws for parliamentary approval. Comforted by these words, the senators replied that Pétain ought to have the authority to govern by decree until a new constitution was drawn up in consultation with parliament. Apparently the marshal then exclaimed, 'That is a proposal. Let me see a text.' Within 24 hours the senators were back with a draft document embodying the suggestions which they had floated the previous day.[60]

Also on 7 July the marshal was confronted with a second, and more radical, plan produced by Flandin, one of Laval's former ministerial colleagues. As everyone was agreed on a Pétain government, he saw little point in changing the constitution. The simple solution was for the President to resign and for the marshal to take his place. He would then govern with powers similar to those previously granted to Daladier and Reynaud during the *drôle de guerre*. As with the senators, Pétain gave his blessing to this scheme and encouraged Flandin to pursue the matter. He soon ran into problems. Lebrun, supported by Jeanneney and Herriot, saw no need to resign and on 8 July Flandin admitted defeat.[61] None the less, that day saw the emergence of a third proposal framed by Vincent Badie, a Radical deputy from the Hérault. Concerned for democracy's future, he drafted an amendment to Laval's text. While this was prepared to grant Pétain full powers until the conclusion of 'a lasting and honourable peace', it explicitly rejected the imputation contained in the preamble of the government's bill that the Republic was in any way responsible for the defeat.[62]

How do we explain Pétain's ambivalent attitude to the above proposals? Apart from the Badie motion, he seems to have given his blessing to each one of the schemes concocted by Laval, Taurines and Flandin. It has since been speculated that he was playing a double or triple game, fending one group off against another.[63] Others have argued that he was genuinely won over by the various suggestions but that Laval then convinced him of their defects. It is more likely that he was biding his time. Never one to be seen openly politicking or seeking power via a conspiracy, he continued to wait on events, confident in the knowledge that whatever happened he would ultimately be granted the right to rule without recourse to parliament.

This confidence was witnessed in his handling of Taurines' proposal. When on 7 July the senators presented him with their plan, he told them that they must now consult with Laval who was the 'government's representative in the matter'. Not surprisingly, the Deputy Prime Minister refused their text, which Taurines decided to propose as an amendment to the government's bill. Having seen off the senators, Laval was determined to consolidate his own position and asked Pétain for a letter pledging his support for the government motion. Without this, he would not go before the National Assembly. Pétain, in turn, was happy to oblige,[64] perhaps aware that Laval was best able to convince the National Assembly of the need for constitutional change. Yet it is doubtful whether his support for Laval was whole-hearted. So long as he was granted full powers, Pétain was happy with whichever scheme won the vote.

On 9 July the National Assembly held a preliminary meeting where it agreed on the necessity of constitutional reform. Wishing to curtail any further discussion that day, Laval proposed that the two chambers should meet together in a secret session the next morning where they would discuss matters informally before voting in the afternoon. It was at this early session of 10 July, held in camera, that Laval announced a modification to the government's bill: the future constitution would not be ratified by the assemblies it had established, but by 'the nation' as a whole. Laval might have introduced this change to allay the worries of the ex-service senators. If so, the ploy failed; they remained determined to move their amendment. This prompted Laval to read out the letter which Pétain had granted him on 7 July. He then made a speech which focused on his usual themes: the foolishness of the Republic in declaring war; the mistakes of the Popular Front; the treachery of Britain; and the feebleness of parliamentary democracy. He concluded by invoking the need for discipline and recalled the prestige of Pétain.

At the public session that afternoon, Laval had other tactics at hand to ensure that he won the vote. In a procedural motion it was decided to vote on the government's bill first, ahead of the two main amendments put forward by Badie and

Taurines. It was also decided that, as the assembly was meeting in unusual circumstances, the government only required a simple majority and not the constitutionally agreed majority of all members entitled to attend.[65] Victory was now assured, and in the ensuing vote the government's motion was carried by 569 votes to 80 with 17 abstentions. The Third Republic had been pronounced dead.

In explaining the size of this majority, historians have ventured a number of interpretations. Some still cling to the idea of a Pétain–Laval conspiracy. Others have argued that parliament was assassinated by Laval. Certainly, in the days before the vote, terror was his favourite weapon. At Pétain's trial, Blum recalled how on 9–10 July an atmosphere of fear had gripped the parliamentarians: a fear of Doriot's gangs in the street; a fear of Weygand's troops at Clermont-Ferrand; and a fear of the Germans nearby at Moulins.[66] Indeed, Laval had no hesitation in threatening recalcitrant deputies with sanctions. Those parliamentarians who had left on the *Massilia* and since returned to metropolitan France were denounced as traitors. Even so, it is important not to exaggerate the Auvergnat's influence. The overwhelming impression is that the National Assembly was already willing to grant Pétain full powers; it needed little persuading by Laval. Contrary to what Baudouin had predicted, parliament was ready to commit suicide.

Evidence to support this view stems from an analysis of parliament itself. First, it should be remembered that the Chamber of 1940 was not the Popular Front Chamber of 1936.[67] Since 1938 the balance of power had shifted rightwards, a move which was even more pronounced after the exclusion of communist deputies in October 1939. Without doubt, this centre-right majority was more amenable to an authoritarian regime, although it should not be forgotten that many left-wing deputies were also prepared to concede constitutional changes. Second, it appears that pacifism had a bearing on the vote of 10 July. Although most parliamentarians had rallied round the war effort, not all had overcome their repugnance for war. For the pacifists on the left, the vote of 10 July was less a move to alter the constitution than an attempt to secure a long-lasting peace. For the pacifists on the right, the vote was not necessarily an indication of their empathy for fascism; it was, instead, an opportunity to reach an accommodation with an hereditary enemy which possessed superior resources.

Third, several deputies acknowledged that they would have to relinquish some of their powers to a cabinet which was operating in extraordinary circumstances. To a degree, French politicians were already accustomed to doing this. During the Great Depression and *drôle de guerre*, they had regularly delegated their authority to government. Between 1 September 1939 and 10 May 1940 parliament only voted for 29 laws; by contrast the government took 644 decrees. Fourth, it is possible that some deputies were relieved that they had the opportunity to jettison a regime which had been in place for the past 70 years. This did not necessarily denote an antipathy for liberal democracy. Rather, in the 1930s, a growing number of parliamentarians had become convinced that the Republic was beyond reform and was incapable of meeting the challenges of the twentieth century. Military defeat had been its ultimate failing.

There is, then, considerable evidence to support the view that parliament committed hara-kiri. Yet it is doubtful whether it would have impaled itself on the sword of Laval's motion had it not been for the prestige surrounding the marshal. Nearly everyone was agreed that he was the right man for the moment, the only person who could secure peace with Germany and maintain internal stability. After all, he was a marshal of France; a well-loved leader of men; the 'Victor of Verdun'; the 'Republican' general; France's 'noblest and most humane soldier'; the supreme example of sacrifice; the embodiment of the nation's honour. Few recognized that he did not possess the virtues accredited to him.

Pétain, too, was unaware of his weaknesses. Observers were quick to note the delight which he took on being accorded full powers. Shortly after the vote, Serrigny found his friend in talkative mood; he was no longer the 'silent marshal' who rarely said more than three words.[68] Passing Pétain in the corridors of the Hôtel du Parc, du Moulin de Labarthète noted a similar change. The grey old man who had responded to Reynaud's call on 17 May was now walking tall with a sharp gaze and colour in his face.[69] These comments are important as they help lay to rest the claim made by some of Pétain's supporters that the old soldier was already senile in 1940, and was thus incapable of understanding what was happening. Certainly age was beginning to take its toll. Several people commented that he appeared hard of hearing – although, as Spears commented, his deafness was selective, depending on the subject of conversation.[70] It is also true that his personal doctor and private secretary, Bernard Ménétrel, gave him shots of amphetamine to heighten his spirits. Yet, contrary to what is sometimes claimed, he was never the dreamy Reaganesque figure who fell asleep in cabinet meetings, 'le conquistador' (le con qui se dort) as Mandel christened him.[71] While he tired easily, throughout his time at Vichy he retained a remarkable alertness;[72] and, as Laval discovered to his cost, a formidable will of his own. Pétain was only mentally old in the sense that his 'preconceptions had become even more firmly entrenched than before'.[73] He did not understand that they fitted ill with the harsh realities of occupation.

. . .

NOTES AND REFERENCES

1. Pétain quoted in M. Séguéla, *Pétain-Franco. Les secrets d'une alliance* (Paris: Albin Michel, 1992), pp. 44–5.
2. J.F. McMillan, *Twentieth-Century France. Politics and Society, 1898–1991* (London: Edward Arnold, 1992), p. 125.
3. J.-L. Crémieux-Brilhac, *Les français de l'an 40*, vol. 1 (Paris: Gallimard, 1990), p. 284 and E. Weber, *The Hollow Years. France in the 1930s* (New York: Norton, 1994), p. 267.
4. McMillan, *Twentieth-Century France*, p. 125.
5. Ibid.
6. Crémieux-Brilhac, *Les français*, vol. 1 pp. 407–11 and vol. 2 pp. 425–48.
7. Among the many comparisons of French and German forces, see P.M.H. Bell, *The Origins of the Second World War in Europe* (London: Longman, 1985), p. 167; Crémieux-Brilhac, *Les français*, vol. 2 pp. 347–55; J.-B. Duroselle, *L'abîme. Politique étrangère de la France, 1939–1944* (Paris: Imprimerie Nationale, 1982), pp. 20–2; and R. Frankenstein, *Le prix du réarmement français, 1935–1939* (Paris: Publications de la Sorbonne, 1982), pp. 303–19.
8. P. Jackson, 'Recent Journeys Along the Road Back to France, 1940', *Historical Journal*, 39 (2) 1996, pp. 497–9.
9. R. Griffiths, *Marshal Pétain* (London: Constable, 1970), p. 221.
10. M. Alexander, 'Maurice Gamelin and the Defeat of France, 1939–1940', in B. Bond (ed.), *Fallen Stars. Eleven Studies of Twentieth-Century Military Disasters* (London: Brassey's, 1991), p. 111.
11. M. Alexander, *The Republic in Danger. General Maurice Gamelin and the Politics of French Defence, 1933–1940* (Cambridge: Cambridge University Press, 1992), p. 379.

12. Alexander, 'Maurice Gamelin', pp. 119–24; Duroselle, *L'abîme*, pp. 51–7; and D. Porch, *The French Secret Services. From the Dreyfus Affair to the Gulf War* (London: Macmillan, 1995), pp. 159–61.

13. Alexander, 'Maurice Gamelin', p. 111. This essay provides a succinct guide to allied strategy in 1939–40. See too J.A. Gunsburg, *Divided and Conquered. The French High Command and the Defeat of the West, 1940* (Westport, Conn.: Greenwood, 1979), pp. 119–46.

14. Gunsburg, *Divided and Conquered*, p. xxii and R. Young, *In Command of France. French Foreign Policy and Military Planning, 1933–1940* (Cambridge, Mass.: Harvard University Press, 1978), p. 247.

15. A. Horne, *To Lose a Battle. France 1940* (London: Macmillan, 1969), pp. 361–86.

16. M. Ferro, *Pétain* (Paris: Fayard, 1987), pp. 29–30.

17. Griffiths, *Pétain*, p. 227.

18. W. Churchill, *The Second World War*, vol. 2 (London: Cassel, 1949), pp. 108–9.

19. P. Baudouin, *Neuf mois au gouvernement, avril–décembre 1940* (Paris: Editions de la Table Ronde, 1948), p. 86.

20. E. Spears, *Assignment to Catastrophe*, vol. 1 (London: Heinemann, 1954), p. 223.

21. Griffiths, *Pétain*, p. 230.

22. G. Warner, *Pierre Laval and the Eclipse of France* (London: Eyre & Spottiswoode, 1968), p. 162.

23. Ibid.

24. Baudouin, *Neuf mois*, p. 90.

25. Griffiths, *Pétain*, p. 230.

26. P. Reynaud, *La France a sauvé l'Europe*, vol. 2 (Paris: Flammarion, 1947), p. 260. See too Warner, *Pierre Laval*, p. 164.

27. Baudouin, *Neuf mois*, p. 130.

28. C. de Gaulle, *Mémoires de guerre*, vol. 1 (Paris: Plon, 1954), p. 60.

29. Among the many accounts of this meeting, see Baudouin, *Neuf mois*, pp. 135–8; Churchill, *The Second World War*, vol. 2 pp. 136–8; A. Eden, *The Eden Memoirs*, vol. 2 (London: Cassel, 1965), p. 115; de Gaulle, *Mémoires de guerre*, vol. 1 pp. 53–4; Spears, *Assignment to Catastrophe*, vol. 2 pp. 133–59; and Reynaud, *La France*, vol. 2 pp. 297–311.

30. Churchill, *The Second World War*, vol. 2 p. 139.

31. Eden, *The Eden Memoirs*, vol. 2 p. 117.

32. On this meeting, see Baudouin, *Neuf mois*, pp. 147–52; Y. Bouthillier, *Le drame de Vichy*, vol. 1 (Paris: Plon, 1950), pp. 54–9; C. Chautemps, *Les cahiers secrets de l'armistice* (Paris: Plon, 1963), pp. 125–9; A. Lebrun, *Témoignages* (Paris: Plon, 1945), pp. 75–6; and Reynaud, *La France*, vol. 2 pp. 313–6.

33. Warner, *Pierre Laval*, p. 168.

34. Ibid., pp. 168–9 and Reynaud, *La France*, vol. 2 p. 319.

35. This note is in R. Aron, *Histoire de Vichy* (Paris: Fayard, 1954), p. 21.
36. Baudouin, *Neuf mois*, p. 166.
37. Griffiths, *Pétain*, p. 238.
38. This letter is in H. Noguères, *Le veritable procès du maréchal Pétain* (Paris: Fayard, 1955), p. 107
39. Warner, *Pierre Laval*, p. 176.
40. Griffiths, *Pétain*, p. 239.
41. Warner, *Pierre Laval*, p. 177.
42. Speech of 17 June 1940 in J.-C. Barbas (ed.), *Philippe Pétain. Discours aux français, 17 juin 1940–20 août 1944* (Paris: Albin Michel, 1989), pp. 57–8.
43. Griffiths, *Pétain*, p. 241.
44. Speech of 20 June 1940 in Barbas (ed.), *Discours*, pp. 59–60.
45. See C. Rimbaud, *L'affaire du Massilia, été 1940* (Paris: Seuil, 1984), pp. 68–96.
46. Warner, *Pierre Laval*, p. 181.
47. Ibid., p. 184 and Aron, *Histoire de Vichy*, p. 72.
48. H.R. Kedward, *Occupied France. Collaboration and Resistance, 1940–1944* (Oxford: Basil Blackwell, 1985), p. 2.
49. Warner, *Pierre Laval*, p. 188.
50. J. Cairns, 'Along the Road Back to France', *American Historical Review*, LXIV (3) 1959, p. 84.
51. Speech of 25 June 1940 in Barbas (ed.), *Discours*, pp. 63–6.
52. G. Miller, *Les pousse-au-jouir du maréchal Pétain* (Paris: Seuil, 1975), p. 45.
53. M. Cointet-Labrousse, *Vichy et le fascisme* (Brussels: Editions Complexe, 1987), pp. 26–7.
54. M. Cointet-Labrousse, *Vichy capitale* (Paris: Perrin, 1993), pp. 17–21.
55. Ibid., p. 60.
56. Warner, *Pierre Laval*, p. 193.
57. This memorandum is in Ferro, *Pétain*, pp. 125–6.
58. Laval quoted in Baudouin, *Neuf mois*, p. 219.
59. Ibid., pp. 227–8.
60. Aron, *Histoire de Vichy*, p. 122 and Warner, *Pierre Laval*, p. 199.
61. Warner, *Pierre Laval*, p. 201.
62. Ibid., p. 205.
63. Aron, *Histoire de Vichy*, p. 122.
64. Noguères, *Le veritable procès*, p. 162.
65. Warner, *Pierre Laval*, p. 208.
66. Testimony of Léon Blum, 27 July 1945, in *Procès du maréchal Pétain. Compte rendu officiel in extenso des audiences de la Haute Cour de Justice* (Paris: Louis Paliente, 1976), p. 103.
67. Cointet-Labrousse, *Vichy et le fascisme*, pp. 29–35.
68. B. Serrigny, *Trente ans avec Pétain* (Paris: Plon, 1959), p. 179.

69. H. du Moulin de Labarthète, *Le temps des illusions. Souvenirs, juillet 1940–avril 1942* (Geneva: Le Cheval Ailé, 1946), p. 17.
70. Spears, *Assignment to Catastrophe*, vol. 2 p. 183.
71. M. Larkin, *France Since the Popular Front* (Oxford: Clarendon Press, 1986), p. 83.
72. Du Moulin de Labarthète, *Le temps*, p. 90.
73. Griffiths, *Pétain*, p. 250.

Chapter 5

LE CHEF, 1940–2

At Pétain's trial in 1945, controversy raged over the nature of his powers during the Occupation. Reluctant to advance a plea of senility, the defence claimed that he had been divested of any real authority by the Nazis. What little freedom he retained had been used to save the French from further suffering. In the words of Jacques Isorni, the ablest of the defence team, Pétain had been the 'shield' of France and de Gaulle the 'sword'. Although this argument was designed to turn the tables on the prosecution and embarrass the Provisional Government, there is no doubt that the marshal genuinely cared for his countrymen. Nor is there any disputing the enormous pressures that the Germans placed on his government. None the less, Isorni carefully ignored the old soldier's political ambition and desire to build a new France. He also played down the autonomy which Vichy had enjoyed in the unoccupied zone. As German archives have demonstrated, during the period from July 1940 to early 1942 Hitler cared little about what went on in this area so long as the German military position remained secure.[1] What, then, was the true extent of Pétain's powers, and how did he use his influence?

. . .

In voting for the suspension of the 1875 Constitution, many deputies believed they were merely investing Pétain with the extraordinary powers he would need until the conclusion of a peace and the return of government to Paris, as foreseen in the armistice agreement.[2] They had not bargained on the intentions of his associates, who sought nothing less than the destruction of liberal democracy. On 11 July 1940, cabinet was presented with three constitutional acts. Drafted by Alibert, in consultation with Laval, these laid the legal foundations of Pétainist rule.[3] Only too happy to allow others to do his dirty work for him, the marshal was delighted with this new-found authority. It went far beyond what he could have originally hoped for when he took over as Prime Minister on 16 June, and vindicated his decision not to have become embroiled in the manoeuvrings that led to the destruction of the National Assembly.

Published in the *Journal Officiel* on 12 July, each one of these laws began with the declaration, 'Nous, Philippe Pétain, Maréchal de France'. Hereafter, the royal 'we' would preface all legislation, thus underlining the monocratic nature of the new regime. No longer did the source of power emanate from the people, but from the person of the marshal. According to constitutional act number one, he was head of the French state, *chef de l'état français*. At the same time, the office of President, a key element in the 1875 Republican constitution, was abolished. In future, all coins, banknotes, stamps and official notepaper would bear the legend 'état français' and the profile of the marshal. Only in the dying days of the Vichy regime did the word 'Republic' begin to reappear on official documents as foresightful civil servants, mindful of their careers, sought to prove their democratic credentials.

The second act of 11 July 1940 amplified Pétain's functions. Among other responsibilities, he possessed the right to nominate ministers, appoint government officials, initiate laws, command the armed forces, negotiate treaties, and grant pardons and amnesties. Thus the old distinction between judicial, executive and legislative powers, an important characteristic of the Republican regime, had gone: all authority was now invested in one man. The only restriction on his position was that he could not declare war without 'the prior assent of the legislative assemblies', a provision which was to prove valuable in later dealings with the Germans.

To be sure, Pétain was only supposed to enjoy these powers until the introduction of a new constitution. The third act of 11 July 1940 looked ahead to the formation of fresh assemblies. In the meantime, the existing Senate and Chamber were to be adjourned; only the marshal was authorized to reconvene them. In the event, he never bothered. Thus, for the first time since 1789, France possessed no national representative body. Nor was there any hurry to establish a new constitution.

Although a National Council was created in 1941 with the task of looking into this matter, it announced that it could not act until the conclusion of peace.[4]

A fourth act, approved on 12 July 1940, settled the question of a succession. Originally the marshal had intended that this would be decided by cabinet; in the event, he named Laval. It is possible that he bowed to Laval's argument that only a civilian would allay fears of a Weygand take-over. It might also be that he wanted to reward his deputy for having steered through the destruction of the National Assembly. Afterwards the newly appointed dauphin liked to flatter the elderly marshal by telling him that he had more power than Louis XIV. In practice, Vichy was never a personal dictatorship in which one man ruled the roost. How, then, did government operate under the *état français?*

True to his authoritarian leanings, Pétain relied heavily on a personal entourage which he saw more frequently than he did his ministers.[5] This body advised on policy and helped compose his speeches. Its members included life-long friends: General Laure; Charles Brécard; Major Bonhomme; and Ménétrel, his personal physician. A vicious antisemite, Ménétrel soon acquired a reputation as an *éminence grise* protecting the marshal from unwanted visitors. Others in the entourage were men whom Pétain had known in Spain. Du Moulin de Labarthète, a former financial attaché in Madrid, was made head of his *cabinet civil*, and Major Gorostarzu entered his *cabinet militaire*. The most prominent newcomer among this clique was René Gillouin. A Protestant sympathizer of the Action Française, in 1941 he was shocked by Vichy's antisemitism and carefully distanced himself from the regime.

Although this entourage was undoubtedly important, key legislative matters, especially those concerning foreign policy, were taken by a team of leading ministers known as the *petit conseil.* Meeting every morning in a room adjoining the marshal's office in the Hôtel du Parc, this inner council initially comprised Pétain himself; Laval; Alibert; Baudouin; Bouthillier; Darlan; and Weygand. In 1941, when Darlan replaced Laval as the marshal's principal minister, government was run as a so-called 'Directorate' in which key decisions again remained the task of an inner council.

Wider administrative matters were the province of the full cabinet which assembled at the Pavillon Sévigné. To begin with, this met once a week; but, as it framed domestic legislation, it soon convened on a more frequent basis. The upshot was that the policies of the National Revolution were often determined more by the personalities and ideologies of individual ministers than by the marshal and his advisers. Nor did Pétain have complete control over ministerial appointments. As in the Third Republic, cabinets frequently came and went. The background to these changes will be considered in the context of Franco-German relations, but it should be emphasized that, before 1944, the Germans forced resignations but rarely: Weygand in September 1940; Xavier Vallat in May 1942; and a number of those involved in the plot against Laval of 13 December 1940, notably Alibert, de la Laurencie and Peyrouton.[6] Otherwise, the instability of personnel may be put down to inter-ministerial rivalries and the failure of government policies.

Pétain's first ministry, that of 17 June to 12 July, was essentially the rump of Reynaud's old cabinet, and it was no surprise that the marshal wanted to include his own people. Thus a reshuffle of 12 July brought in yet more military figures and representatives of the traditional right. The only member of the left was René Belin, a high-ranking official in the Confédération Générale du Travail (CGT), whose pacifism and belief in corporatism drew him to the Vichy camp where he became Minister of Industrial Production and Labour. Significantly, Pétain did not include any of the prominent *liguers* who soon found the atmosphere at Paris more congenial than Vichy. Fearful of their German backers, he looked on these people as potential rivals. Nor did he wish to employ former parliamentarians, and in a second reshuffle of 6 September he dismissed Marquet and introduced another batch of traditionalists: Vallat at Veterans' Affairs and Georges Lamirand in charge of Youth. The one parliamentarian to survive was, of course, Laval, who managed to add Information to his other responsibilities. On 24 October he even succeeded in taking over Foreign Affairs, the post he had long coveted. Yet he ought to have seen the writing on the wall, and on 13 December he was dismissed in a third reshuffle. Ironically, his place was filled by another ex-parliamentarian, Flandin. The one other change was the inclusion of Jacques Chevalier at Education. A devout Catholic and political reactionary, this academic philosopher further strengthened the position of the traditionalists.

By the beginning of 1941 the marshal had largely been successful in filling his cabinet with like-minded individuals, and it is significant that this period coincided with the high-point of the National Revolution. However, on 9 February 1941, Pétain was forced to undertake a fourth reshuffle thanks to the resignation of Flandin, who was disappointed that he had been unable to make headway in his negotiations with the Germans. That same day Pétain named Darlan as Deputy Prime Minister, and entrusted him with Foreign Affairs and Defence as well. The next day the admiral became *dauphin* and, on 17 February, added Information to his other responsibilities. The emergence of Darlan clearly marked a diminution of Pétain's own authority. Not only did Darlan combine more posts than Laval, he had little time for the traditionalists in cabinet, describing them as 'virgin altar boys'.[7] His preference was for technocrats, young *dirigistes* who believed that the efficient running of the state was a matter for the state itself.[8] The practice of recruiting 'experts' to help run government had been initiated by the Third Republic; yet never before had their influence been so pronounced as under Vichy. Typical of Darlan's recruits was Pierre Pucheu, a former official of the Cartel des Forges, who took charge of Industrial Production. On 11 August 1941 a fifth major reshuffle saw the traditionalists again lose out. Pucheu moved over to the Interior; his place at Industrial Production was taken by François Lehideux, Louis Renault's nephew. The influence of these men undoubtedly troubled Pétain, yet he tolerated Darlan as the man most capable of achieving concessions from Berlin. As will be seen, it was largely this quest for a breakthrough in Franco-German relations that led in April 1942 to the recall of Laval and the extinction of much of Pétain's remaining authority.

What should not be overlooked is that changes in government organization and personnel were being replicated at a local level. On 12 October 1940 elected departmental councils were abolished; their place was taken by appointed administrative ones.[9] On 16 November 1940, Vichy was permitted to nominate mayors for all towns with a population over 2,000. Municipal councils in such communes were, in turn, to be chosen by the new mayor. Ultimately, it was the dream of the traditionalists in Pétain's entourage to replace the administrative units of the Third Republic with the provinces of medieval France, thus providing the nation with a link to an organic past. Given Hitler's plans to dissect France, this remained a pipe-dream. Meanwhile, Vichy contented itself with a large-scale *épuration* of Republican officials. Not surprisingly, out went the elected representatives of 'the classic Third Republic small-town left – the radical and moderately socialist local school-teachers, lawyers, and merchants who formed the "republic of pals".'[10] In came Pétainist disciples.

The marshal himself liked to call these appointees the 'défenseurs naturels' of France;[11] more commonly they are referred to as the 'notables'. Recent research has shown that they were drawn from local business, small industry, finance, landed property and professions such as medicine and law.[12] Significantly, each of these groups had a vested interest in reversing the social changes introduced by the Popular Front. As has been remarked, this did not mean that the notables were a political minority. It is often forgotten that nearly half of an all-male electorate voted against Blum in 1936. Had there been an election in 1940, it probably would have produced a right-wing landslide: 'Pétainism, in a sense, was that landslide.'[13] Thus the country was prepared to accept that socially con-servative groups should occupy the key positions of power. The result was that for the first time since the Second Empire, France possessed a uniformity of political control at both a national and local level. In the long term this proved a weak-ness as it meant that many areas, especially towns with left-wing traditions, were governed by people out of touch with local sentiment.[14] Slowly but surely, the French recognized that the government under Vichy was even more remote than under the Third Republic.

To be fair, Pétain's advisers were conscious that the emerg-ing structures of the Vichy state, in particular the constitu-tional acts of July 1940, did not provide a link between *le chef* and his people. One means of forging this bridge was through the many tours which Pétain conducted in the unoccupied zone. In 1941 alone, he visited Saint-Etienne, Le Puy, Grenoble, Vienne, Pau, Lourdes, Tarbes, Montluçon, Commentry, Limoges, Roanne, Aix-en-Provence, Auch, Nérac, Agen, Les Alpes, Lyon and Beaujolais.[15] Each of these appearances brought thousands on to the streets, scenes that were eloquently described by the hagiographer, René Benjamin.[16] At Vichy itself, crowds gathered in the afternoons to watch Pétain take his regular walk from the Hôtel du Parc to the nearby square where he would chat with old soldiers and play with small children.[17] These were the techniques of fraternizing that he had used so effectively in the trenches. By avoiding over-familiarity and by retaining an aloofness worthy of his position, he presented himself as a leader the people could trust. He was also one they could listen to. His frail voice, 'interrupted by dry coughs',[18] was often to be heard on the radio, lecturing the French on the need to change their ways. As in the past, the old soldier called on his *nègres* (ghost-writers) to draft his broadcasts for him. This team included some curious individuals. It has not gone unnoticed that one of his most famous speeches, that of 25 June 1940, in which he evoked simple peasant values by declaring 'the earth does not lie', was written by Emmanuel Berl, a half-Jewish Parisian intellectual who later fled France for fear of falling victim to Vichy's antisemitic legislation.[19]

A further means of establishing a bridge between the marshal and the people was through the establishment of a single party, an option favoured by other authoritarian regimes. Déat suggested this solution when he visited Vichy in July 1940.[20] The proposal was quickly rejected. Not only were the Germans opposed to the idea, so too was Pétain. Having decried the Republic as a 'regime of parties' and self-interested compromise, he had no wish to be seen heading a party himself. Moreover, there was the fear that such a party would fall into the wrong hands. Rather, the marshal looked to the organizations of the National Revolution – the Chantiers de la Jeunesse, the Secours National, the Corporation Paysanne – to act as a 'transmission belt' between himself and the population.[21] The workings of these bodies will be discussed later, but some mention must be made of the veterans' association, the Légion Française des Combattants, as this linked Pétain to the men with whom he felt most empathy, and was the nearest Vichy ever came to creating a political party. As Laure declared, 'The Légion is not a state within a state: it is the state since it includes in its ranks and at its head the *chef de l'état.*'[22]

In essence, the Légion was an amalgamation of the many ex-servicemen organizations that had existed before 1939.[23] Forbidden by the Germans to operate in the occupied zone, by 1941 it had still managed to recruit 1,700,000 members. Anxious to inculcate loyalty to the Vichy regime, these former soldiers distributed propaganda and organized receptions for the marshal as he toured southern France. Often *légionnaires* were given privileged positions in local government. From there, they kept a watch on the public, denouncing any subversive behaviour. Inevitably, these activities angered some prefects who felt that their own responsibilities were being undermined. In the event, prefectoral authority remained intact and the influence of the Légion declined, reflecting the loss of public confidence in Vichy. By 1942 the regime had been forced to open its membership to any supporter of the National Revolution, regardless of whether he had served in the armed forces. Ominously, in 1943 the more active *légionnaires* helped found the Milice Française, a security force designed to combat the Resistance.

The growth of internal dissidence marked a clear challenge to the authority of both Vichy and the marshal. Yet Pétain's supporters drew reassurance from the fact that he continued to command enormous popular support. Indeed, in this respect, his authority did resemble that of Louis XIV. As under the *ancien régime*, the public was disinclined to blame its sovereign. Opprobrium was heaped instead on his evil ministers, notably Laval. Why, then, did Pétain enjoy such popularity? To answer this question, it is necessary to examine further the cult of marshalship.

In 1940 it was difficult to avoid the cult of the marshal. Within government buildings, his bust replaced that of Marianne. Within schools, special lessons were devoted to his honour and the classroom walls reverberated to sounds of, 'Maréchal, nous voilà', a song specially composed for children. Within churches, his portrait frequently stood behind the altar. Within the countryside, peasants dug up clods of their land which they then sent in caskets to their leader. Within people's homes, a photograph of the marshal often hung on the wall. In October 1941 the government announced that sales of Pétain's portrait and other memorabilia had totalled 16,848,000F, the profits of which were to be used for the relief agency, the Secours National.[24] Pétain thoroughly enjoyed this hero-worship. Whereas in 1916 he had been no Joffre, devoting hours to his fan-mail, in 1940 he took enormous pleasure in receiving gifts from his countrymen. When du Moulin de Labarthète warned against this, he replied, 'But it gives them so much pleasure.'[25]

Given the various manifestations of this cult, some historians have spoken of there being 40 million Pétainists in the summer of 1940.[26] This is clearly an exaggeration. First, it should be remembered that there were always dissenting voices, even at the time of the armistice. For example, on 17 June 1940, the day before de Gaulle broadcast from London, Edmond Michelet, a prominent Christian Democrat, typed an appeal to the inhabitants of Brive-la-Gaillarde, a small town deep in the heart of rural France, urging them to continue the fight.[27] Elsewhere, other individuals were taking similar initiatives out of which would emerge a resistance movement. Second, it is clear that there was a regional dimension to Pétain's popularity. Crudely speaking, it appears that this was strongest in the unoccupied zone. This was because the marshal's ruralist image, carefully constructed by Vichy propagandists, was better suited to the social structure of the south than to the north.[28] It was also because the north was occupied from the very beginning, thus limiting the scope of Vichy propaganda. It is especially noticeable that Pétainism never had a tremendous appeal in the annexed zone of the Nord-Pas-de-Calais, where it was difficult to portray the marshal as a saviour; here, Gaullism was quick to take a hold.[29] Interestingly, Pétainism also proved popular in French Algeria, 'an area which never saw German troops during the war and where, consequently, Pétain was little tainted by associations with defeat and invasion'.[30] Third, historians have made a distinction between a 'passive' form of Pétainism and an 'active' one.[31] 'Active' Pétainists were those ideologically committed to the National Revolution, for example the 'notables' and members of the Légion. 'Passive' Pétainists, the majority of the population, tended to be those men and women who looked upon the marshal as a figurehead. Their loyalty was to the man himself, not to his government.

The strength of the marshal's cult has been explained in various ways. Some writers have suggested that the demoralized men and women of France were manipulated by Vichy propaganda, in particular the patriotic language of the National Revolution.[32] Certainly Vichy, like all authoritarian regimes, was anxious to influence public opinion, yet historians today are increasingly convinced that Pétainism came as much from below as it did from above.[33] Had it simply been the work of propagandists, it is doubtful that throughout the Occupation over 2000 people a day would have written personally to the marshal.

The spontaneity and depth of this loyalty has already been explained in terms of the public's disenchantment with the

Third Republic in general and the Popular Front in particular. It is also necessary to recall the shock of defeat. The speed with which the French armies collapsed in June 1940 left public opinion in a bewildered state. That bewilderment had been compounded by the *exode*. In a desperate attempt to escape the advance of the Panzers, between six and eight million refugees took to the roads. Seemingly abandoned by government officials and stranded in unfamiliar surroundings in southern France, they looked for a figure of hope amid the confusion, and out of that chaos stepped the marshal.

The depth of public loyalty to Pétain may be further explained by reference to the cult of marshalship that had been born out of the First World War. In this respect, it helped that in the 1920s and 1930s Pétain had rarely commented on national affairs. This silence not only distinguished him from excitable Republican politicians, it also meant that 'he had become a blank image, ready to be stamped with each Frenchman's conception of a saviour'.[34] To ex-soldiers, he was the hero of Verdun, France's most compassionate general, a man who would make no more wars. To the peasantry, he was one of their own, an honest leader of unpretentious habits, who would promote the interests of the countryside. To Catholics, especially among the episcopacy, he was the 'homme providentiel', a product of the *école libre*, who would reverse the past 60 years of state secularism. To left-wing sympathizers, he was the most Republican of the High Command, a man who would check the reactionary impulses of Weygand and others. To Vichy 'notables', he was the personification of all those traditional values that had made France great. As in the 1930s, those who mocked Pétain tended to be drawn from the irreverent right which now openly embraced the German cause.[35]

Although each man and woman had their own concept of a saviour, Vichy propaganda, the marshal's own speeches and those of his supporters also articulated a philosophy of Pétainism. Great stress was laid on his gifts of leadership. There were few limits to his abilities: he was frequently heralded as 'le chef', 'le père', 'le médecin'. Some, including many Catholics, spoke of his divine qualities. At Lyon, the regional prefect, Pierre Angeli, used the occasion of a prize-giving to instruct children to follow the marshal as the Hebrews had followed the signs in the desert.[36] One of the most outlandish religious tributes came from Georges Gérard who, echoing the cult of

Joffre, rewrote the Lord's Prayer in Pétain's honour.[37] Others compared Pétain to great figures in French history, notably Joan of Arc. Carefully avoiding the ambiguity which surrounded the Maid of Orléans as a figure of resistance, play was made of the way in which both Joan and Pétain had united France at a time of crisis.[38] Thus the marshal's leadership qualities were presented in an anti-historical manner; they were attributes that transcended time. Rarely did Vichy propaganda refer to specific events in his life; the press was even told not to label him as 'Victor of Verdun' as this drew attention to his age.[39] Instead, references were made to his good health – his upright figure, his broad shoulders and piercing blue eyes.

In addition, Pétainism was projected as a form of patriotism. This was not the Jacobin nationalism of the Revolutionary tradition. Nor was it the xenophobic nationalism of fascism. Instead, it was the patriotism of a traditional right, epitomized by such writers as Maurras, Bainville, and Barrès. Accordingly, Pétainism rejected all those things which were deemed to have made France less than a nation: individualism; intellectualism; parliamentary democracy; socialism; communism; freemasonry; and Judaism. In their place, the marshal offered the traditional and simple virtues which had once made France great. These were the values of discipline, order, and hierarchy which stemmed from the soil, the family and Catholicism. To emphasize the marshal's own commitment to such values, reference was made to his military upbringing. As Pétain himself believed, the army was the supreme embodiment of the nation and a key instrument in the re-education of the people. This explains why he was almost invariably portrayed in his uniform, addressing rallies of *anciens combattants*.[40]

Finally, Pétainism was represented as a form of social conservatism. His hagiographers were quick to remind their readers that the marshal came from peasant stock; that he was the fourth child of a family of seven; and that his family had lived in the Artois for generations. No reference was made to the fact that in 1919 he had decided against retiring to his birthplace and had chosen to buy a house in the south. Instead, he was presented as the protector of a traditional society which was based on the land. As well as being the 'chef de l'état français' he was often described as 'le chef de la terre française'. His own speeches lauded the merits of the peasantry, representing the humble *paysan* as one of the healthiest and most vibrant elements in French society. In so doing, Pétain stood as a bulwark of stability who would defend the countryside from the corrosive effects of industrialization and the influence of a left-wing proletariat whose power had recently been demonstrated in the Popular Front victory of 1936. Viewed in this light, it is not difficult to see why Pétainism has been interpreted as a reaction against the recent inroads of the left and trade unionism.[41]

Given the irrational hold which the cult of Pétainism exerted over the people, few dared question the marshal's attributes. It was widely accepted that he had made the right choices. To ignore this self-evident truth was a brave decision which invited mockery and scorn. The initial impact of Pétainism was, therefore, to immobilize choice.[42] Small wonder there were few 'resisters of the first hour'. Ultimately, however, the cult of marshalship may have proved counterproductive. Although hero-worship can lead to emulation and imitation, too much eventually stultifies action.[43] This possibly explains why the public quickly lost enthusiasm for Pétain's National Revolution. Yet several other problems undermined this experiment in political and social engineering.

· · ·

After the war, former Vichyites were quick to suggest that the National Revolution had been foisted on a reluctant France by a victorious Germany. This was not the case. Although Vichy did draw inspiration from other authoritarian regimes – Salazar's Portugal rather than Hitler's Reich – its programme for renewal was very much a French experiment. This has led some historians to suggest that the National Revolution was a triumph of traditional right-wing values. Some of the marshal's supporters, eager to portray their hero as a 'resister of the first hour' and play down the persecution of the Jews, have also claimed that it was little more than an expression of conservative views.[44] On closer inspection, however, the intellectual bases of Vichy's internal policies appear extremely eclectic, reflecting the wide body of opinion within government. As already noted, by early 1941 the traditionalists, prominent in the opening months of the Occupation, were losing ground to the technocrats, men who sought inspiration from the ideals of nineteenth-century positivism. In any case, few historians today believe that the National Revolution took place in some kind of intellectual vacuum. It needs to be situated in its political and economic context. As has been remarked, 'it was the expression of indigenous French urges for change, reform, revenge, nurtured in the 1930s and made urgent and possible by defeat'.[45] This is why many people from different sides of the political spectrum were initially enthusiastic about Vichy's schemes for recovery. Before long, it became clear that these plans were little more than a front for the expression of vested interests, especially those of the propertied classes. By early 1941, public disenchantment was already setting in.

At the forefront of the National Revolution were attempts to reform education. Schooling had, of course, been a pet subject of Pétain's in the 1930s, and it was no surprise that in 1940 he should return to familiar themes. In conversation with William Bullitt, the US ambassador to Vichy, he blamed defeat on the schoolteachers.[46] To ensure that the custodians of the nation's young became loyal servants of the regime, left-wing teachers were removed from positions of authority and the teacher-training colleges of the old Republic were dismantled. In October 1940 the teachers' union, the Syndicat National des Instituteurs (SNI), was outlawed, to be replaced by a number of state-run associations. These reforms achieved little. Poorly paid, badly treated and under-valued, teachers had little desire to become the 'black hussars' of the marshal.

Their mistrust was heightened by changes within the classroom itself. To rectify the alleged 'bookishness' of Republican education, the syllabus of both primary and secondary schools was extensively revised. History and geography textbooks were purged of their alleged left-wing bias; technical lessons were given a boost; and housecraft classes became compulsory for girls. Under the newly created Ministry of Sport, directed by the former Wimbledon tennis champion Jean Borotra, sporting facilities were vastly improved. Undoubtedly, many pupils enjoyed this new emphasis on outside activities, yet several educational officials, used to the academic rigour of the Republican curriculum, were less enthusiastic. Nor were such officials entirely happy about attempts to invoke spiritual values in education. These moves reached a high-point under Chevalier, who, in January 1941, reinstated religious instruction as a compulsory subject in the state-school timetable. Fearing an anti-clerical backlash, this law was quickly amended by Chevalier's successor, Jérôme Carcopino, the great classical scholar. Ironically, from April 1942 onwards educational policy was in the

111

hands of a non-believer: Abel Bonnard, the homosexual writer renowned for his fascist sympathies. His tenure of office was marked by its negativism and contempt for clerical interests.[47]

During the first two years of the Occupation, however, religion formed a central plank of the National Revolution. While not a fervent Catholic, Pétain maintained that the nation's recovery could only be achieved by a return to Christian values. Thus he was happy to see a reversal of many of the secular laws of the 'godless' Republic. On 3 September 1940 monks and nuns recovered the legal right to teach once more; on 2 November 1941 private elementary schools were granted state subventions, albeit on a temporary basis; and on 8 April 1942 the law on associations was revised, making it easier for religious orders to seek legal recognition. Left to his own devices, Pétain would probably have gone much further. Catholic and Protestant leaders were frequent guests at his dinner table in the Hôtel du Parc. In 1941 the marshal even submitted his 'Principes de la Communauté', a credo of National Revolution beliefs, to the papacy for approval.[48] There was also talk of a new concordat betweeen church and state, although negotiations came to naught, largely because the Vatican came to view Vichy as a temporary regime.

Nor were all Pétain's ministerial colleagues eager to satisfy Catholic interests. There was a worry that extreme pro-clerical policies would reawaken sectarian divisions at a time when France needed unity. Accordingly, the National Revolution proceeded tentatively in religious affairs. This caution was welcomed by the Protestant churches, which generally adopted a reserved attitude towards Vichy, but caused disappointment among the Catholic hierarchy. Although Catholic prelates did eventually relinquish something of their early enthusiasm for Vichy, most could not hide their continuing admiration for Pétain. In 1941, the Assembly of Cardinals and Archbishops (ACA) urged the nation to 'venerate' the *chef de l'état* and practise a loyalty towards his government.[49] In so doing the Church, along with the Légion, served as a vital pillar of support for Pétainism. Yet it is doubtful whether members of the laity and lower clergy heeded the ACA's advice. Many were alienated by the authoritarian nature of the regime and understood that the men who filled the marshal's cabinet in 1941 – Darlan, Pucheu, Lehideux – were no friends of the Church. Eventually events in 1942, notably the stepping-up of measures against Jews, forced a majority of Catholics to relinquish their enthusiasm for Vichy, if not for Pétain. A few Catholics, drawn largely from the pre-war Christian Democrat parties, the Church's youth movements and the religious orders, even joined the Resistance. At the Liberation, the actions of such resisters redeemed the action of those bishops who had never shaken off their affection for Pétain, and discouraged the Provisional Government from undertaking a wholesale *épuration* of the episcopate.[50]

The National Revolution had, of course, its own youth movements. To the disappointment of the collaborators in Paris and the relief of Catholics, who were anxious to retain the autonomy of their own organizations, Vichy's intention was never to create *une jeunesse unique* similar to the Hitler Youth. As with a single political party, there was a fear that such an organization would end up in the wrong hands. Instead, the regime established a multiplicity of organizations, served by leadership schools such as that at Uriage, whose task it was to produce the future leaders of the nation's young. Eschewing the fascist example, Vichy's organizations drew heavily on the scouting ideals of service to the community. The Baden-Powell ethic was clearly discernible in the Compagnons de France, a voluntary movement for adolescents, and the compulsory Chantiers de la Jeunesse, headed by the former scout, General de la Porte du Theil. Initially established as an emergency measure to provide basic work for men of draft age, by January 1941 the Chantiers had become a form of national service, reflecting Pétain's belief that the military was the school of the nation. Performing a variety of physical tasks, its members received a meagre wage and a generous dollop of National Revolution rhetoric. Yet the military uniforms of the Chantiers were enough to awake the suspicions of the Germans, who banned all of Vichy's youth movements from operating in the occupied zone. Had it been the intention of the Chantiers to become a clandestine army, it might have been a more attractive prospect to conscripts. Although some were taken by its ideals of community, others were put off by its naive moralism and the fruitless tasks they had to perform. By 1943 most people's illusions about the Chantiers were shattered when its camps were turned into departure points for those leaving for work service in Germany, the Service du Travail Obligatoire (STO).

Although no organization of similar stature existed for women, the National Revolution was eager that they too should do their bit for France's renewal. Their task was to remain at home where they would raise large families. Worries about a static birth-rate were, of course, nothing new. This had been a perennial concern of the Third Republic, which took a series of pro-natalist measures, the most famous being Daladier's Family Code of 1939. In Vichy's eyes, these policies had been undermined by the Republican climate of individualism. The National Revolution invoked a new morality in which 'breeding became a sacred duty'.[51] To facilitate this, women were discouraged from going to work; divorce laws were tightened; and subsidies were provided for women who stayed at home. Emphasis was also placed on Mother's Day, another opportunity for Pétain to speak on the radio.[52] To the more perceptive of his audience, such speeches must have seemed strange coming from a childless *roué* who had married a divorcée. Indeed, it seems that few women were taken in by the National Revolution's pro-natalist propaganda. Home life was austere. The unavailability of basic materials and foodstuffs ensured that women had to spend even longer hours performing domestic chores such as washing, cooking and queueing. At the same time, Vichy's subsidies failed to cover the costs of rearing a family in a period of rampant inflation; many mothers were forced to face official stigma by seeking paid work. Eventually, in 1943, Vichy itself recruited female labour to replace those men who had been dispatched to Germany. The fact remains, however, that the Occupation witnessed a surge in the birth-rate. Although this owed something to Vichy's improved provisions for post-natal care and its extension of Daladier's Code, other factors played a part. Apart from the usual argument that the curfew made bed a welcome refuge in the long evenings, the post-1918 baby boom meant that there were now more marriageable people living in France. For their part, women have suggested that 'in the darkest days of the Occupation a baby was a sign of hope'.[53] Ironically, the introduction of STO may have provided a further boost to the birth-rate as fathers with large families could claim exemption from conscription.

A similar gulf between Vichy rhetoric and economic reality undermined the National Revolution's policies on agriculture. Like other conservatives, Pétain had become increasingly concerned about France's declining rural population, believing that a self-supporting peasantry was vital for social stability. In a message of 10 October 1940 he promised to halt the exodus from the countryside, and proclaimed that family agriculture would form the economic and social base of the new France.[54] To this end, Vichy celebrated peasant folklore. On a more practical level Pierre Caziot, Vichy's Minister of Agriculture from July 1940 to April 1942, attempted to boost production by providing loans for the improvement of farm buildings and by encouraging the consolidation of scattered small-holdings. Peasants even had their own Charter of December 1940. This, in turn, established the Corporation Paysanne, whose job it was to protect rural producers from the pitfalls of free-market competition by organizing them into corporations. To curb the fall in the rural population, Caziot initiated the 'Return to the Soil', whereby subsidies were granted to families who took over abandoned farms.

Peasants were undeniably grateful for Vichy's attention. Throughout the 1930s they had believed themselves the victims of government neglect, and had struggled to make their political presence felt. Ultimately, they judged the Pétain government by results. These were few and far between. While the regime could supply peasants with song-sheets reviving forgotten rustic tunes, German requisitioning meant it could not provide fertilizers, machinery and better veterinary care for their animals.[55] In this situation, there were few incentives to 'return to the soil'; only 1,561 families took up government subsidies for this purpose. More and more, the regime seemed distant from rural concerns. The Corporation Paysanne appeared to be a club for large-scale producers, essentially concerned with urban markets.[56] Thus by 1942 the small-scale farmer felt abandoned by Vichy. Laval did not help matters when, the following year, he removed the exemptions from STO enjoyed by particular groups of rural workers.

By 1942 Vichy's policies for industry also lay in ruins. Initially, Pétain and his traditionalist advisers had hoped to build a corporatist society which freed the economy from the pressures of class struggle and the competition of capitalism. His speeches, notably that of 10 October 1940, denounced the dangers of free enterprise and underscored the need for unity between labour and management. Belin, his first Minister of Industrial Production, shared similar aspirations. To this end, in August 1940 the regime abolished national trade unions and business organizations. In their place, it established Organization Committees (OCs). Here, employers supervised and coordinated strategy in their respective sectors of the economy. In August 1941 Vichy published its long-awaited Labour Charter which promised a new era in industrial relations. The traditionalists, however, did not have it all their own way. By early 1941, the influence of the technocrats was coming to the fore. They sought to use their power and the 'temporary submissiveness of their stunned countrymen to reinvigorate France and make it a respected partner in Hitler's Europe'.[57] Accordingly, Pucheu and Lehideux closed down inefficient firms and established the Délégation Générale à l'Equipement National (DGEN). This body framed a ten-year plan for the economy, foreshadowing the kind of planning which France would witness after the Liberation.

The incoherent nature of Vichy economic policy managed to alienate virtually everyone. Labour was particularly disgruntled. It did not go unnoticed that the OCs had no trade union equivalents. Nor did it go unremarked that the Labour Charter did little for workers' rights. Strikes were prohibited; unions above a regional level were outlawed; and worker participation was limited to *comités sociaux*, local committees which merely dealt with pension rights and recreational affairs.[58] Representatives of small enterprises also had their worries about the reorganization of industry, believing that Vichy's plans only served the interests of big business, a belief bolstered by the influence of the technocrats. In 1941 there were rumours that an international synarchy of business magnates had taken over the economy. In truth, big business was far from in charge, and may well have been irked both by the corporatism of the traditionalists and the *dirigisme* of the technocrats.[59] Ultimately, Germany controlled the French economy, ensuring that it served Nazi interests. The only real authority which Vichy enjoyed in economic matters was the power to organize labour and management.

Controversy also surrounds the autonomy which Vichy enjoyed in racial affairs. While Germany was busy implementing a range of antisemitic policies in the occupied zone, the Pétain government introduced its own discriminatory legislation: on 12 and 17 July 1940 anyone not of French parentage was debarred from holding public office; on 22 July the state undertook a revision of all naturalizations conducted since 1927; on 27 August restrictions on antisemitism in the press were lifted; and on 3 October the first *Statut des Juifs* was introduced, banning Jews from many positions of authority in both the public and private sectors. The following year saw the establishment of a Commissariat Général aux Questions Juives (CGQJ) under the direction of Vallat, the former head of Veterans' Affairs. An ardent xenophobe who believed Jews to be unassimilable in French culture, he was responsible for the second *Statut des Juifs* of June 1941. This limited further the types of jobs which Jews could perform. The following month he undertook the seizure of Jewish property and businesses. As will be seen, Vichy ultimately became a willing participant in the 'Final Solution'.

Ever since the Liberation, Vichyites have claimed that the above laws were imposed on France by the Nazis. Yet German archives indicate that there was no pressure on Pétain to undertake an antisemitic programme. Other apologists have suggested that the regime did indeed initiate discriminatory legislation, but only in an attempt to outwit Hitler. By introducing measures known to please Berlin, it was hoped to keep German interference in French affairs to a minimum. There is some truth in this argument. Laval, never an antisemite of conviction, appreciated that racial policies emphasized his government's autonomy, especially in the occupied zone. Recent research, however, has demonstrated that the National Revolution contained an indigenous antisemitism which had long been present in French society. Even this finding has been turned into a defence of Vichy. It has been suggested that the regime's xenophobia was less overt than that of Hitler's Germany. Vichy, it is maintained, only followed the Nazi path in 1942 when the unashamedly racist Darquier de Pellepoix replaced Vallat. To be sure, the traditionalists – prominent in Pétain's cabinets of 1940 – demanded cultural conformity, not the total destruction of the Jewish race. This is why the government was prepared to exempt Jewish war veterans and long-established families from the full rigours of the law. None the less, it is clear that even in 1940 Vichy's definition of a Jew was a racial one. The Germans themselves noted with satisfaction that the regime's antisemitic legislation largely mirrored their own.

As the horror of Vichy's xenophobia has become clear, attention has focused on the role which Pétain himself played in his government's racial programme. Reflecting on his silence during the Dreyfus Affair, his supporters argue that he was no

117

racist, pointing out that he had no hand in framing Vichy's discriminatory legislation. The whole affair was the work of others, it is claimed. As proof of this, we are reminded that the marshal displayed particular concern for the welfare of Jewish ex-servicemen and often acted to save the lives of individual Jews, especially those known personally to him. Nor did he ever mention Jews in his public speeches. The fact that his first Minister of Colonies, Henry Lémery, was a black from Martinique is also seen as significant. This evidence points not to the marshal's open-mindedness, but to the type of racism he espoused. His years in the military and hours spent reading the newspapers of the Action Française had inculcated a xenophobia similar to that of other conservatives. This chauvinism had become so ingrained that he displayed an unthinking and indifferent attitude towards racial affairs. It was an indifference which proved tragic. As already noted, in 1940 there was no German pressure to implement an antisemitic programme. Nor was French public opinion clamouring for racist measures. Despite an upsurge in xenophobic sentiment before the war, the shock of the defeat had left the population in a bewildered state, concerned above all with private issues.[60] In this situation, the fanatics at Vichy had their chance. This was the essence of 'Pétain's crime': it was not that he initiated the persecution of the Jews, but that he did nothing to stop it. In his mind, racial discrimination was perfectly legitimate if its intention was to rid France of 'unassimilable elements'.

The persecution of the Jews remains the most sordid aspect of the National Revolution. Yet, in other respects, this crusade had caught the mood of the age: 'a greater provision for outdoor activities and sport, more concern for the welfare of old people, more family legislation, more state interference in the running of the economy, and a greater reliance on appointed experts rather than elected representatives'.[61] After the war, the Fourth Republic built on these developments. In the long term, however, the marshal failed in his attempts to create a nation loyal to the values of *travail, famille, patrie*. Through the Contrôle Technique – a system by which state officials opened people's mail and eavesdropped on their telephone conversations – it was learned, as early as summer 1941, that the National Revolution was largely perceived as a failure.[62] It was testament to Pétain's political naivety and vanity that he believed he could overhaul his country's institutions when

France was under enemy occupation. This has led to questions whether the whole experiment might have been successful had circumstances been different, yet such speculation ignores the fact that the National Revolution owed its existence, and ultimately its success or failure, to the unique conditions produced by the defeat.[63] It also diverts attention away from the repression which Vichy deployed in pursuing its schemes for renewal. By autumn 1941 the pages of the *Journal Officiel* were no longer filled with projects for renewal. Instead, they detailed the creation of special commissions to deal with Jews, special courts to handle Gaullists, special police forces to combat communists, special tribunals to try democratically elected representatives of the old Republic. As Léon-Paul Fargue remarked, 'Travail, Famille, Patrie' had given way to 'Tracas, Famine, Patrouilles' (Bother, Hunger, Surveillance).[64]

. . .

From the outset, it was anticipated that the Vichy regime would be authoritarian in nature. After all, this was a wartime government operating in exceptional circumstances. During the *drôle de guerre*, even the Third Republic had curtailed civil liberties, setting up internment camps for foreigners and suspending the PCF. Vichy went much further than this, laying the foundations of a police state. As with the anti-Jewish legislation, it has been claimed that this development was the result of direct German interference. A more plausible argument was that outlined by Isorni and other Pétainists in 1945. By ensuring that the nation's discipline was maintained by French officials rather than German ones, Pétain and his associates asserted Vichy's independence and saved their country from 'Polonization', an allusion to the brutal subjugation of that country by the Nazis. This argument ignores the fact that the marshal always believed that tough measures were necessary both for the success of the National Revolution and the maintenance of internal order. It also underplays the extent to which Vichy was prepared to prostrate itself in front of Germany.

In the summer of 1940 Pétain's overriding priority was the success of the National Revolution. In order to succeed, this needed to overcome the forces of the 'anti France'.[65] Although he never named the elements behind this conspiracy, it was widely understood that he was thinking of Jews, foreigners, freemasons, communists and free-thinkers, all those groups that had supposedly undermined traditional French values. Early

Vichy legislation reflected his concerns. On 13 August, the regime abolished masonic lodges, and required public officials to declare that they had never been a member of a secret society. After the raid on Dakar of 20 September, special courts were set up to deal with Gaullists accused of treason. De Gaulle himself was sentenced to death *in absentia* by a military tribunal at Clermont-Ferrand. The other dark force working against the values of *travail, famille, patrie* was, of course, communism. Pétain had encountered this 'evil' in 1917, 1925 and 1936. Now it was time again to do battle. Building on Daladier's earlier measures, close surveillance was kept on party militants. Those considered most dangerous were imprisoned or placed on the infamous Liste S, a secret dossier which contained the names of those who were to be arrested in the event of public disorder.[66] Before long, communist conspiracies were spotted everywhere, reflecting Pétain's belief that Bolshevism posed the most serious threat to internal order.

Spring 1941 witnessed a further round of repressive measures. On 27 January 1941 secretaries of state, high civil servants and dignitaries were required to swear an oath of allegiance to the *chef de l'état*.[67] On 14 April this requirement was extended to the army and magistrature, thus limiting the independence of the judiciary. The Darlan Directorate also established regional prefects, responsible for the distribution of food and maintenance of order, and the Groupements Mobiles de Réserve (GMR), a special police force designed to root out internal dissidence. Before long, the préfectures of southern France were teeming with lists of potential subversives, a process aided by a sophisticated system of political surveillance. As well as listening into people's telephone calls and opening their mail, Vichy encouraged a process of anonymous denunciations whereby the public were invited to inform on 'subversives'. Popular targets were state schoolteachers. Despite Vichy's attempts to turn them into loyal agents of the National Revolution, the *instituteurs* were still viewed with suspicion by the Légion and the Catholic Church.

The regime also reinforced its powers of persuasion. Although Vichy had enjoyed some success in promoting a cult of Pétain, this had not been especially difficult given the marshal's underlying popularity. Elsewhere the regime's propaganda apparatus failed to function smoothly. Some semblance of order was achieved on 28 October 1940 with the creation of a

Secrétariat Général à l'Information, yet the responsibilities of this body remained ill-defined and often overlapped with those of other agencies such as the Légion. Eager for greater efficiency, in March 1941 Darlan delegated the Information portfolio to Paul Marion. An ex-communist and PPF sympathizer, Marion had some success in extending state controls over the press, radio and cinema. However, his authoritarian tone did little to quell public disquiet that Vichy was succumbing to German domination, and in 1942 he stood down. All in all, Vichy had no fewer than 15 ministers/secretaries of state for Radio and eight for Information. This ministerial instability not only revealed the importance which the Pétain government attached to propaganda, it also demonstrated the difficulties of manipulating public opinion at a time when France was under enemy occupation.

Indeed, the growing authoritarianism of the regime in spring 1941 was an indication that not all was well in Vichy France. Although Pétain continued to command people's loyalties, the popularity of his government was rapidly waning. Clearly different factors influenced different people at different times and, as befitted a country as regionally diverse as France, different areas responded in different ways. None the less, it is still possible to outline a number of issues that were troubling public opinion. The nightmare caused by the *exode* continued to haunt thousands of people, unable to return to their homes in the north. The material circumstances of the Occupation were also starting to bite. Rationing was severe, compounded by German requisitioning. It was not just foodstuffs that were restricted, but tobacco, clothes, shoes and fuel. Townspeople and the poor were especially hit. By contrast the peasantry, at least in the southern zone, was less affected. Rural families had the opportunity to produce their own food, and took some satisfaction in the fact that they no longer had to depend so heavily on the towns for their markets. Yet the countryside remained anxious for loved ones held as prisoners-of-war in Germany. As in 1914–18, it was the rural areas that had borne the brunt of conscription.

The wider circumstances of the war were a further cause for concern. At Dakar, Frenchmen had fought Frenchmen, a situation repeated in Syria the following year. At Montoire in October 1940, Pétain had been pictured shaking hands with Hitler. Although the meeting was heralded by Vichy radio as a breakthrough in Franco-German relations, it failed to produce any let-up in the armistice arrangements and raised doubts about Pétain's own patriotism. Nor did the policy of collaboration appear capable of ending the fighting. Having conquered Greece and Yugoslavia, on 22 June 1941 Hitler launched his invasion of the Soviet Union. As de Gaulle recognized, the war was no longer merely a European affair; it was taking on truly global proportions.[68]

The corollary to this growth of public disquiet was the emergence of resistance. Although the numbers of 'active' resisters were always tiny, by 1941 protest was no longer the work of isolated individuals. Thanks to the German presence, the movements in the occupied zone – Organisation Civile et Militaire, Libération Nord, Ceux de la Résistance and Ceux de la Libération – were small and precarious in nature, carrying out occasional acts of sabotage and distributing clandestine newspapers. In the unoccupied zone, groups such as Combat, Libération Sud and Franc Tireur were more expansive, establishing escape networks for allied airmen and collating intelligence information. They also tended to be urban-based. Not only were material shortages most keenly felt in the towns, it was here that the printing presses were based and it was here that the best hiding places were to be found.[69] The one movement to operate across both zones was the communist-dominated Front National which emerged in the wake of the German attack on the Soviet Union. Although several communists had already joined the Resistance on an individual basis, in June 1941 the party now placed its considerable underground networks on the allied side.

The entry of the communists into the Resistance was accompanied by an intensification of 'terrorist' acts, and prompted Vichy to march further down the path of repression. Pétain was especially troubled. Social disorder had always been his worst nightmare, and was one of the principal reasons why he had signed the armistice. As de Gaulle had observed, only such a settlement would forestall the re-emergence of the Paris Commune. Yet in autumn 1941 the marshal's mind was fixed not so much on 1871, but on the mutinies of 1917. Such concerns became clear in a broadcast of 12 August 1941.[70] Here, he referred to 'un vent mauvais' ('an evil wind') sweeping through France. Laced with military imagery, his speech complained that the authority of government was being questioned by the troops of the *ancien régime*. Recalling the 'gift of his person' to the nation, Pétain spoke of how he had quelled dissent in 1917 and had avoided total disaster in 1940. Once again, he planned to save his country from ruin.

Who were the 'mutineers' of 1941?[71] Clearly Pétain had in mind the forces of the 'anti France', especially the communists. In his opinion, the Soviet Union's entry into the war had produced the same destabilizing impact as had the February Revolution. The marshal might also have been thinking of parliamentarians. Even though the National Assembly was prorogued, he believed that France was still paying the price for the selfishness of liberal democracy. As will be seen, at the preliminary hearings of the Riom trials Daladier and others were busy criticizing his government, just as the deputies had chastised the High Command in 1917. Another possibility is that the marshal included the Paris collaborators among his list of 'mutineers'. In autumn 1941 they were especially active in denouncing the failure of Vichy to rally behind the New Order.

As in 1917, Pétain believed the solution to internal contamination lay in his mixture of firmness and compassion. Thus in his message to the nation of 12 August, the longest of all his radio broadcasts, he outlined a number of tough measures: the suspension of political parties, more or less a *fait accompli*; the suppression of parliamentary immunity; a further crusade against secret societies; a reinforcement of the powers of the Légion; an extension of police authority; and a promise to punish those responsible for the defeat. These promises were quickly translated into legislation. On 20 September a Tribunal d'Etat was created to strike against potential subversion; on 4 October the oath of loyalty was extended to all public servants; later in October separate police forces were created to deal with Jews, communists and freemasons. Among the conciliatory gestures announced in the speech of 12 August, Pétain called for the quick promulgation of the Charte du Travail; a curtailing of the influence of big business on the OCs; and the establishment of *commissaires du pouvoir*, officials who would check on bureaucratic abuses of power. Soon after, Pétain introduced the Francisque, 'an emblem combining a gallic axe and a marshal's baton, to reward loyal service'.[72]

1941 was not 1917. To begin with, Pétain had misjudged the nature of dissent. Although in 1917 he had succumbed to the same political prejudices as the High Command, he understood that the causes of the mutinies were essentially military in origin. In 1941 he was not oblivious to people's everyday concerns, but was transfixed by the dangers of internal dissent. Furthermore, his proposed solutions were impractical. In 1917 he had been in a position to adopt a series of concrete measures to improve the morale of his troops. In 1941, blinded by his belief in himself as a saviour, he failed to see that the circumstances of the Occupation prevented him from taking any real actions to alleviate the suffering of a civilian population. As a result, the reactionary measures of autumn 1941 outstripped the conciliatory ones.

For the Germans, Vichy's repression had not gone far enough. Two issues, in particular, needed addressing. The first was the punishment of leading figures of the Third Republic. Vichy itself had initially set out to do this. Constitutional act number five of 30 July 1940 promised that the state would try those officials responsible for the defeat. This was the beginning of the infamous Riom trials. Pétain was especially excited at the prospect of seeing leading figures of the Popular Front era, among them Blum, Gamelin and the hated Daladier, in the dock. Matters did not go as planned. The Germans were angered that the accused were to be charged with having lost the Battle of France, not with having started the war. There was also anger at the tardiness of French justice. By autumn 1941 the trials had not yet started. The preliminary hearings remained in session, and had already provided opportunities for the defendants to turn the tables on their prosecutors.

It was a wish to speed matters up, coupled with his desire to stem contamination from the interior, that prompted the marshal, in his speech of 12 August 1941, to promise that he would personally judge the Third Republic's leaders. He was true to his word. On 29 September he announced the creation of a special council of political justice to advise the court at Riom. As with the courts martial of 1917, he envisaged a quick verdict which would reassert the state's authority. To guarantee this, he handpicked the judges, who, in any case, had recently sworn the oath of loyalty. A close personal friend, de Peretti della Rocca, selected the jury. Leaving nothing to chance, in a speech of 16 October 1941 the marshal even suggested what the outcome ought to be.[73] Once again, events did not run smoothly. The presiding judge at Riom refused to toe the Vichy line, and struggled to assert his independence. In the courtroom itself, the prosecution failed to pin down the defendants. Daladier, in particular, demonstrated how the military unpreparedness of France owed much to Pétain's strategic thinking. Enraged by this bungling, in March 1942 Hitler ordered the suspension of the trials. In 1943 Vichy surrendered the accused to Germany.

The other matter that irritated Berlin was the maintenance of law and order in the occupied zone. It will be recalled that the Germans cared little about what went on on the Vichy side of the demarcation line so long as the Reich's military security was not compromised. Occupied northern France was different. Although the French police force was allowed to operate in this area, discipline was also maintained by the German military command at Paris. (The Nord-Pas-de-Calais was, of course, governed by the military command at Brussels.) It was not long before the other agencies of the Nazi state arrived at Paris, notably the SS and Gestapo. None the less, the combined powers of these forces could not prevent the sharp rise in the number of 'terrorist' acts that took place during autumn 1941. On 21 August Alphonse Moser, a German naval cadet, was gunned down in the *métro*. Unwilling to wait on the French police, the occupying authorities reacted with characteristic brutality, demanding 100 hostages, of whom 50 were to be shot. These executions would be avoided, Vichy was informed, so long as the French instituted a Paris 'Special Section' to deal with terrorist and communist activities. This tribunal, it was further stipulated, should immediately execute six communists held in prison for infraction of the decree of September 1939 dissolving the party. Vichy readily agreed, hoping this act would discourage others. The assassinations continued. On 27 August Paul Colette, a young French officer, wounded Déat and Laval. On 3 September another German soldier was killed in the Gare de l'Est. On 20 October the Feldkommandant at Nantes was shot dead. In retaliation for this spectacular act, the Nazis decided on executing hostages and presented Pucheu, as Minister of the Interior, with a list of names.

Given his authoritarian leanings, Pucheu readily accepted that executions would have to take place. Yet the German list troubled him on two counts. First, it contained the names of several *anciens combattants*. Better to execute communists and other 'subversives' than former soldiers, the natural supporters of the marshal. Second, the list was a clear signal that the Germans were usurping the role of the French police in the occupied zone. Thus, in an attempt to reassert Vichy's autonomy, Pucheu argued that the French should be allowed to choose their own hostages for execution. In the event, the Germans merely supplied another list, mainly comprising communists. This had to be accepted, and by 25 October 98 executions had gone ahead. Thereafter, much to Pucheu's dismay, the Germans resorted to yet further hostage-taking without consulting Vichy. As has been observed, it is ironic that in 1944 the Provisional Government at Algiers executed Pucheu for something he had tried to do and failed.[74]

How did Pétain respond to these events? In August he had approved of the shooting of the six communist prisoners. With his mind again set on 1917, he believed that such a limited reprisal would act as a deterrent to others. He was disgusted, however, by the numbers killed in October 1941. At the time of the mutinies, there had only been 49 executions; now the Germans had carried out 98 in two days alone. As a response it was it was decided that he should travel to Paris where he would offer himself up as a hostage. Before his departure, he planned to make a speech in which he would announce his decision and call on Hitler to stop the killing. Whether Pétain himself dreamt up this scheme remains doubtful. It may well have been suggested by Laure or du Moulin de Labarthète.[75] In the event, his cabinet colleagues, notably Darlan and Pucheu, dissuaded him from going, and his message of protest was never aired. Thus Vichy made no formal protest against the killing of innocent civilians. In a speech of 22 October, Pétain merely condemned the assassination of German soldiers.[76] An opportunity to muster public support had been lost.

Why Pétain chose to stay remains a matter of debate. It may be, as Otto Abetz, the German ambassador, believed, that the original plan was a bluff on the part of the marshal's entourage.[77] It seems more likely, however, that Pétain's decision was dictated by two other considerations. First, he remained enthusiastic for collaboration. Despite recent setbacks in Franco-German relations, he remained confident that he could produce a diplomatic success. He was also excited by the German invasion of the Soviet Union. As he explained in a letter to Hitler of 20 October 1941 – the anniversary of Montoire – France and Germany shared a common interest in the defeat of

Bolshevism.[78] Thus the marshal was reluctant to antagonize Berlin, and may even have come round to Pucheu's belief that the recent assassinations and reprisals were only minor incidents in a much broader conflict. Second, it appears that Pétain was troubled that his surrender would lead to the appointment of a Gauleiter and the further subjugation of France. This eventuality would, of course, mean that he could no longer claim to be the saviour of his people. Similar reasoning would, in November 1942, keep Pétain at Vichy when the Germans occupied the southern zone.

No doubt in October 1941 Pétain believed he was acting in France's best interests by remaining at the helm of government. His compassion for the French people and outrage at German actions was sincere. Yet he remained capable of appalling lapses of humanity. This has been seen in his callous indifference over the fate of the Jews. It was further apparent in his attempts to root out the 'anti France' and quell internal dissidence. Now his lack of moral judgement was exposed by the attempts of his ministers to preserve French autonomy. He did not realize that by sticking closely to the terms of the armistice, Vichy was at risk of doing the Germans' dirty work for them. It was thus in danger of 'Polonizing' itself. If he had been more astute, he would also have seen how this so-called 'shield' philosophy was likely to lead to the extinction of his own powers. To explain why he lost much of his remaining authority, it is necessary to move away from the domestic sphere and examine his fruitless quest for collaboration.

. . .

NOTES AND REFERENCES

1. R.O. Paxton, *Vichy France. Old Guard and New Order, 1940–1944* (New York: Columbia University Press/Morningside Edition, 1982), p. xi. Subsequent references to Paxton's *Vichy France* are taken from the 1972 edition published by Alfred A. Knopf, New York.
2. P. Burrin, *La France à l'heure allemande, 1940–1944* (Paris: Seuil, 1995), p. 77.
3. M. Prelot, 'La révision et les actes constitutionnels. La figure politique et juridique du chef de l'état français', in Fondation Nationale des Sciences Politiques, *Le gouvernement de Vichy, 1940–1942* (Paris: Armand Colin, 1972), pp. 23–36.
4. Paxton, *Vichy France*, p. 192.

5. R. Griffiths, *Marshal Pétain* (London: Constable, 1970), p. 252.
6. Paxton, *Vichy France*, pp. 199–200.
7. Darlan quoted in H. du Moulin de Labarthète, *Le temps des illusions. Souvenirs, juillet 1940–avril 1942* (Geneva: Le Cheval Ailé, 1946), p. 347.
8. Griffiths, *Pétain*, p. 281.
9. Paxton, *Vichy France*, p. 196.
10. Ibid., p. 197.
11. See Y. Durand, 'Les notables', in J.-P. Azéma and F. Bédarida (eds), *Vichy et les français* (Paris: Fayard, 1992), pp. 371–81.
12. H.R. Kedward, *Occupied France. Collaboration and Resistance, 1940–1944* (Oxford: Basil Blackwell, 1985), p. 23.
13. Ibid.
14. Ibid., p. 24.
15. M. Cointet-Labrousse, *Vichy capitale* (Paris: Perrin, 1993), pp. 218–19.
16. R. Benjamin, *Le maréchal et son peuple* (Paris: Plon, 1941).
17. Kedward, *Occupied France*, p. 20.
18. A. Koestler, *The Scum of the Earth* (London: Jonathan Cape, 1941), p. 168.
19. R. Vinen, 'Vichy: Pétain's Hollow Crown', *History Today*, 40 (1990), p. 14.
20. M. Déat, *Mémoires politiques* (Paris: Denoël, 1989), p. 549.
21. Paxton, *Vichy France*, p. 190.
22. Laure quoted in D. Peschanski, 'Encadrer ou contrôler?', in L. Gervereau and D. Peschanski (eds), *La propagande de Vichy, 1940–1944* (Paris: Collection des Publications de la BDIC, 1990), p. 13.
23. Kedward, *Occupied France*, p. 26.
24. AN F^{17} 13319, circular of 15 October 1941.
25. Pétain quoted in du Moulin de Labarthète, *Le temps*, p. 101.
26. H. Amouroux, *La grande histoire des français sous l'occupation*, vol. 2 (Paris: Robert Laffont, 1977), p. 11. This second volume of Amouroux's ten-volume history is entitled *Quarante millions de pétainistes, juin 1940-juin 1941*.
27. W.D. Halls, *Politics, Society and Christianity in Vichy France* (Oxford: Berg, 1995), p. 204 and Kedward, *Occupied France*, p. 48.
28. Vinen, 'Pétain's Hollow Crown', p. 17.
29. J.-M. Flonneau, 'L'évolution de l'opinion publique de 1940 à 1944', in Azéma and Bédarida (eds), *Vichy et les français*, pp. 506–22.
30. Vinen, 'Pétain's Hollow Crown', p. 18.
31. Y. Durand, *La France dans la 2e guerre mondiale, 1939–1945* (Paris: Armand Colin, 1989), pp. 70–1.
32. See especially G. Miller, *Les pousse-au-jouir du maréchal Pétain* (Paris: Seuil, 1975).

33. H.R. Kedward, 'Patriots and Patriotism in Vichy France', in *Transactions of the Royal Historical Society*, 5th series, 32 (1982), p. 177.
34. Paxton, *Vichy France*, p. 35.
35. Ibid.
36. J. Duquesne, *Les catholiques français sous l'occupation* (Paris: Grasset, 1966), p. 37.
37. This prayer is quoted in M.-P. d'Argenson, *Pétain et le pétinisme* (Paris: Editions Créator, 1953), p. 170. For a similar prayer in honour of Joffre, see M.-M. Huss, 'Virilité et religion dans la France de 1914–1918: Le catéchisme du poilu', in M. Cornick (ed.), *Beliefs and Identity in Modern France* (Loughborough: ASMCF/ ERC, 1991), p. 140.
38. N. Atkin, 'The Cult of Joan of Arc in French Schools, 1940–1944', in R. Kedward and R. Austin (eds), *Vichy France and the Resistance. Culture and Ideology* (London: Croom Helm, 1985), p. 267.
39. Kedward, *Occupied France*, p. 19.
40. Vinen, 'Pétain's Hollow Crown', p. 17.
41. R. Kedward, 'Introduction', in Kedward and Austin (eds), *Vichy France and the Resistance*, p. 1.
42. Kedward, *Occupied France*, p. 19.
43. W.D. Halls, *The Youth of Vichy France* (Oxford: Clarendon Press, 1981), pp. 226–7.
44. K. Munholland, 'Wartime France: Remembering Vichy', in *French Historical Studies*, 18 (3) (1994), pp. 804–5.
45. Paxton, *Vichy France*, p. 143.
46. Pétain quoted in ibid., p. 37.
47. N. Atkin, *Church and Schools in Vichy France, 1940–1944* (New York: Garland, 1991), pp. 31–2.
48. Du Moulin de Labarthète, *Le temps*, p. 96. The text of the *Principes* may be found in J.-C. Barbas (ed.), *Philippe Pétain. Discours aux français, 17 juin 1940 – 20 août 1944* (Paris: Albin Michel, 1989), pp. 363–5.
49. ACA declaration of 24 July 1941 in *La vie catholique. Documents et actes de la hiérarchie catholique. Années 1940–1941* (Paris: La Bonne Presse, 1942), p. 65.
50. M. Larkin, *Religion, Politics and Preferment in France since 1900* (Cambridge: Cambridge University Press, 1995), p. 175.
51. Kedward, *Occupied France*, p. 25 from where much of this information on women has been taken. See too F. Muel-Dreyfus, *Vichy et l'éternel féminin* (Paris: Seuil, 1996).
52. See Pétain's speech of 25 May 1941 in Barbas (ed.), *Discours*, pp. 133–4.
53. Kedward, *Occupied France*, p. 25.
54. Message of 10 October 1940 in Barbas (ed.), *Discours*, pp. 86–94.
55. Kedward, *Occupied France*, p. 24.

56. Paxton, *Vichy France*, pp. 208–9.
57. R. Kuisel, *Capitalism and the State in Modern France* (Cambridge: Cambridge University Press, 1982), p. 132.
58. Paxton, *Vichy France*, p. 217.
59. See R. Vinen, *The Politics of French Business, 1936–1945* (Cambridge: Cambridge University Press, 1991).
60. A. Cohen, *Persécutions et sauvetages. Juifs et français sous l'occupation et sous Vichy* (Paris: Cerf, 1993), pp. 191–240. See too M. Marrus and R.O. Paxton, *Vichy France and the Jews* (New York: Basic Books, 1991) for a full discussion of Vichy's antisemitism.
61. Kedward, *Occupied France*, pp. 30–1.
62. Peschanski, 'Encadrer ou contrôler?', p. 22.
63. Kedward, *Occupied France*, p. 31.
64. Léon-Paul Fargue quoted in P. Bourget, *Un certain Philippe Pétain* (Paris: Casterman, 1966), p. 235.
65. P. Pétain, 'L'éducation nationale', in *La Revue des Deux Mondes*, 15 August 1940. This article is reprinted in Barbas (ed.), *Discours*, pp. 350–3.
66. Kedward, *Occupied France*, p. 29.
67. Griffiths, *Pétain*, p. 282.
68. C. de Gaulle, *Mémoires de guerre*, vol. 1 (Paris: Plon, 1954), p. 193.
69. H.R. Kedward, 'The French Resistance', *History Today*, 34 (1984): Special Supplement, pages not numbered.
70. Message of 12 August 1941 in Barbas (ed.), *Discours*, pp. 164–72.
71. M. Ferro, *Pétain* (Paris: Fayard, 1987), p. 339.
72. Paxton, *Vichy France*, p. 225 outlines these measures.
73. Speech of 16 October 1941 in Barbas (ed.), *Discours*, pp. 201–3.
74. Paxton, *Vichy France*, p. 225.
75. Griffiths, *Pétain*, pp. 292–3.
76. Speech of 22 October 1941 in Barbas (ed.), *Discours*, pp. 203–4.
77. Griffiths, *Pétain*, p. 291.
78. This letter is cited in Ferro, *Pétain*, p. 350.

Chapter 6

THE COLLABORATOR, 1940–2

Like other aspects of his life, Pétain's relations with the Germans have been interpreted from so many self-interested points of view that it is difficult to unearth events as they happened at the time. Usually, the marshal's supporters argue one or both of two defences. First, they maintain that, in his role as the 'shield of France', he sought to save the French from further suffering by parrying German demands. If anyone at Vichy was keen on cooperation with the Nazis, then that person was Laval. Second, the marshal's apologists deploy the 'double-game' argument. Behind his silent façade, Pétain was secretly working for the deliverance of his country. It is testimony to the enduring strength of the cult of marshalship that these arguments remain alive today despite the release of both French and German archives demonstrating how collaboration was a French initiative in which Pétain gladly participated.[1] It was, however, an initiative that saved France little and cost Pétain a great deal. By April 1942 collaboration had secured no German concessions of any worth, but had undermined the marshal's own standing both in government and in the country.

· · ·

For Pétain, collaboration was always a necessity, never an option.[2] Having weighed up the military situation and having plumped for an armistice, he believed that France had little choice other than to do business with the Germans. After all, Britain would not remain in the war for long; following Mers-el-Kébir, Pétain may have taken some pleasure in looking forward to the day when perfidious Albion was humbled by the Nazis. By then, Pétain hoped to have accomplished some relaxation of the armistice terms with Germany, notably the

131

release of the 1,500,000 prisoners-of-war. In this sense, he was attempting to 'shield' his countrymen from further suffering. Yet collaboration also had a political dimension. It would provide the breathing-space in which to launch the National Revolution. Ultimately, Pétain calculated that collaboration would secure his place in posterity. Once the terms of the armistice had been revised and French institutions reinvigorated, he was confident that the Germans would concede a favourable peace treaty, just as they had done after the Franco-Prussian war of 1870. Once that treaty was signed, Pétain would be lauded as the man who had saved France from the worst disaster in its history. Admittedly, this would not be a military triumph such as he had achieved in 1916. It would instead be a 'diplomatic Verdun', a moral triumph over the forces of despair that had overcome the nation in June 1940.[3]

Befitting his vanity, this dream of a moral victory would never desert Pétain, not even in the dark days of 1942–3 when the Germans openly scoffed at French requests for concessions. By then, collaboration had increasingly become a fruitless quest to justify the decisions he had made in June 1940. Indeed, throughout the Occupation, Pétain was uncertain how best to achieve a breakthrough in Franco-German relations. In 1940 he calculated that only a top-level meeting between himself and Hitler would suffice. To secure this, he despatched a number of personal envoys to Berlin. Betraying his naive belief that the Germans were 'comrades in arms', the marshal typically chose military men as his representatives: Colonel Fonck, a First World War flying ace, and Georges Scapini, a veterans' leader.

At the same time, Pétain dearly valued Laval's attempts at collaboration. It will be recalled that the Auvergnat's inclusion in government was largely an acknowledgement of his negotiating skills. The marshal could also draw reassurance from the fact that several of Laval's views on foreign affairs coincided with his own. Both saw collaboration as an inevitability; both were contemptuous of Britain's chances; both sought a definitive peace treaty with Germany; both were optimistic of a settlement. Yet, while Laval was never a 'lone wolf' in his dealings with the Nazis, he did have an agenda of his own. Unlike Pétain, he never saw collaboration as a route towards moral recovery. Nor did he view himself as a spiritual leader whose foreign policy would lead France out of the darkness. Rather collaboration was a means of securing his long-held dream of Franco-German *rapprochement*. This reconciliation would banish the spectre of renewed Franco-German conflict, free France of its ties with Britain and, most importantly, rid Europe of the menace of Bolshevism. Pétain, too, was frightened of communism. It was, in part, the fear of a Paris Commune that had led him to call for an armistice. Yet it was not until summer 1941, after Hitler had invaded the Soviet Union and resistance had begun to mount in France, that anti-communism came to occupy a central position in his thinking on foreign policy.

Laval's methods of working also differed from those of the marshal. He was critical of Pétain's armistice negotiators for not having exploited France's remaining strengths to have achieved a more favourable settlement. These assets, notably the navy and colonies, could now be used to put pressure on Berlin. Nor did he have much time for the discreet diplomacy being pursued by Pétain. Confident of his own abilities, Laval attempted to open every possible line of communication with the Germans, even enlisting the services of those French fascists who preferred to congregate at Paris rather than Vichy.

These fascists were an eclectic bunch. Each possessed a competing vision of how France should take its place in the New Order. What united them was a shared admiration of Nazi Germany and a belief that the Occupation could further their own careers. Some were intellectuals such as Robert Brasillach, novelist and editor of *Je Suis Partout*, and Alphonse de Chateaubriant, editor of *La Gerbe* and founder of the literary circle, Groupe Collaboration. Others were journalists, for example Fernand de Brinon and Jean Luchaire, who had enjoyed close links with Germany before the war, notably through the Comité France-Allemagne, an organization devoted to Franco-German collaboration. Then there were the *liguers* of the 1930s: Marcel Bucard, head of the Franciste which enjoyed something of a revival in the occupied zone; Jacques Doriot, whose PPF continued to be the most successful of the fascist movements; and Marcel Déat who, with German backing, established in 1941 the Rassemblement National Populaire (RNP). Déat had hoped that the RNP, the first political party to be founded under the Occupation, would become the nucleus of a single collaborationist organization, but the jealousies and ideological rifts that had shaped the relationships between the French fascists in the 1930s continued to produce division.

Ironically, the Germans were also suspicious of Déat's projects, fearing that a single party might rejuvenate French nationalism.[4]

Further suspicions of the collaborationists were harboured at Vichy. It will be recalled that in summer 1940 Pétain rejected the idea of a *parti unique*, worried lest this should form a rival power base. In 1941 a similar concern ensured that the RNP was banned from operating in the non-occupied zone. Historians have since distinguished betweeen the collaboration of Vichy and that of the Paris fascists by coining the term 'collaborationism' to denote the ideological empathy which Déat and others felt towards Hitler's Germany. While this distinction is useful, it blurs the interrelationship between the two French capitals. Vichy was always prepared to use the Paris collaborators for its own ends. This was especially true of Laval. He quickly forged an association with Déat, and employed de Brinon and Luchaire as messenger boys between the two zones. In 1941 former members of the PPF, Pucheu and Marion, were appointed to Darlan's cabinet. By 1943 Vichy included large numbers of fascists in its ranks, providing a unity that had been absent from earlier cabinets.

There also existed an ideological affinity between Vichy and Paris. Although most collaborationists bemoaned the traditionalism and clericalism of the National Revolution in its early phase, Doriot proclaimed himself a 'man of the marshal' and heralded the Hitler–Pétain meeting at Montoire as the start of a new relationship with Germany. Pétain, remembering the way in which Doriot had criticized his handling of the Rif war, was clearly embarrassed by this support,[5] but could not help feeling a certain sympathy for the overall aims of the collaborationists, especially their anti-communism. This was evidenced in 1941 when he sent a personal message of support to the newly formed Légion des Volontaires Français contre le Bolchévisme (LVF), an organization which recruited Frenchmen to fight on the eastern front.[6] Later, he claimed that he signed this letter, which was published in Doriot's newspaper *Le Cri du Peuple*, without having read it beforehand. Its true author, he maintained, was de Brinon. Whatever the truth of this, Pétain had been identified with the ideals of French volunteers fighting in German uniforms.[7]

How, then, did the Germans view collaboration? Hitler himself was determined to resist French demands. Concessions could well rejuvenate French nationalism, and threaten his overall plans for France. In the long term, he intended to partition the country, a policy apparent in the annexation of Alsace Lorraine, the placing of the Nord-Pas-de-Calais under the High Command at Brussels, and the creation of 'reserved' and 'prohibited' zones in the north and east of France.[8] In the medium term, as he prepared to invade Britain, he sought to exploit France economically, a policy reflected in demands for raw materials and the imposition of astronomical occupation costs. None the less, the Führer appreciated the benefits of keeping France quiescent, recognizing that Vichy could assist Germany in both Africa and the Mediterranean. Thus he was prepared to entertain French overtures of collaboration even though he ultimately intended to reject them.

Hitler's designs were executed by the various Nazi agencies dealing with France: the German delegation at the Franco-German Armistice Commission at Wiesbaden; the German Military Command in France, the Militärbefehlshaber in Frankreich (MBF); and the German embassy at Paris. As elsewhere in Hitler's Europe, the functions of the occupying authorities were not clearly defined, and rivalry soon broke out among the different bureaucracies. None the less, political relations with Vichy were dominated by the embassy under Abetz. Occasionally, the ambassador is portrayed as a francophile who deliberately thwarted the wishes of his masters. The fact that this former pacifist art teacher had a French wife and had spent several long stints in Paris before the war has lent support to such a view. Certainly Berlin was wary of his loyalties,[9] and ensured that he was never entrusted with any real power. Yet, at heart, Abetz was a committed Nazi who was determined to show the French the errors of their ways and the superiority of Nazi culture, a policy he mapped out in an important memorandum of 30 July 1940.[10] He played his role with skill, exploiting the numerous French contacts he had made before the war, and establishing a good rapport with Laval. He was the diplomatic face of the New Order, ready to pretend that Germany was genuinely interested in collaboration when in reality it was not.[11]

Given the Nazi position, it is no surprise that Vichy's early attempts at collaboration resulted in little. For his part, Pétain failed in his task to open a line of communication beyond that of the Armistice Commission at Wiesbaden. In July Ribbentrop ignored an invitation for a top-level conference with the French leader. Two months later Fonck was unable to exploit his influence with Göring to arrange a Hitler–Pétain conference. Meanwhile, Laval was the only Vichy minister to secure a regular pass over the demarcation line. In Paris he was regularly wined and dined by Abetz, yet at the close of September all he had to show for his many visits to the capital was an agreement relaxing the controls governing postal traffic between the two zones.

. . .

This stalemate would have continued had it not been for developments outside Vichy's control: the pro-Gaullist revolts in the French colonies.[12] Since his escape to London, de Gaulle had secured British backing to form the 'Free French', an organization which had particular appeal to colonial officials who felt let down by metropolitan government. By late August 1940 Chad, French Equatorial Africa and the Cameroons had all rallied to the Gaullist cause. The next month, the general himself set sail for Dakar in the hope of winning over West Africa as well. In the event, the raid on Dakar (23–4 September) was resisted by Pétainist forces. This was Vichy's opportunity. Over the next few days, French officials – at Wiesbaden and at Paris – impressed upon the Germans the fact that France had been loyal to the armistice terms; the Germans should now reciprocate by making concessions. Pétain himself took a full part in these attempts to woo Hitler, packing Scapini off to Berlin. On 22 September, the marshal betrayed the depth of his anglophobia by informing a German industrialist that were it not for the armistice he would not hesitate to order active resistance against England.[13] On 10 October he delivered a message to his people, referring to the neglect of Franco-German relations in the past and the importance of these relations in the future.[14] Germany, he declared, could choose between the 'traditional peace of oppression' or 'a new peace of collaboration'.

Hitler was sceptical of these overtures. If he needed new allies, then he was more interested in Spain than in France. He was already ruing his decision not to accept Spanish offers of help back in July, and was now anxious to secure Franco's assistance in the prosecution of the war against Britain. He was further aware that concessions to France might complicate a peace settlement. Both Spain and Italy expected French colonies in the share-out of spoils at the close of the war.[15] None the less, after the raid on Dakar, he appreciated the advantages in treating France as an unofficial ally rather than as a conquered country. With the postponement of the invasion of Britain, he wished to extend the fight against Churchill in the Mediterranean. Hitler was also looking ahead to the Soviet campaign, and was anxious to secure Germany's rear. Thus he appreciated how some formal working arrangement with France, which enabled Vichy to defend its overseas empire, could be advantageous.

To resolve these conundra, Hitler undertook a tour of Latin Europe, starting with a meeting with Mussolini on 4 October in which the German leader floated the idea of a European coalition comprising France, Spain and the Axis powers. Such a coalition would prevent Gaullism from gaining a foothold in North Africa and would test Britain's resources. France, however, would not be allowed to recover its pre-war standing and Italy would still get former French colonies. A hesitant Mussolini admitted the scheme was worth exploring, and Hitler's entourage set off for Hendaye to discuss matters with Franco. As the journey took the Führer's special train through France, it was decided to meet with French leaders both going and returning.

These meetings were held at the little railway station of Montoire-sur-Loir. It was there that a surprised Laval, anticipating an interview with Ribbentrop, was brought to Hitler on 22 October 1940. After an inconclusive and incoherent exchange of views, the Führer suggested he should meet with Pétain. Laval welcomed this offer and a further conference – to coincide with Hitler's return journey from Spain – was arranged for two days' time. At this meeting, which Laval also attended, the marshal expressed a desire for Franco-German reconciliation and regretted that this had not been achieved before the war.[16] Yet there was still time to regain what had been lost. In response, Hitler underscored his commitment to collaboration. Looking to the future, he reassured his French visitors that as England was the main culprit in the war it would bear the brunt of the material costs of the fighting. Meanwhile, it was necessary to build both a European and extra-European community against Britain. France, he added enigmatically, needed to study whether it should join and work with this community. Anxious lest Germany should seek French entry into the war, Pétain replied that he was not in a position to define the exact limits of Franco-German relations. Laval, fearing that Pétain was sending out the wrong signals, interjected that, while the marshal was unable to declare war without referring the matter to the National Assembly, France would defend its empire against British aggression. Here discussions petered out. Both sides agreed on nothing more than a general statement on the mutual need for collaboration. The handshake between Hitler and Pétain that accompanied the meeting merely acknowledged the mutual benefits of collaboration; it did not confirm any hard-won agreements.

Because of their vagueness, much discussion has centred on the Montoire meetings. On the German side, it has been suggested that Hitler was seeking France's entry into the war. Documents from the German Foreign Ministry archives support such a contention,[17] yet these were never handed over to the French. Hitler preferred to leave the Montoire meetings open-ended. Why was this? First, he appears to have been happy with the response of the French leaders. He was struck by Pétain's determination to defend the colonies and may well have reasoned that this attitude would lead to *de facto* hostilities between France and Britain. Second, he retained suspicions of France. Although Pétain had impressed him, he regarded Laval as an untrustworthy politician. Third, it should be remembered that Hitler saw collaboration as part of a wider design involving Italy and Spain. Yet both these countries expressed doubts about working with Vichy, doubts that resurfaced at Hitler's meeting with Franco on 23 October. Indeed, the Spanish dictator was so unaccommodating that Hitler later remarked that he would prefer to have teeth extracted rather than go through the ordeal of negotiating with Franco again.

On the French side, the marshal's apologists have claimed that the Montoire meetings are proof that it was Laval, not Pétain, who was working for collaboration. Much is made of the fact that it was Laval who first met Hitler; Pétain, we are reminded, was reluctant to journey to Montoire. This hesitancy was mere bluff; as already seen, the marshal had long sought direct talks with Hitler. To support the 'double-game' argument, it has been claimed that while the French leader was busy avoiding making commitments at Montoire, his representative, Professor Louis Rougier, was in London where he allegedly concluded a series of 'secret agreements' with Churchill.[18] These looked towards the relaxation of the British blockade of French ports; the watering-down of BBC radio attacks on Vichy; the safeguarding of the French empire; and the reining-in of de Gaulle. Rougier, it is suggested, even explored the possibility of France re-entering the war on the allied side. Certainly, both London and Vichy were anxious to retain a line of communication. Yet the claims made for the Rougier mission, largely by Rougier himself, should be treated with caution.[19] Although the professor was in London at the time of Montoire, this was coincidence. There is no evidence to show that he enjoyed the confidence of either Pétain or Churchill. Rather he was acting largely on his own initiative, and left London empty-handed.

Pétain's real intentions at Montoire are better observed through his speech to the French people of 30 October.[20] Here he announced that he had freely accepted the Führer's invitation: 'I did not have to put up with any diktat or pressure from him. A collaboration has been envisaged between our two countries. I have accepted the principle of it.' Thereafter, he outlined the main objectives of his policy towards Germany. By taking the path of collaboration, French unity would be preserved and its empire upheld. Collaboration would also reduce the plight of the nation: prisoners would be released and occupation costs reduced. Only history, he concluded, would tell whether his policy was correct. By looking to the future, Pétain betrayed his hope that collaboration would secure his place in posterity. Yet in other respects the speech was one of his more restrained broadcasts. Gone was the self-satisfaction of the past.[21] This may have been because he was troubled by reactions to the Hitler interview. Weygand, whose criticisms of Laval had in September led to his dismissal as Minister of National Defence and subsequent posting to North Africa, warned the marshal that Montoire might well give encouragement to the Paris fascists. Indeed, the collaborationist press heralded the meeting as a step towards the integration of France into the New Order. Such interpretations – often accompanied by the photograph of Pétain shaking hands with Hitler, which also appeared in the authorized Vichy press – clearly unsettled public opinion. A growing number of people were beginning to appreciate the extent to which France had capitulated to Germany. The appeal of Pétainism was starting to weaken.

In the event, Montoire accomplished little. If the Nazis had ever hoped that France would declare war on Britain, they were soon disappointed. Montoire was not followed by renewed Anglo-French hostilities in Africa. As to the French, the expected gains of the Hitler talks never materialized. Given Italian and Spanish doubts about collaboration, the Führer saw little need to grant concessions to Vichy. One of the first German actions after Montoire was to expel French inhabitants living in Lorraine! Then there was considerable delay in arranging the Laval–Ribbentrop meeting which was supposed to thrash out the details of the agreements reached in principle at Montoire. Sidetracked by the Italian campaign in Greece, Ribbentrop would not meet with French leaders until the new year, by which time Laval was gone. By late November, the only concession which Vichy had obtained was a protocol providing for the provisional release of certain categories of prisoners-of-war.

. . . .

One Vichy minister was undaunted by the lack of progress: Laval. On 24 October he had added Foreign Affairs to his other portfolios, following the resignation of Baudouin, who was angered at the cavalier way in which he had been treated during the Montoire negotiations. Now that he enjoyed titular as well as practical control over Franco-German relations, Laval was even less willing to brook interference than before, and took a number of decisions on his own initiative. In November, the cabinet was surprised to learn that French shares in the Bor copper mines in Yugoslavia had been handed over to Germany. It was also astonished to hear that Belgian gold reserves, entrusted to France for safekeeping, had been transferred to Berlin. While Laval believed these to be trivial matters, his colleagues were furious they had not been consulted. As winter approached, the talk at Vichy was of Laval's removal. Yet when this came on 13 December 1940, it still took everyone by surprise. Why did Pétain rid himself of his leading minister, and what were the consequences of this action?

Like a refrain, Pétain's supporters argue that Laval was dismissed because of his solo quest for collaboration. In addition to surrendering shares in the Bor copper mines and the handing-over of the Belgian gold, it is alleged that he was over-eager to build on Montoire by engaging in an offensive operation against the British and Free French in Africa. Certainly in early December Vichy was holding talks with Germany over a possible attack on Chad. Yet Laval was not alone in making such suggestions. Darlan and Huntziger were far more agressive.[22] Pétain, too, favoured, a tough position: vigorous defence of the colonies was unlikely to produce war with Britain, but might secure German concessions. Thus in December 1940 Vichy was keen on more collaboration, not less.

Nor may it be maintained that Laval was sacked because he was jeopardizing Pétain's double-game strategy. On 6 December Pétain is alleged to have concluded a further 'secret agreement' with the British. After the war, Chevalier claimed that he had received a note from Lord Halifax, the British Foreign Secretary, sent via the intermediary of the Canadian ambassador, Jean Dupuy.[23] Addressed to Pétain, this document supposedly outlined a *modus vivendi* in which Vichy and London would maintain the illusion of tension but, behind the scenes, would agree to cooperate. To be sure, contacts were made; yet they merely highlighted the differences between the two countries. Rather than material aid, Churchill promised military support if Pétain left for North Africa.[24] When confronted with the offer, the marshal remarked, 'We have not received it.' There is no record of any agreement signed thereafter.[25]

The real reason behind Laval's sacking is to be found in his relationship with Pétain. It will be recalled that the marshal had always been distrustful of his deputy. Contemptuous of his parliamentarianism, Pétain had been angered by Laval's mockery of the National Revolution and lack of deference for authority, typified by the way in which he billowed cigarette smoke into the marshal's face. Pétain had put up with this so long as his minister produced results. After Montoire, Laval had accomplished little. In this situation, Pétain had become increasingly intolerant of Laval's secretive methods of working, and was fearful that he might be plotting against him.

Pétain's resolve to dismiss Laval was hardened by members of his cabinet. Alibert noted with disdain that Laval was the one parliamentarian to have survived the 6 September reshuffle. Bouthillier was aggrieved at Laval's secrecy, especially the way in which he had handled the Bor copper mines and Belgian gold reserves. Peyrouton was troubled that the Auvergnat had eyes on his own portfolio at the Interior. British agents may also have fuelled rumours that Laval was bent on more power. Although Laval had no immediate plans for further office, he did little to assuage the fears of his colleagues when he remarked to Baudouin that he was not able to govern.[26]

It is against this background of mounting suspicion that Pétain composed a letter to Hitler laying out the reasons why he had chosen to replace Laval with Flandin. Drafted on 9

December, this message was never delivered, possibly because Pétain changed his mind. Indeed, Laval would probably have survived in office, at least for the time being, had it not been for an episode which brought to a head many of Pétain's doubts about his deputy.[27] In a goodwill gesture, Hitler decided to send the ashes of Napoleon's son, the Duc de Reichstadt, to Paris from Vienna. The reinterment ceremony was planned for 15 December, and an invitation was issued to the marshal. News of this invitation reached Vichy on 12 December and was accompanied by a phone call from Laval, then in Paris, who underscored the need for Pétain to attend. The marshal was determined to stay put. It has subsequently been claimed that this decision was due to a desire not to be seen shaking hands with any more Germans. In truth, he would have shaken hands with as many Germans as necessary if such gestures brought about an improvement in Franco-German relations. Rather his refusal stemmed from fear. Once in the occupied zone he believed Abetz would force him to surrender his powers to Laval. The latter would then form a new government comprising Déat, who had recently published several attacks on the National Revolution in his newspaper, L'Oeuvre.

Furious at the marshal's stubbornness, Laval arrived at Vichy on 13 December. There he got Pétain to change his mind. As news of this decision percolated through the corridors of Vichy, members of the government decided to act. Late in the afternoon a delegation comprising Bouthillier, Peyrouton, Darlan, Alibert, Baudouin and du Moulin de Labarthète persuaded the marshal to sack Laval. Thus at the evening cabinet meeting Pétain (in the style of the Third Republic) asked for a collective letter of resignation from all of his ministers. Thinking that this was a ploy to dismiss Belin, Laval duly signed. Within minutes, he was startled to learn that only his resignation and that of Ripert, the Minister of Education, had been accepted. There followed a sharp exchange of words before Laval left the room, soon to discover that he was under house arrest, as was Déat in Paris. The following evening Pétain went on the radio to announce that Flandin was the new dauphin.[28]

What was the wider significance of Laval's dismissal? On the French side, it was hoped little had changed. The objectives of Vichy foreign policy remained the same: to exact concessions from the Nazis and to cooperate as an equal within Hitler's Europe. None the less, the regime did recognize that there was a need to reassure the Germans of its good intentions. Thus Pétain's representatives – among them Scapini, Huntziger and Doyen – made known to Hitler that Laval's dismissal was purely an internal affair; it had no bearing on Franco-German relations. Collaboration was to continue. Flandin also did his bit to placate the Germans. A prominent pre-war conservative and active appeaser, he was confident that he could re-establish good relations with Germany. He soon discovered that Abetz was not in an accommodating mood.

On the German side, it was undoubtedly Abetz who was most affected by the events of 13 December. Much of his policy rested on the relationship that he had built up with Laval, and he understood that the appointment of Flandin put both that policy and his own position in jeopardy. Reminiscent of a gunslinger bursting into a saloon, on 16 December the ambassador travelled to Vichy accompanied by ten heavily armed SS men. The next day, in a series of meetings with Pétain, he employed his bullying tactics to the full, betraying the primeval National Socialist urges he had kept hidden in the suave salons of Paris. Among other things, he demanded the return to power of Laval; the setting up of a Directorate comprising Laval, Darlan, Huntziger and Flandin; and the dismissal of a number of pro-clerical and anti-German ministers. Otherwise collaboration would stop. At one point in the meetings, he secured the release of Laval, who was brought over from nearby Châteldon. Laval was in even less control of his emotions than was Abetz, and accused the marshal of being a 'puppet' and 'windbag'. Although Pétain agreed to the proposal of a Directorate, he shrugged off these insults and refused to take back Laval. Instead, he composed a letter to Hitler promising that he would investigate events leading up to the sacking of his deputy. On Christmas Eve, Darlan delivered a further letter to an angry Führer in which Pétain made clear that there was no chance of Laval's reinstatement.[29]

The German leader's displeasure is significant as it signals that it was not just Abetz – after all only a minor player in Franco-German relations – who was affected by the events of 13 December. Admittedly Hitler cared little about Laval himself. Only a few days before his dismissal, Berlin had approved Operation Attila, which foresaw an immediate occupation of the southern zone in the event of a British invasion of the Continent, a sure sign that the Führer had no confidence in

Vichy's collaborationist overtures. None the less, Hitler was aggrieved by the marshal's behaviour. He had taken Pétain's refusal to attend the Reichstadt ceremony as a personal insult. To make matters worse, Vichy had interpreted his goodwill gesture as a device to ensnare its head of state. To Hitler this was conclusive evidence of French untrustworthiness. Thus the mistrust generated by 13 December had given Berlin cause – or at least an excuse – to avoid making any further concessions to France.

Unnerved by Flandin's inability to break the impasse, Pétain met with Laval and discussed his reinstatement. He also made known to Abetz that he was willing to take on Laval as part of the Directorate. Two factors conspired to prevent the Auvergnat's return. The first was the attitude of Laval himself, who had no wish to rejoin a government that had betrayed him; only when the leading conspirators had been purged would he return. Thus, when offered a ministerial post, he made a number of unreasonable demands which would have severely curtailed the marshal's powers. Second, Berlin was not keen on Laval's reinstatement. It was now calculated that he would be more use in Paris than in Vichy. If the Pétain government ever needed coercing, then Germany could threaten to establish a rival Laval regime in the occupied zone. Accordingly, Ribbentrop reined in Abetz who, on his own initiative, had been pressing for Laval's reappointment. Instead, the ambassador was to make it clear that the Germans had a new favourite: Darlan. Not only had Berlin been impressed by the admiral's anticlericalism, it had also been struck by his tough stance against the Anglo-Gaullists in Africa.

Ultimately, it was Pétain, not Ribbentrop, who decided to appoint Darlan. As discussed in Chapter 5, when on 9 February Flandin withdrew, the admiral was named Deputy Prime Minister, and took over Foreign Affairs and Defence to boot; the next day he became dauphin. Pétain was clearly troubled by vesting Darlan with so much power. The admiral's lukewarm support for the National Revolution and dislike of traditionalists was well known. Yet in early 1941 he seemed the man most capable of re-establishing the links with the Germans which had been damaged by the 13 December. Not only was he known to Abetz, he had met with Hitler on Christmas Eve 1940. By reinvigorating Franco-German relations, Pétain further calculated that Darlan's appointment would forestall any plans Berlin might have for a rival Laval government in Paris. Thus, in sacrificing something of his own authority, the marshal believed Darlan would safeguard Vichy's independence.

. . .

Given the way in which Darlan rallied first to Vichy in 1940 and then to the Americans in 1942, he has often been characterized as a shameless opportunist who sought power for its own sake. On closer inspection, it may be seen that his position was more consistent than has previously been recognized. Through his many pre-war posts at the Ministry of the Navy, he had become a skilled diplomat with an appreciation of geopolitics which almost rivalled that of de Gaulle.[30] In early 1941, both men foresaw how the war was likely to become a truly global affair. Out of this conflict, Darlan predicted the emergence of two camps: a European bloc, also comprising Africa, which would be dominated by Germany, and an American bloc, supported by a gravely weakened Britain. Those keen to rehabilitate Darlan argue that he sought to steer a neutral path between these two sides. Rather the consistency of his position lay in his preference for Germany.[31] A fervent anglophobe, a believer in an authoritarian Republic and a callous antisemite, he had little sympathy for the Anglo-Saxons. It was only when a German victory looked less likely that he contemplated abandoning Vichy for the Allies.

On taking office in spring 1941, Darlan's diplomatic skills were deployed in framing his so-called 'Grand Design'. This policy endeavoured to provide France with a naval and imperial role within a new continental system. This would have numerous advantages. First, it would lead to a speedy peace between France and Germany, thereby removing the spectre of internal dissent, a growing problem for Vichy in 1941. Second, it would safeguard the empire and navy from British clutches. Indeed Darlan, whose great-grandfather had supposedly fought at the Battle of Trafalgar, eagerly looked forward to the day when Britain was a spent power. Third, it would provide a bulwark against Bolshevism, another of Darlan's pet hatreds. In many ways, these objectives were similar to Laval's. Yet the methods of the two men were different. Although Laval was willing to make concessions to Germany, he understood that something had to be kept in reserve; otherwise there would be nothing left to bargain with. In his fruitless attempts to collaborate, Darlan found himself conceding more and more,[32] and almost took France back into the war on Germany's side. The admiral's policies also troubled Pétain, who was reluctant to see further bloodshed. The marshal only tolerated Darlan in the belief that he was the man best able to achieve a break-through in Franco-German relations.

The fundamental problem confronting Darlan in February 1941 was the same as that which had faced both Laval and Flandin: how to interest the Germans in collaboration? On one level, this was to be facilitated by closer economic coopera-tion. To the technocrats among Darlan's cabinet, such a policy also offered a chance to revitalize French industry. Thus, in early May, Jacques Barnaud, Vichy's chief economic nego-tiator, negotiated a deal with Germany for joint aluminium production. That same month, Jean Berthelot, the Minister of Communications, visited Paris with plans for the rebuilding of Europe's roads and railways. On another level, Darlan hoped to promote collaboration by adopting a far stiffer attitude towards Britain than was expected of him. Negotiations with London to relax the British blockade were abruptly halted. On 15 March Darlan requested permission to use French naval vessels for convoying, a request that was eagerly granted by the Armistice Commission, which hoped that Franco-British relations would take another turn for the worse. Indeed, by the spring of 1941 Britain and France were virtually involved in an undeclared naval war.[33] Berlin remained unimpressed. Even Abetz, usually eager to do business with the French, gave Darlan the 'cold shoulder'.

Once again, the situation changed thanks to events beyond Vichy's control. Just as the Gaullist rebellions in the colonies paved the way to Montoire, the April revolt by Rashid Ali-al-Gailani against the British in Iraq made possible a further top-level Franco-German conference. Having just conquered Yugoslavia and Greece, Hitler saw how he could exploit this colonial crisis for his own purposes. Yet to get to Iraq his troops needed to pass through French Syria. Thus at the beginning of May Abetz informed Darlan that Hitler wished to see him. This time, the ambassador explained, collaboration would be on different terms. In return for German concessions, France would provide clandestine support to the Iraqi rebels and allow the Luftwaffe to use Syrian air-bases.

Darlan seized this as an opportunity to realize his Grand Design, an occasion to achieve the major Franco-German settlement that had eluded Laval. After all, Darlan would be meeting Hitler not at some obscure railway station but at Berchtesgaden, the Führer's private retreat. Here, on 11 May, the Nazi leader was in uncompromising mood.[34] Germany, Darlan was told, did not need France in order to win the war. On the other hand, the assistance of France could shorten hostilities. If France cooperated, concessions could be contemplated. If it did not, the consequences would be dire, involving a loss of territory. Such threats left the desired impression. Three days later, Darlan informed the Vichy cabinet that this was the last chance to achieve a *rapprochement* with Germany. Should France favour Britain, it would be crushed and dismembered. His colleagues, including Pétain, agreed. Although in April the marshal had declared in a radio broadcast that France would never take action against its former allies,[35] he took reassurance from Darlan's claims that aid to Germany in the Middle East would largely be economic in nature. Nor would it involve a declaration of war against Britain. Accordingly, Pétain authorized his deputy to conduct further negotiations with the Germans, out of which stemmed the protocols of Paris of 28 May.

All in all, there were four protocols. The first granted Germany the use of Syrian air-bases; in addition, Vichy agreed to fuel and rearm German planes. By the second, Rommel's Afrika Korps were given permission to deploy the Tunisian port of Bizerte as a supply route. The third looked ahead to the establishment of a German submarine-base at Dakar. In return for the Syrian part of the bargain, Germany promised to reduce occupation costs, release certain categories of POWs, and ease passage over the demarcation line.[36] There was also a promise of more concessions to come. A fourth complementary protocol envisaged some degree of political collaboration should France find itself at war with either Britain or the United States of America. Significantly, on the German side, this last protocol was only recognized by Abetz, who remained more indulgent to the French than his Berlin masters.

Although Darlan hailed the protocols as the start of a new era in Franco-German relations, in the event they were never signed by Pétain. Traditionally it has been argued that it was Weygand who prevented their formal ratification.[37] Worried lest France was about to re-enter the war, on 2 June he returned from Africa to argue against the Germans terms. The way to avoid these commitments, he suggested, was to demand much broader concessions which were bound to be refused by Berlin. Indeed, some credit may be given to Weygand for hardening the resistance of certain cabinet members and for sowing the seeds of doubt in Pétain's mind. Until early June, the marshal had gone along with Darlan's strategy, partly because he was ill-informed as to what was happening, and partly because he remained desperate for a foreign-policy success. Now he was afraid that Darlan was moving too fast at the risk of achieving nothing.

Recent study has further suggested that Darlan himself may have sabotaged the protocols.[38] It has been speculated that he agreed to the fourth complementary protocol knowing full well that this would cause consternation on the part of his colleagues, who would subsequently refuse to go along with the military agreements. Given the way in which Darlan struggled to reawaken German interest in the Paris agreements during the remainder of 1941, this explanation seems unlikely.

Ultimately, it was Berlin that relinquished the protocols. On 14 July it signalled its intention of abandoning the agreements. This was due to the wider developments of the war. On 8 June Anglo-Gaullist forces, aware that German planes were refuelling at Palmyra and Aleppo, invaded Syria. Despite heavy resistance by Vichyite troops, on 14 July Syria fell, thus ending any interest which Germany had in assisting Rashid Ali-al-Gailani. Meanwhile, Rommel had enjoyed success against the British in Egypt, reducing his need for supplies through Tunisia. Most importantly, on 22 June Germany began its invasion of the Soviet Union. Thereafter, the Syrian affair was little more than a sideshow.

Had the protocols been ratified, they would inevitably have taken France back into the war on the German side. Public opinion, of course, did not know this but was perturbed by the fact that in Syria, as at Dakar, Frenchmen had fought Frenchmen. There was also concern at the invasion of the Soviet Union, a sure indication that there was no prospect of an early peace in sight. Against this backdrop, the Vichy regime seemed incapable of securing any let-up in the armistice arrangements. As befitted his semi-regal status, the public was disinclined to blame Pétain for this lack of success. Discontent was focused instead on his malevolent minister, Darlan, who seemed even more remote from people's everyday concerns than Laval had been. Yet Pétain could draw little comfort from the recognition that his popularity outweighed that of his government. It was no coincidence that Vichy's latest foreign-policy failure was followed by his speech of 12 August complaining that 'un vent mauvais' was sweeping through France.

. . .

Despite the setbacks over Syria and the growth of internal dissent, Pétain remained sanguine about the prospects of collaboration. If anything, he was more enthusiastic than before. In large measure, this optimism derived from the invasion of the Soviet Union. Although a dislike of the left had always been a part of Pétain's ideological make-up, he now calculated that closer cooperation with Germany would not only save the French people from the worst defeat in their history, it would also free them from the menace of Bolshevism. Thus in late 1941 anti-communism added an extra zest to Vichy foreign policy, just as it provided a new repressive edge to the National Revolution.

The perennial problem was how to open a dialogue with the Nazis. One thing was certain: Pétain had no wish to give offence to Hitler. This, of course, was why he failed to make a spirited protest over the shooting of French hostages. This self-restraint was not, however, acknowledged by the Germans. When on 12 November Hitler replied to Pétain's letter of 20 October, congratulating Germany on the crusade against Bolshevism, the Führer fulminated against the French for the recent assassinations of German personnel and recalled the harsh treatment of German POWs in 1918.[39] Nor had the marshal resolved how far collaboration should extend. Although he kept faith with Darlan, he was apprehensive about the admiral's offers of military cooperation.

Confident of Pétain's support, in autumn 1941 Darlan set out to relaunch his Grand Design. This was to be achieved by an aggressive policy both at home and abroad.[40] At home, he hoped that the tough measures outlined in the marshal's message of 12 August would demonstrate to the Germans that Vichy was serious in crushing communist and Gaullist dissent. Abroad, he made it known to Abetz that France was willing to contemplate military action in support of the Germans. When these overtures failed, he decided on a dramatic ploy designed to fulfil a long-standing German demand: the dismissal of Weygand.

Since becoming Pétain's Special Representative to North Africa in September 1940, Weygand had maintained a strictly *attentiste* approach, building up French forces should they be required to defend the empire at some point in the future. Although he had not hidden his germanophobia, nor had he shown any sympathy for the Anglo-Gaullists. This impartiality had not impressed Berlin. It was rumoured that he had been behind the plot to dismiss Laval, and was using his position to blackmail Pétain by threatening to place the North African forces at the disposal of de Gaulle. For good measure, Abetz blamed Weygand for the failure of the Paris protocols. Thus in German eyes he was more than a mere irritant.

Darlan, too, held Weygand responsible for sabotaging his Grand Design, but it remains unclear whether his desire to be rid of this troublesome general stemmed solely from a desire for closer collaboration. Ideologically, the general's traditionalist values were anathema to Darlan. Weygand had also opposed Darlan's plans to become Minister of Defence, a post he eventually acquired on 11 August 1941.

Mystery also surrounds the reasons why Pétain ultimately agreed to dismiss Weygand. While he had no personal liking for his fellow soldier, a dislike that dated back to the jealousies of the First World War, he welcomed the general's support for the National Revolution. It may be that the marshal was impressed by Darlan's claims that collaboration could not continue while Weygand remained in place. After all, Hitler had said as much in his letter of 12 November. Yet it is doubtful whether such threats would have worked had not Germany offered the prospect of a top-level meeting between Pétain and Göring. Promised in early November, this enabled Vichy to present the German removal of Weygand, accomplished on 18 November, in a less humiliating light.

In removing Weygand, Pétain had miscalculated in two respects. First, he had misjudged the unease it would create among his natural supporters. In government, du Moulin de Labarthète, Carcopino and Bergeret all threatened to resign. In the country several *anciens combattants* wrote to the Hôtel du Parc, clearly worried that Weygand's dismissal represented a German triumph.[41] Second, the marshal had misjudged what he could obtain from Göring. Pétain's belief in 'the comradeship of arms' remained strong, and he was sure that he would be able to do business with the German officer just as he had done in the 1930s. Thus, in preparation for the meeting, various Vichy ministers drew up a dossier outlining the economic, social and political steps that needed to be taken to improve Franco-German relations. As with Dakar and Syria, Pétain failed to see that Berlin's desire to renew talks with Vichy sprang from outside events. Recent victories on the part of the British in North Africa had made Rommel's access to Bizerte important again.

Given this background, it is small wonder that the Pétain–Göring interview, held on 1 December at Saint-Florentin, was a fiasco. According to some reports it degenerated into a shouting match, with Göring exclaiming, 'Who are the victors, you or us?' Apparently Pétain replied that 'he had never felt more profoundly than in the course of this interview to what extent France had lost the war', and stuffed his memorandum of French demands into Göring's pocket. Whether Pétain behaved with such determination or not remains unclear.[42] What is certain is that Germany had no intention of bowing to French requests: all Berlin was interested in was French military aid in Africa. Subsequent events vindicated Göring's intransigence. Despite much huffing and puuffing, in early January Vichy provided military equipment to Rommel through Tunisia. Admittedly, the Germans did not establish permanent bases in the French empire, notably at Bizerte, yet this was largely because the British failed to push Rommel west on to French territory.

Shortly after the failure of the Saint-Florentin interview, French hopes for collaboration suffered a more serious blow: on 7 December 1941 Germany declared war on the United States of America. In July 1940 Vichy had greatly welcomed American neutrality and recognition of the *état français*. American business techniques had also been a source of inspiration for many of Vichy's technocrats. Pétain, too, was an admirer of the USA and had a number of American friends, notably the Pardees. In the First World War he had enjoyed far more convivial relations with Pershing than he had with Haig. In 1931 he had made an official visit to America and was impressed by what he saw. In 1940 he had gone out of his way to cultivate William Bullitt, the US ambassador to Vichy. Now that the USA was a belligerent nation, Pétain understood that Washington would no longer display the same kind of cordiality to his government. Although Roosevelt did not immediately break off diplomatic relations with France, intense pressure was put on

Darlan to ensure that French bases in the Caribbean did not fall into German hands.[43] For its part, Berlin countered by demanding that Vichy should refuse to cooperate with American requests. Caught in a cleft stick, in January 1942 the French government contemplated severing its links with the USA. Jacques Bénoist-Mechin, Vichy's representative at Paris, and Abetz, both keen to revive their flagging fortunes, even discussed the possibility of France entering the war on the German side.[44] In the event, Darlan, himself eager to re-establish his position and protect what was left of the French empire, attempted to play off both the Americans and Germans with reassurances of French neutrality in the Caribbean.

It is against this background that moves began for the return of Laval. For their part, the Germans, frustrated with Darlan, made known in late February that if Laval was not reinstated a Gauleiter would be appointed. Aware of this pressure, Laval encouraged the collaborationist press to campaign on his own behalf. In March he arranged a meeting with Helmut Knochen, a key SS man. Here he voiced concern over the deteriorating state of Franco-German relations, and expressed a desire to meet with someone of importance on the German side. As Göring was about to visit Paris, an interview was hastily arranged. In what Laval later described as a 'monologue', Göring delivered a long attack on French duplicity and warned Laval not to rejoin a government that faced the prospect of subjugation; clearly, not everyone at Berlin was keen to see the Auvergnat back in harness.[45] The meeting was supposed to have been confidential yet Laval let it be known to Vichy what had been said, and arranged an interview with Pétain, which took place on 25 March in the forest of Randan. Laval stressed the danger of Darlan's policies and the possibility of Germany imposing a Gauleiter.[46]

Pétain was in a dilemma. On the one hand, he wished to be rid of Darlan, who had repeatedly failed in his efforts to improve Franco-German relations. On the other hand, Pétain had no wish to recall Laval, who remained as untrustworthy as ever and was known to want those powers that had been denied him in January 1941. That is why the former dauphin turned down an offer, made immediately after the Randan meeting, of a place in Darlan's cabinet. Relieved at this decision, Pétain now believed that the way was open to press ahead with the creation of a new government which would breathe new life into the National Revolution and relaunch Franco-German relations. The proposed cabinet would comprise traditionalists and military men as well as a smattering of experts. The leading minister was to be Joseph Barthélemy, formerly a Minister of Justice and scourge of the left. Clearly, then, in spring 1942 Pétain was seeking to recover something of the authority that he had relinquished to Darlan.

The marshal did not understand that his freedom of action was now severely curtailed. Having devised his new list of ministers, copies were sent to both the Germans and the Americans. Washington, aware that pressure was mounting for Laval's reinstatement, made known that the Auvergnat's return would lead to the breaking off of diplomatic relations. This had the opposite effect to what had been intended, as it intensified German demands for Laval's return. Sources differ over whether Hitler issued an ultimatum declaring that he would judge France's willingness to collaborate by the presence or absence of Laval, but this is what Abetz wished Vichy to believe.[47]

Thus Pétain was ultimately caught between Laval's return and American displeasure.[48] Fearful of a Gauleiter and still convinced that collaboration was desirable, Pétain decided that he wanted good relations with the Germans more than he did with the USA. Thus in early April the marshal relinquished his plans for a traditionalist cabinet, and considered how best to bring Laval back into government. Various solutions were considered, with Darlan, anxious to retain something of his authority, offering his own suggestions. Eventually, it was one of Darlan's ideas that was accepted: Laval would become Deputy Prime Minister and the admiral Commander-in-Chief of all the armed forces.

When the new government was announced on 18 April, Pétain could take some satisfaction in what had happened. He had a new cabinet; he had succeeded in reducing Darlan's importance; he had secured fresh German contacts. Yet he had lost much. Despite the recall of Laval, a peace settlement with Germany seemed no closer than it had been in 1940. The armistice terms remained in place; many of the colonies had been lost; and friendships overseas had been relinquished. While Pétain had never wished for a Franco-British rapprochement, he was disappointed that on 24 April 1942 the USA carried out its threat to break off diplomatic relations. The reasons for the lack of success were patent. Pétain, and indeed

Laval and Darlan, never understood the ways in which Berlin–Vichy relations were shaped by the totality of the French defeat, the uncompromising stand of Hitler and the wider developments of the war. Yet driven by a curious mixture of compassion, ambition and naivety, Pétain remained certain that he could produce a 'diplomatic Verdun'. Few thanked him for his efforts. Each stage in the tortuous road of Franco-German relations – Montoire, Syria and Saint-Florentin – had cost him friends in both government and the country. Each stage had also marked a reduction in his own authority. With the return of Laval, the omens were not good for what remained of his powers.

· · ·

NOTES AND REFERENCES

1. The first study to make extensive use of German archives was E. Jäckel, *Frankreich in Hitlers Europa. Die Deutsche Frankreichpolitik im Zweiten Weltkrieg* (Stuttgart: Deutsche-Anstalt, 1966).

2. H.R. Kedward, *Occupied France. Collaboration and Resistance, 1940–1944* (Oxford: Basil Blackwell, 1985), p. 32.

3. Ibid., p. 32. The term 'diplomatic Verdun' was first used by the ardent Pétainist Louis-Dominique Girard in his *Montoire. Verdun diplomatique* (Paris: André Bonne, 1948).

4. Kedward, *Occupied France*, p. 43.

5. H. du Moulin de Labarthète, *Le temps des illusions. Souvenirs, juillet 1940 – avril 1942* (Geneva: Le Cheval Ailé, 1946) p. 327.

6. M. Ferro, *Pétain* (Paris: Fayard, 1987), pp. 330–2.

7. Kedward, *Occupied France*, p. 41.

8. The 'reserved zone', which existed within the main zone of German occupation (see map), was designated for German settlers. The 'prohibited zone', which existed within the 'reserved zone', was designed as a buffer between the main zone of occupation and the Nord-Pas-de-Calais. See W.D. Halls, *The Youth of Vichy France* (Oxford: Clarendon Press, 1981), pp. 228–33.

9. F. Taylor (ed.), *The Goebbels Diaries, 1939–1941* (London: Hamish Hamilton, 1982), pp. 185–6.

10. CDJC LXXXI–28, 'Politische Arbeit in Frankreich', Salzburg, 30 July 1940.

11. Kedward, *Occupied France*, pp. 12–13. See too N. Atkin, 'France's Little Nuremberg', in H.R. Kedward and N. Wood (eds), *The Liberation of France. Image and Event* (Oxford: Berg, 1995), pp. 197–208.

12. G. Warner, *Pierre Laval and the Eclipse of France* (London: Eyre & Spottiswoode, 1968), p. 222.

13. R.O. Paxton, *Vichy France. Old Guard and New Order, 1940–1944* (New York: Alfred A. Knopf, 1972), p. 72.
14. Message of 10 October 1940 in J.-C. Barbas (ed.), *Philippe Pétain. Discours aux français, 17 juin 1940–20 août 1944* (Paris: Albin Michel, 1989), pp. 86–94.
15. Hitler's concerns discussed in Warner, *Pierre Laval*, pp. 225–6.
16. The Hitler–Pétain interview is followed in Ferro, *Pétain*, pp. 187–191.
17. DGFP, Series D, vol. X1, no. 207 unsigned memorandum, and no. 208, draft protocol, pp. 348–51. See too Warner, *Pierre Laval*, pp. 239–40.
18. L. Rougier, *Mission secrète à Londres. Les accords Pétain–Churchill* (Paris: La Diffusion du Livre, 1946).
19. R. Frank, 'Vichy et les britanniques, 1940–1941: double jeu ou double langage?', in J.-P. Azéma and F. Bédarida (eds), *Vichy et les français* (Paris: Fayard, 1992), pp. 146–50.
20. Message of 30 October 1940 in Barbas (ed.), *Discours*, pp. 94–6.
21. R. Griffiths, *Marshal Pétain* (London: Constable, 1970), p. 271.
22. Paxton, *Vichy France*, pp. 72–3.
23. J. Chevalier, 'Un témoignage sur deux points d'histoire', in *Ecrits de Paris*, 19 July 1953, pp. 22–9.
24. This offer was made in early December 1940 and early January 1941. See R.T. Thomas, *Britain and Vichy* (London: Macmillan, 1979), pp. 79–80.
25. Ibid., p. 80.
26. P. Baudouin, *Neuf mois au gouvernement, avril–décembre 1940* (Paris: Editions de la Table Ronde, 1948), p. 403.
27. Griffiths, *Pétain*, p. 272.
28. Message of 14 December 1940 in Barbas (ed.), *Discours*, p. 101.
29. Warner, *Pierre Laval*, pp. 262–7.
30. H. Coutau-Bégarie and C. Huan, *Darlan* (Paris: Fayard, 1989), p. 732.
31. R. Frank, 'Pétain, Laval, Darlan', in J.-P. Azéma and F. Bédarida (eds), *La France des années noires*, vol. 1 (Paris: Seuil, 1993), pp. 311–27.
32. J.-B. Duroselle, *L'abîme. Politique étrangère de la France, 1939–1944* (Paris: Imprimerie Nationale, 1982), pp. 281–301.
33. Paxton, *Vichy France*, p. 116, who also gives details of the Barnuad and Berthelot initiatives and who remains the best authority on Darlan's 'Grand Design'.
34. Ferro, *Pétain*, p. 312.
35. Speech of 7 April 1941 in Barbas (ed.), *Discours*, pp. 120–2.
36. Paxton, *Vichy France*, p. 118. See too R.O. Paxton, 'La collaboration d'état', in Azéma and Bédarida (eds), *La France des années noires*, vol. 1, pp. 332–61.

37. A similar view is repeated in a recent biography of the general:
    B. Destrumeau, *Weygand* (Paris: Perrin, 1989), pp. 685–92.
38. Coutau-Bégarie and Huan, *Darlan*, pp. 396–7.
39. These letters are cited in Ferro, *Pétain*, pp. 350–1.
40. Paxton, *Vichy France*, p. 124.
41. Ferro, *Pétain*, pp. 358–61.
42. Ibid., pp. 361–5.
43. Paxton, *Vichy France*, p. 130.
44. Ibid., pp. 387–90.
45. Warner, *Pierre Laval*, p. 284 gives details of the Göring–Laval
    meeting.
46. Ibid., p. 285.
47. Ibid., pp. 287–8 and Griffiths, *Pétain*, p. 299.
48. Griffiths, *Pétain*, p. 299.

Chapter 7

THE FIGUREHEAD, 1942–3

Most writers agree that Pétain's powers declined markedly in the remaining two years of the Occupation. Laval's recall in April 1942, the occupation of all of France in November that year, the intensification of German demands in 1943 and the allied invasion of 1944 severely curtailed the marshal's freedom of action. No longer the fountainhead of power, he had become a figurehead.[1] None the less, contrary to the claims of those who seek to dissociate him from the blackest phase of Vichy's history, he was not completely lacking in authority, and cannot be exonerated from all that was done in his name. He retained an appeal in the towns and villages of rural France, a popularity that was critical in propping up the mouldering edifice of the Vichy regime. Nor, despite his tremendous age, had he lost his appetite for wheeler-dealing. Accordingly, at moments of crisis – for example, November 1942 and December 1943 – he again occupied centre stage, and was determined to exercise his influence to the full.[2]

. . .

It will be recalled that in February 1941 Laval had insisted upon extensive powers as a precondition for his return to government, knowing that these would not be granted. In April 1942 he understood that they could not be refused. By constitutional act no. 11 of 18 April, he became *chef du gouvernement* or Prime Minister, responsible only to the *chef de l'état*; no longer was he the deputy premier. Admittedly, he was not the dauphin; that honour rested with Darlan, who was now Commander-in-Chief of all the armed forces. Even so, Laval received the following key portfolios: Foreign Affairs, the Interior and Information. In practice, this latter post was occupied by the journalist René Bonnefoy.

Through these changes Pétain had lost much of the authority granted to him by constitutional act no. 2 of 10 July 1940.
Marc Boegner, head of the Fédération Protestante, observed
that the *chef de l'état français* now had even less power than the
President of the Third Republic, a post the marshal had
despised because of its limited functions.[3] In April 1942, real
power rested with Laval, who possessed the right to choose
ministers and initiate policy. Only two sanctions were open to
the marshal if he wished to keep a check on his leading minister. First, he could refuse to sign laws put before him; yet he
knew that he would need to muster tremendous tenacity of purpose if he sought to oppose Laval. In any case, he often found
himself in broad agreement with the Prime Minister's strategy.
Second, he could dismiss Laval. It was recognized, however, that
this course of action was likely to invite another visit from Abetz
and a possible German take-over of Vichy. Pétain was, then,
boxed into a corner, a situation which depressed him. On 20
April 1942 he held a dinner for outgoing members of his cabinet. Here, he was overheard to remark to his aide, Bonhomme,
how on 13 December he had given Laval a good kick up the
backside. When the guests were leaving, Pétain's pessimism
resurfaced as he confessed that he was nothing more than a
man overboard.[4]

The cabinet reshuffle that accompanied Laval's return
marked a further dent in Pétain's authority. Admittedly the
marshal retained some of his trusted friends, notably Romier,
Benoist-Méchin and Barthélemy. Yet out went 'the men of 13
December' – Bouthillier, Belin and Caziot – as well as a number of Darlan's experts. Out, too, went some of Pétain's inner
circle of advisers. Although Ménétrel (who it was rumoured
had discovered a secret cure for ageing) remained, du Moulin
de Labarthète was forced to resign.[5] Thereafter the marshal
became increasingly isolated, with few friends who could inform him of the latest gossip, a dangerous state of affairs given
Laval's methods of working.[6] Certainly Pétain could not con-
fide in the new ministerial appointees. They included fascist
sympathizers such as Bonnard and the ex-syndicalist Hubert
Lagardelle; technocrats such as Jean Bichelonne, Jacques le
Roy Ladurie and Max Bonnafous; and, inevitably, former parliamentarians such as Pierre Cathala. Space would have been
made for more of these ex-deputies, including Marquet, yet
they were either too greedy in their demands or knew when

not to join a sinking ship. As in 1940, Laval did not include any of the Paris collaborationists. Their presence would have restricted his dealings with the Germans and threatened his own position. Instead, he had plumped for his trusted cronies, men who would not plot another 13 December.[7]

Confident of cabinet backing, Laval set out to devise policy and, in so doing, further undermined the marshal's standing. Pétain's pet love remained the National Revolution even though this experiment had, by April 1942, run out of steam. Laval's return ensured that in future only lip-service would be paid to the ideals of *travail, famille, patrie*. This lack of enthusiasm is most clearly witnessed in educational and youth affairs, once the engine-room of the National Revolution. Apart from giving technical schools a boost, Bonnard (the new minister) devoted little energy to educational matters, and spent most of his time in Paris entertaining writers and artists. His salon life-style, blatant homosexuality and Nazi sympathies earned him the reproach of many at Vichy, including Pétain's wife, who named him 'la Gestapette', a word derived from 'Gestapo' and 'tapette', French slang for 'queer'.[8] Ominously, the only domestic policies to be extended were those designed to quell internal dissidence and persecute minorities.

Now that the National Revolution had been put out to grass, Laval believed he could devote his talents to his first love: foreign policy. Yet, thanks to a radically altered international landscape, he discovered that his room for manoeuvre was more limited than in 1940. Previously the navy and colonies had been his most valuable assets when dealing with Berlin; in 1942 their worth was rapidly deteriorating. By early that year both Syria and French Equatorial Africa had gone over to the Gaullists. Moreover, Soviet and American participation in the conflict meant that the war had become truly global. Laval especially rued Washington's involvement. One of his long-term goals had been to make France a bridge between Europe and the USA. However, as 1942 wore on, it became apparent that Roosevelt had little interest in retaining Vichy's goodwill. In April Admiral Leahy, the US ambassador to France, was called home, leaving only a *chargé d'affaires*; in May the State Department supported the British invasion of the French colony of Madagascar; in July Roosevelt accredited an official representative to the Gaullist Committee of National Liberation; and in autumn considerable pressure was placed on Admiral Robert, the High Commissioner in the French West Indies, to ensure that French ships and ordnance did not fall into Nazi hands.[9]

In view of these developments, it is small wonder that Darlan began to lose faith in a German victory. By contrast, Laval remained sanguine about Hitler's prospects. After all, in summer 1942, German armies were in the heart of the USSR; Rommel was enjoying fresh success in North Africa; and the Japanese had taken over much of the Far East. Thus Laval's first speech to the nation since his recall to power returned to his favourite topic of Franco-German reconciliation. Broadcast on 20 April, he spent little time dwelling on internal matters, emphasizing instead that in these 'hours of peril' it was the duty of the French people to work towards a *rapprochement* with Germany. This was the only means of securing long-term peace on the continent and of thwarting Bolshevism. Significantly, he avoided using the word 'collaboration', preferring instead the epithet 'entente', an acknowledgement that in the days ahead he would have some difficult decisions to sell to the French people.[10]

As ever, the success of Laval's policies depended on the flexibility of the German position. This proved less compromising than before. Berlin retained considerable suspicions about Laval, which were intensified by the Giraud affair. On 17 April the former commander of the Ninth Army escaped from the castle of Königstein on the Elbe, where he had been held prisoner since May 1940, and made his way to Vichy where he was warmly welcomed. Hitler, who mistakenly believed Giraud to be the real author of de Gaulle's *Vers l'armée de métier*, was fearful that the general might now become head of the French resistance overseas. Thus various people, including Abetz, Laval and eventually Pétain, attempted to persuade a bewildered Giraud to return to captivity. The failure of their efforts resulted in a German clampdown on concessions to French prisoners-of-war and the temporary disgrace of Abetz, who was perversely blamed for the whole episode.

Laval's task was made no easier by the fact that Berlin's displeasure over the Giraud affair coincided with its need for foreign workers. By spring 1942 the Russian campaign was beginning to take its toll, and the German economy found itself confronting the demands of total war. Albert Speer, Minister of Armaments Production and soon to become head of the National Economic Planning Organization, sought to shift these demands on to the peoples of occupied Europe. Fritz Sauckel, a one-time sailor, Nazi of the first hour and Gauleiter of Thuringia, was thus assigned the job of recruiting foreign labour for the Reich. Given that the supply of Polish and Russian workers was drying up, it was inevitable that he should have looked westwards, particularly to France. A prisoner there during the First World War, Sauckel despised all things French. It was, then, with some relish that in May 1942 he demanded 250,000 French workers by the close of July.

Aware that Order No. 4 of 7 May 1942 entitled Sauckel to use force to obtain labour, Laval's response was to haggle and procrastinate. The result of his negotiations was the infamous Relève scheme by which one French prisoner-of-war was to be released in return for every three French workers who enlisted to work in Germany. In the event, this arrangement never enticed enough skilled volunteers to board the train for Germany, and on 4 September a Vichy law, imposed by Abetz, allowed the compulsory recruitment of certain categories of skilled workers, a prelude to the introduction of full-blown conscription in February 1943. These developments lay in the future. Meanwhile, on 22 June 1942 Laval took to the airwaves in a bid to sell the Relève to the nation, and outwit the Paris fascists who maintained that he was too tepid in his support for the Nazi war effort. It was in this broadcast that he declared, 'I desire the victory of Germany for without it Bolshevism would tomorrow install itself everywhere.' Laval will always be remembered for this comment. It has become more renowned than any of Pétain's speeches, and probably secured the Auvergnat's place in front of a firing-squad in 1945.[11] Yet, in essence, there was little new in what he announced. He had expressed the same sentiment several times before and, indeed, had used a virtually identical phrase some 11 days earlier when addressing leaders of the Légion Française des Combattants.[12] It was the timing that was inappropriate. As Laval himself later acknowledged, the words would be like a 'drop of sulphuric acid on the skin of suffering people'.[13]

Certainly Pétain was aware of the impact of the speech on public opinion. This explains why, in 1945, the marshal used the occasion of his pre-trial hearing to dissociate himself from Laval's sentiments by maintaining that he had objected to the speech when it was discussed at the following cabinet meeting.[14] There is no evidence to support this claim; rather he may well have approved the text beforehand. At Pétain's trial proper, Laval recalled how the marshal had disliked his original phrase, 'I believe in the victory of Germany'.[15] The soldier had pointed out to the politician that, not being a military man, he had no right to 'believe' as he did not understand the matters at stake; so the phrase was altered to 'I desire the victory of Germany'. Once Laval vacated the witness box, Pétain made one of his infrequent interjections to denounce this testimony.[16] The affair was settled when the prosecution produced written evidence from an eye-witness, Charles Rochat, permanent head of the Vichy Foreign Ministry, to corroborate Laval's version of events.[17] Indeed, Laval's story sounds authentic, particulary given Pétain's anti-communism. Unable to find anything wrong with the so-called policy being pursued by his deputy, it was typical that the marshal should have insisted on a pedantic stylistic change.

In addition to having to cope with the marshal's textual corrections, Laval had to contend with a more serious matter. Hard on the heels of German demands for French labour, Berlin insisted on the deportation of Jews. At the Wannsee Conference of January 1942, the Reich tidied up the remaining details of the 'Final Solution'. In France, as elsewhere in Hitler's Europe, there had been forewarnings of this strategy. In May 1941 the Paris police had cooperated in the first mass internment of foreign Jews. In December that year, the Nazis decided on a different form of reprisal for the assassination of German soldiers. Instead of shooting hostages (of whom many had been Jewish) they arrested 743 Jewish intellectuals and imposed a fine of one billion francs on the occupied zone. Those caught in this round-up embarked on trains destined for the east; they were soon joined by others, also arrested in retaliation for attacks on German servicemen. These piecemeal measures were nothing compared to the barbarity of what was to follow. In an attempt to isolate future deportees, from 7 June 1942 all Jews in the occupied zone had to wear the yellow star of David on an outer garment, a measure Vichy had previously resisted; four days later the Germans demanded the regime hand over 100,000 Jews for deportation; on 23 June, the government learned that all Jews were to be transported from France.[18]

Although no antisemite of conviction, Laval had little sympathy for Jews. This callousness was evidenced in the sordid policy he devised in July 1942, stipulating that Vichy would deliver 10,000 foreign Jews from the unoccupied zone on the understanding that French Jews living in the occupied zone would only be deported if the total of foreign Jews fell short of German quotas.[19] In this way, Laval hoped to protect both French nationals and Vichy's autonomy. Thus the French police, under the direction of the former prefect René Bousquet, took a full part in the *grands rafles*. The first of these was on 16 July when some 13,000 foreign Jews, among them 4,000 children, were deposited in the Vélodrome d'Hiver, a large indoor sports arena in Paris. From there many were sent to Drancy, a half-finished housing estate to the north-east of the capital. Shortly afterwards, the first convoys from the unoccupied zone made their way to this camp before setting out on the sorry journey to the east. When in November 1942 the Germans crossed the demarcation line, it became increasingly difficult for Laval to resist demands for all categories of Jews. By August 1944, some 75,000 would have left France for the death camps; of this number, barely 2 per cent returned alive.

The savagery which lies behind these statistics raises a further question concerning Pétain's role in Vichy's persecution of the Jews. His supporters maintain that in 1942 he continued to protect the lives of individual Jews, and was largely ignorant of what was going on in the camps. To his credit, he did intervene to protect personal acquaintances and war veterans; yet the plea of ignorance is a dubious one. As 1942 unfurled, various agencies – notably the Protestant and Catholic churches – informed him of the horrors that were being being perpetrated at Drancy and elsewhere.[20] In September 1942 the Vatican made a belated protest. Still Pétain did not act. Admittedly, it would have been difficult to have resisted Laval, and it should be remembered that the policy of bartering foreign Jews for French ones was Laval's invention, not Pétain's. None the less, all the indications are that the marshal approved of the broad strategy being pursued by Laval. While he might have baulked at the brutality of the methods employed, the old soldier had no liking of foreigners. If French nationals could be saved by the surrender of outsiders, then the sacrifice was worth making. Pétain must therefore bear a significant portion of moral responsibility for the deportations.

Overall, there is little that can be said in support of the 'shield' philosophy devised by Laval in the summer of 1942 and supported by Pétain. While it might have protected France from the full horrors of Nazism, it was based on the belief that certain categories of people were more expendable than others, and ignores what would have happened if Vichy had given the occupiers no help whatsoever in their antisemitic policies.[21] In mid-1942 the German police agencies were woefully under-manned in France and were largely ignorant of the urban and rural landscape. Thus the assistance of the French authorities proved vital in the hunting out of Jews. Struck by this, several historians have contrasted the Vichy 'shield' with the position adopted by the Italians. From November 1942 to July 1943, Mussolini's troops occupied a small corner of south-eastern France which provided a safe haven for thousands of Jews escaping deportation. Although the *duce* himself frequently caved in to Nazi pressure, his administrators were prepared to resist both Berlin and Vichy.

Unfortunately, Pétain and Laval clung to the illusion that their 'shield' was working, and remained keen to maintain good relations with Berlin. Early in summer 1942 Pétain made clear to the German embassy in Paris that he was willing to instigate Franco-German preventative measures should the Allies make further attacks on French colonies. This sugges-tion arose once more in August when British and Canadian troops launched an abortive raid on Dieppe. According to some accounts, the attack prompted Pétain to write to Hitler and the German Commander-in-Chief in the west congratulating the Reich on its success.[22] Whether these letters are genuine or forgeries perpetrated by de Brinon is open to doubt, although it does appear that some contact was made with Hitler. What-ever the truth of the matter, Pétain was anxious that France should play a part in its own defence. Within weeks that anxiety would express itself again.

.   .   .

On the evening of 7 November 1942 American and British troops landed in Morocco and Algiers as part of Operation Torch. Four days later German soldiers crossed the demarca-tion line to occupy all of France. These developments posed a dilemma to Pétain. Should he stay at Vichy or leave for North Africa? Had he chosen the latter course of action, it is likely that the political history of post-war France would have been very different. Given the unscrupulous way in which the Ameri-cans used both Giraud and Darlan, it seems probable Pétain would have become head of the resistance overseas and might even have emerged as the first leader of a liberated France. Whether de Gaulle would have allowed this to happen is, of course, a further matter of speculation. In the event, Pétain remained at Vichy. With hindsight, this decision was not an unexpected one, especially given the attitudes that he had displayed in June 1940 and October 1941.

The November crisis broke at approximately 3 a.m. on the 8th, when news of the allied *débarquement* reached Vichy. An hour later Roosevelt sent a personal message to the marshal explaining the American position. It is a reflection of Pétain's loss of influence that he was not awoken immediately to be informed of the news. Instead Laval and Ménétrel drafted a reply, and considered an offer of German air support ventured by Krugg von Nidda, the Reich's foreign ministry representative at Vichy. When Pétain surfaced at 7 a.m. he approved Laval's response to Roosevelt. This expressed indignation at what had happened and spelt out France's determination to defend itself. Shortly afterwards, instructions were issued to French representatives in North Africa ordering them to repel the invasion. The marshal also met the American *chargé d'affaires* to vent his anger over the landings; however, according to eye-witnesses, the old man seemed far from unhappy with the situation and even hummed a little tune![23] His supporters claim that this pleasure stemmed from his tacit support of the American action. In truth, he was furious at the infringement of French territory, but delighted to be back in the thick of the action.

As 8 November dragged on, Vichy's position grew ever weaker. That morning the cabinet learned of an attempted Gaullist *coup* in Morocco, and heard that Giraud had issued an appeal to all French forces in North Africa urging them to side with the Allies.[24] German pressure was also mounting. There remained the unresolved offer of German air support. After consultation with Darlan (currently on a tour of inspection of French Africa) Laval fudged the issue. Worried about French sovereignty, he requested that the Luftwaffe should be used only against allied shipping, not against ground troops, and that it should fly from its bases in Italy, not French aerodromes in North Africa. Then in the afternoon Germany insisted on Vichy breaking off all contacts with the USA. Unwilling to make a concession without a trade-off, Laval promised that he would consider this so long as Germany agreed to guarantee the integrity of the French empire. Always suspicious of Vichy's intentions, Hitler now decided to test the regime's resolve and made a demand for France to declare war on the USA and Britain. Typically, Laval played for time and asked for a meeting with Hitler.

Meanwhile, Pétain sought the advice of Weygand. Preoccupied with internal dissent, he argued that the surest means of ensuring stability was to side with the Americans. The marshal rejected this counsel. Instead, Laval and Pétain, working largely independently of one another, had, by the evening of 8 November, concocted a common policy designed to placate both the Americans and Germans. To please Hitler, it was decided that the Americans had, by their actions, severed relations with Vichy. To conciliate Roosevelt, an outright declaration of war was avoided; instead, French troops would merely continue to resist the landings. This ramshackle policy was destined to fail.[25] By the evening of 8 November General Juin, with Darlan's blessing, had already been forced into negotiations for a ceasefire in Algiers. Shortly after midnight, Hitler insisted that Axis planes should have the right to use French bases in Tunisia and Algeria; Vichy had no alternative but to accede to this demand.

On 9 November negotiations were in a state of 'suspended animation' while the participants of the drama mulled over their options.[26] At Berchtesgaden, Hitler rehearsed his doubts about enlisting French support. Driving to meet the Führer (appropriately enough, through thick fog), Laval was thinking of the concessions that could be wrung from Germany. In Algiers, General Juin accepted an armistice, and Darlan considered American terms for a ceasefire throughout all of North Africa. At this stage, he was still undecided whether to go over to the Americans or seek German support. He had, however, agreed to Laval's request that he would not make any decision on his own, and dutifully transmitted the ceasefire proposals to Vichy. And here at the Hôtel du Parc waited Pétain, debating his next move.

The overriding question was whether he should take off for North Africa. Several of his closest advisers were already urging him to head for Algiers. Yet he resisted this pressure, informing one supplicant that he was too old to fly, a dubious claim given that he had flown to the Rif at the age of 69 in an open cockpit! According to his apologists, the decision to stay was based on the double-game he was playing with the Germans.

Great play is thus made of a telegram he sent on the morning of 8 November informing Darlan that he enjoyed his 'confidence'; this, it is argued, was really designed to give the admiral the freedom to negotiate a settlement with the Americans.[27] Employing a naval code unknown to the Germans, in the days ahead Pétain is believed to have sent, via Admiral Auphan, a series of further cables, the infamous 'secret telegrams', which were again designed to encourage Darlan to do a deal with the USA.[28] It has even been speculated that the admiral's presence in North Africa was more than mere coincidence. To be sure, he had been in contact with the Americans, yet he knew nothing of Operation Torch. He had merely taken advantage of a tour of inspection of French Africa to visit his sick son in Algiers. Moreover, not too much importance should be attached to the 'secret telegrams'. As with the message of 8 November, it is difficult to believe that these were designed to give Darlan *carte blanche* in his relations with the Allies.[29] All the contemporary evidence suggests that Pétain remained furious at the American action and was determined to preserve the inviolability of the empire.

The marshal's supporters are on surer ground when they argue that his decision to stay at Vichy was based on compassionate grounds. Aware that the Allies were not going to invade France, he believed that to leave his country was to abandon its people to the fate of 'Polonization'. He had, after all, expressed such worries before the landings took place. It is now known that in the autumn of 1942 two of his former ministers, Pucheu and General Begeret, urged him to take refuge in North Africa. While Pucheu did not know of an imminent allied *débarquement*, Bergeret almost certainly did.[30] Adopting a fatherly attitude, Pétain turned down their requests, reminding them of the needs of the French people and the 1,500,000 prisoners-of-war. Yet Pétain's motives for remaining on metropolitan soil were not all altruistic. Like Weygand, he was haunted by the spectre of communism, and feared what might happen if he was no longer at the helm. Nor could he willingly relinquish office and his plans for a National Revolution. Having been sidelined by Laval, he was again at the heart of power and revelled in his new-found importance, hence his good humour when he met the American *chargé d'affaires* on 8 November. And, of course, he still dreamt of being France's saviour. One day, he believed, his countrymen would thank him for his sacrifice.

Thus a curious mixture of motives kept him at the Hôtel du Parc: a love of the French people; a fear of disobedience; a craving for power; and a desire to be seen as a saviour. Although it is impossible to know which of these factors was most important in shaping his decision, they were much the same considerations that had dictated his behaviour in June 1940 and October 1941.

If Pétain's behaviour was predictable, so too was that of the Germans. On 10 November, the day on which Darlan bowed to American pressure and surrendered all of North Africa to the USA, Hitler demanded that Axis troops should be allowed to land in Tunisia. When this ultimatum arrived at Vichy on the evening of the 10th, Pétain complained that Laval had given in too easily to this request, and even spoke of repeating the '13 December coup'.[31] This fighting talk was mere bravado, and an order was given telling French troops not to resist the German and Italian forces. Unknown to Vichy, Hitler had also given the command for the occupation of all of France and, at 4 a.m. on 11 November, the first German troops crossed over the demarcation line. At 5.30 a.m. Krugg delivered a letter to Pétain from Hitler claiming that the invasion was necessary to prevent an allied invasion of southern France. By the time Pétain awoke at 7 a.m. the German take-over was largely complete.

What was Vichy's response? On 10 November, with Darlan away, Pétain had taken over as Commander-in-Chief. His orders to Darlan, issued that day, were to carry on fighting the Allies in North Africa, although the double-game theorists would have us believe that the marshal countermanded this request through the first of the 'secret telegrams'.[32] Pétain's orders to troops in France were to resist any invasion of the southern zone. Thus when he awoke on 11 November, his first reaction was to believe that France was at war with Germany as the armistice terms had been broken. Yet while the marshal had slept his ministers had given the order not to repel the Germans. It would have been a futile, albeit heroic gesture. Even so, Pétain was determined to do something. Weygand argued that Darlan should be instructed to cease fire in North Africa; others warned against this, fearing German reprisals. In the event, the government decided to wait on Laval's return. It did, however, appoint General Noguès, Resident General of Morocco, Pétain's sole plenipotentiary in North Africa, necessary now that Darlan was in American custody. Apparently, this order was accompanied by a further secret cable. It is difficult to see how this second 'secret telegram', any more than the first, was designed to allow Darlan leeway in his negotiations with the Allies.[33]

Reluctant to wait for Laval, at 10.40 a.m. on 11 November Pétain summoned Field Marshal von Rundstedt, the German army commander in western Europe, to his office. Here, he asked that Nice not be occupied by the Italians and that Toulon be left unoccupied to signal the neutrality of the French navy.[34] He then read out a letter of protest drafted by Weygand. This expressed indignation at the invasion which was in breach of the armistice negotiations. Despite German attempts to block the airwaves, the letter was broadcast repeatedly on the radio, accompanied by a personal message from Pétain to the French people. 'Have confidence in your marshal', he exhorted, 'who is only thinking of France.'[35]

Much has since been made of this protest. At least he had taken action, which is more than he did in October 1941. His speech also demonstrated something of his genuine concern for a bewildered people waking up to the reality of total occupation. It was, though, a limited act of defiance. His fear of disorder, his love of power, his belief in himself as a saviour prevented him from taking matters any further.

What of the wider significance of the protest? In North Africa it had more bearing on Darlan's actions than did any 'secret telegram'. When the admiral heard of the radio broadcast and learned of the invasion of the southern zone, he issued orders for his troops to resist the German landings in Tunisia and for the fleet to set sail from Toulon to the African coast. In the confusion of events, neither of these orders was obeyed. Nor was Darlan himself resolved whether to go over to the Allies; it would take much American bullying before he eventually changed sides. Even so, his prevarication, coupled with Pétain's message, forced many in North Africa to consider their future allegiance.

Within France, the message certainly convinced a number that their duty lay with the Resistance. Yet a reading of prefectoral reports for November suggests that the public was confused by Pétain's action. Some believed he was playing a double-game with the Nazis. Others thought that he was a prisoner of Abetz and Laval.[36] Most were disappointed that he had not taken firmer action. This disquiet would make it more and more difficult for Vichy propagandists to present the marshal as a saviour. After the total occupation of France, it appears that many men and women spoke of Pétain in an abstract sense. While they retained a respect for his 'person', few celebrated him as the leader of the Vichy regime and author of the National Revolution.[37]

His protest also had repercussions within government. Laval was enraged by the speech and, on returning to Vichy in the afternoon of 11 November, quickly took charge of affairs. Pétain once more faded into the background. Brimming with ideas and boasting of his meeting with Hitler, even though this had resulted in little, Laval convinced cabinet that French forces in North Africa should continue the resistance against the Allies; otherwise there would be German reprisals in France. Pétain agreed, and the necessary commands were issued. The confusion in North Africa was absolute. In a matter of 24 hours, French troops there had received a series of orders and counter-orders. Two things were clear, however. First, there had been no opposition to the German landings in Tunisia. Second, it was obvious the Americans had the upper hand. On 11 November, Noguès was compelled to sign an armistice in Morocco; the next day he was informed that it was American policy to bring Giraud into any overall settlement. On learning this, he cabled Vichy early on 13 November requesting that Darlan be reappointed; this was the only means of keeping the 'traitor' Giraud out of power. The rest of the telegram implied that Darlan, on being reinstated, would then adopt a neutral position.[38]

Before Laval bothered to send a reply, there came another development which further eroded Vichy's authority in the colonies. On the afternoon of 13 November a Franco-American settlement was reached in North Africa. By this, Darlan (at long last won over to the Americans) was to become head of the government of French North Africa; Giraud was to take charge of the armed forces, although for reasons of political amity it was decided to keep this appointment quiet for the time being.[39] Thus when Laval eventually replied to Noguès, little could be done to reassert control. According to Auphan, Pétain agreed to reappoint Darlan; yet apparently Laval refused to issue any statement until there had been further consultation with the Germans. This, it is maintained, prompted Auphan to dispatch a third 'secret telegram' informing Darlan that he continued to enjoy Pétain's *accord intime*. For a long time the very existence of this telegram was doubted, and its recent 'rediscovery' has added an extra zest to the double-game theory.[40] Not too much attention should be paid to this cable. It had no impact on decisions already reached; rather, it appears that Pétain was reiterating his support for Darlan in the struggle against the Americans and Giraud.[41] Perhaps more revealing of Pétain's position was the telegram he issued to Darlan the following day. This strongly worded statement informed the admiral that the actions he had taken ran contrary to the mission with which he was entrusted. Resistance against the American aggression must continue.[42]

Inevitably Laval saw in this situation an opportunity to increase his already considerable powers. How could Darlan remain dauphin now that he was in American hands and on the allied side? Laval's appetite for further authority was whetted by two other factors. First, on 15 November he received another German demand for France to declare war on the USA and Great Britain. This request probably came from Abetz rather than from Berlin, and it appears that what the ambassador sought was not so much a declaration of war as some acknowledgement that a state of war existed.[43] Whatever the case, Laval characteristically believed that he was the only man capable of resolving the matter. Second, he was eager to resolve the North African crisis, which was rapidly jeopardizing his wider plans for collaboration. Also on 15 November, Noguès reported that Darlan was in place and that Giraud had put himself under the admiral's authority. Then came the conflicting and more worrying news that Giraud had given a speech in which he promised to clear both North Africa and France of Axis troops, a task which would be executed in the name of the marshal. Would French forces now side with the Allies? What would the German reaction be? Troubled by these questions, Laval used a cabinet meeting of 15 November to reiterate his faith in collaboration. He argued that France should seek to be treated by the Nazis not as a vanquished nation, but as an ally. This immediately provoked a flood of resignations; there probably would have been more if Laval had not appealed for self-discipline.

The schemer had overstepped the mark, yet he soon recovered his composure and saw how the resignations offered him the opportunity to extend his influence. Although he failed to get the government to recognize that a state of war was in existence (as the lawyer Barthélemy pointed out, only the National Assembly could approve a declaration of war), on 17 November he did manage to secure Pétain's agreement to two new constitutional acts. The first appointed Laval as the marshal's replacement for a period of one month should the *chef de l'état* no longer be able to exercise his functions. At the close of that period, the cabinet would then appoint a definitive successor. Second, Laval was given full powers to promulgate decrees and laws, although he was not allowed to introduce constitutiuonal acts. He had thus become head of state in all but name.

Why did Pétain relinquish much of his remaining power? It has been speculated that this was due to his old age, which could not withstand Laval's constant haranguing. It has also been suggested that the decision was based on a realistic assessment of the situation. With the loss of North Africa and the invasion of the southern zone, he recognized that there would be little opportunity to resist German demands, which were likely to become increasingly severe. Thus it was his duty to stand by the French people in their hour of need. While this compassion may have influenced his actions, it should be noted that the marshal was reluctant to surrender everything to Laval. Nimble-footed as ever, he saw how he could retain the vestiges of power. Accordingly, he only agreed to give in after his Prime Minister had signed a secret pledge. By this, Laval agreed that he would look after the interests of Alsatians and Lorrainers; that he would not use his authority to declare war; that he would protect the spiritual traditions of France, particularly the rights of the family; that he would not attempt to obtain the right to pass constitutional acts; and that he would always submit the names of new ministers for the marshal's approval.[44] In this way Pétain would continue to keep an eye on domestic policy and would remain on the look-out for opportunities to reassert his influence.

It cannot be denied, however, that events in North Africa had brought about a remarkable decline in the authority of both Pétain and his government. According to one historian, November 1942 witnessed the emergence of three Frances: the France of Pétain at Vichy; the France of Darlan at Algiers; and the France of de Gaulle at London.[45] Of the three, the prospects for the marshal's France seemed the most gloomy. At the beginning of the month, Vichy had enjoyed control of a large area of metropolitan territory which remained free of Axis troops. Now all of France was occupied. At the start of November, Vichy had also controlled a large part of its empire; that too had been relinquished. Soon it would lose its other asset, the fleet. Forever mistrustful of French motives, on 26 November the Germans moved in to seize the Toulon enclave. Obeying orders issued by Darlan in 1940, the navy responded by scuttling its vessels. Thus, within three weeks, the regime had been stripped of its key bargaining counters. The prospects for the future looked bleak.

· · ·

In 1940 Laval had flattered Pétain by telling him that he had more power than Louis XIV. After November 1942 the marshal must have considered this remark in poor taste. His position was more akin to that of Louis XVI during the dying days of the constitutional monarchy. Both men had been divested of their authority, both had witnessed their country disintegrate into chaos. At least Louis had tried to reassert his influence by fleeing abroad in the 'Flight to Varennes'. There was no 'Flight to Algiers'. Pétain preferred to stay at Vichy even though it meant handing over power to his leading minister. Thus the marshal was largely an onlooker as Laval revamped his schemes for Franco-German reconciliation. Inevitably, these projects failed to fend off Nazi pressures, which now reached a new intensity, exacerbating internal dissidence. As Vichy struggled to retain control, the regime completed its metamorphosis into a police state. Cast out on the fringes of power, Pétain had little to do with this process, but this does not mean that he was a convert to the allied cause or that he disapproved of what Vichy had become. All the contemporary evidence of his views in 1943 reinforces the impression of an old man clutching at order and the remnants of personal power.[46]

Any profile of Pétain's role during the final months of the Occupation must begin with an assessment of the German pressures on Vichy. Outwardly Hitler liked to maintain that the regime was still sovereign. The armistice was declared to be intact and the demarcation line remained in place until 1943. Neither the German embassy nor the MBF had its authority increased to include the newly occupied zone.[47] In reality Vichy's independence lay in tatters. A series of Gauleiters were soon to stalk the corridors of the Hôtel du Parc and a detachment of guards was stationed at a diplomatic distance outside the capital ready to whisk the regime away should the need arise. Ominously, the powers of the SS were extended throughout the south and, despite an acute manpower shortage, members of the German police began to ensconce themselves in the regional *préfectures.*

The Nazi presence was accompanied by a series of fresh demands on France. Perhaps anticipating such pressure, in December 1942 Laval travelled to Prussia to meet Hitler with an agenda of his own. Here he failed to win any significant concessions in the military and economic spheres. Instead, on his return to Vichy he had to grapple with a German request for an increase in the supply of French labour. Not surprisingly, the Relève had not satiated the unquenchable thirst of the Nazi war machine and, as noted, in September 1942 Vichy introduced the compulsory call-up of certain categories of workers. Unwilling to go over to full-scale conscription, in January 1943 Laval suggested a modification to the Relève. Sauckel told him bluntly that this was not possible and insisted on a further 250,000 bodies. To meet this number, Vichy was forced to modify the September law, and on 16 February 1943 established the Service du Travail Obligatoire (STO), which embarked on the enlistment of whole age-groups. This became the most hated act of the Pétainist regime. By the close of the war, some 650,000 Frenchmen and some 44,000 Frenchwomen had been dispatched to Germany. This figure meant that France had become second only to Poland in the supply of labour to the Reich, and was the leading provider of skilled labour. Even that was not enough. In January 1944 Sauckel informed Laval that he was planning to draft a further 1,000,000 Frenchmen.

Although Laval had little luck in fending off demands for workers, he did have some success in preventing the deportation of further categories of Jews. In summer 1943 there was an unexpected slow-down in the number of deportations. This was partly due to the unreliability of the French police. Although Bousquet remained a willing participant in the Final Solution, his officers were increasingly tied up combating the Resistance and capturing escapees from STO. More importantly, the SS had arrested most of the foreign Jews.[48] Keen to get matters rolling again, in June 1943 the Nazis devised a new scheme. This demanded that Vichy denaturalize Jews of foreign origin who had acquired French citizenship since January 1927.

Although officials went to work preparing drafts of the new law, its introduction was thwarted by Laval. Conscious of recent German military defeats and keen to appease American public opinion, Laval sought to free Vichy's Jewish policy from German influence. Throughout August he held a series of meetings with top SS men in which he rehearsed endless objections to a revision of nationality regulations. He claimed that he had misunderstood the original intention of the German proposals and asserted that he would have to reconsult his cabinet colleagues. He also argued that the law would intensify pressures on the French police and create problems with the Italians. Interestingly, he invoked the marshal's name. As the proposed law had constitutional implications, Pétain's signature would be required, but the head of state was unhappy at the denaturalization of women and children. Troubled by recent church protests over the issue, this indeed was Pétain's position. However, while the marshal can take some credit for obstructing the German programme, it is worth recalling that it was Laval's tactics which carried the day, and that Vichy's CGQJ, under the direction of the zealot Darquier, continued to play an active part in the rounding up of Jews.

Pétain and Laval may well have had another motive for obstructing German plans for changes in the nationality laws: the growth of resistance. Before 1943 this had not posed too serious a threat to public order. Although public disenchantment with Vichy had been quick to set in, only a handful of people had actively become resisters. A majority of the population had accepted that Vichy's tough measures against Jews and Communists were necessary for the common good. In 1942, however, the demands of the Relève, the stepping-up of measures against the Jews and the occupation of all of France brought 'the language of deportation and the facts of authoritarianism into village squares and rural towns which had existed since 1940 in relative isolation from the German Occupation and from state interference'.[49] Persecution now seemed indiscriminate. It affected not just foreigners and minorities, but all French citizens, including women and children. Thus in late 1942 civil disobedience began to spread from the towns to the countryside as many individuals sought to escape the clutches of both French and German officals. STO only made matters worse, forcing large numbers of young people into hiding in the woodlands. Here they established Maquis groups and took on the identity of resistance fighters; no longer were they mere fugitives from the Relève and STO.

1942–3 was also a turning point for resistance outside France 'where the unfolding history of de Gaulle's Free French, now known as La France Combattante, developed into a decisive struggle for recognition by the Allies'.[50] When the Allies invaded North Africa they had chosen not to consult de Gaulle. Although the British acknowledged the National Committee of the Free French as the authentic representative of the French people, the Americans harboured suspicions about the general's dictatorial ambitions. This is why Roosevelt preferred to use first Giraud and then Darlan, who took over as leader of French forces in North Africa. To counter these moves, in late 1942 de Gaulle opened negotiations with internal Resistance leaders and founded the Mouvements Unis de la Résistance (MUR), a loose confederation of non-communist organizations. It has also been suggested that he might have been behind the assassination of Darlan on Christmas Eve 1942, although several other parties had good reason to want the admiral dead. Whatever the case, this event opened a new phase in de Gaulle's struggle for recognition in North Africa. In January 1943 he reluctantly agreed to a joint leadership with Giraud; in June, the Fighting French and Giraud's North African administration merged to become the Comité Français de la Libération Nationale (CFLN). It was not long, however, before de Gaulle took over as the undisputed leader of this organization, which was fast taking on the appearance of a government-in-waiting.

The growth of resistance both within and outside France demanded a response from Vichy. Although there was little that could be done about events in North Africa, there were measures that could be taken closer to home. Since his interview with Hitler in December 1942, Laval had been pressing for the creation of a special police force. Not only would this alleviate the pressure that was overwhelming Vichy's existing law-and-order services, it would also reinforce the appearance of the regime's autonomy. Naturally enough the Germans were suspicious of this request, yet appreciated that their own SS units were undermanned and overworked. Thus on 5 January 1943 they consented to the founding of the Milice. This was created out of the existing Service d'Ordre Légionnaire (SOL), the paramilitary wing of the Légion Française des Combattants, and was headed by Joseph Darnand. A distinguished veteran of the First World War, he boasted an unattractive past, having passed through the ranks of the Action Française, the Croix de Feu, the Cagoule and the PPF. In 1940 he was a Pétainist of the first hour and became head of the Légion in the Alpes Maritimes. In October that year he created the SOL to defend Nice from a possible Italian invasion; later he would serve in the LVF. Impressed by the SOL's ability to root out dissidents, in January 1942 Vichy granted it permission to operate on a national level. For his part, Laval had little liking for Darnand's politics, yet recognized that in early 1943 the easiest means of combating the Resistance was to detach the SOL from the Légion to form the Milice.

The new force went about its task with gusto and, in its brief existence, recruited some 30,000 young toughs. Although the Germans only allowed the Milice to operate in the old southern zone, it proved a reliable ally and was particularly zealous in hunting out Jews, Communists and *réfractaires* from STO. As has been remarked, 'while the ordinary police might be friendly or at least neutral, and the Germans were strangers and might be bluffed, miliciens were sharp, suspicious characters wholeheartedly devoted to the bad cause and only too fully informed.'[51] The activities of Darnand's men reached a high-point in March 1944 when they launched an assault on the Maquis of the Glières plateau. At the Liberation, his cut-throats fought a vicious rearguard action and were responsible for the murders of the Republican politicians, Mandel and Zay. In the event, this brutality only strengthened resistance. Many lost their respect for Vichy justice and expressed sympathy for the Maquis. In the words of one historian, 'Previously law-abiding citizens, and increasing numbers of officials and gendarmes, found themselves taking the first steps towards what must be recognised as an outlaw culture: the belief that natural justice and moral rectitude can no longer be equated with the official process of the law and can only be found outside it.'[52]

Since the war the Milice has come to represent all that was wrong with Franco-German collaboration in the remaining months of the Occupation, and inevitably questions have been raised about its relationship with Pétain. Befitting his marginalized position during the last months of Vichy, the marshal had little to do with the organization's founding. His reservations about Darnand's pro-German sympathies are also well known. In October 1943, the head *milicien* swore an oath of loyalty to Hitler, became an SS Obersturmführer and encouraged other *légionnaires* to enlist in the SS. Later, on 5 August 1944, the marshal wrote a lengthy letter to Laval, conveniently released to the Resistance, complaining of the Milice's activities and deploring the killings of Zay and Mandel.[53] Yet it is significant that Pétain did not raise any other protest about these particular murders. Furthermore, it is telling that he chose to write to Laval and not to Darnand himself. This was not just because Laval was ultimately responsible for police affairs; more importantly, Pétain had no wish to disturb his good personal relations with Darnand. In April 1943 the marshal had issued a message praising the Milice,[54] and in January 1944 welcomed the honorary SS man as Bousquet's replacement as Secretary of State for the Maintenance of Order. Indeed, all the evidence suggests that the relationship between Pétain and Darnand, rather than that between the marshal and Laval, was the more critical in shaping the reactionary police policies of the Vichy regime during its last days of power. Darnand always knew that he enjoyed the marshal's tacit support.

What was the basis of the marshal's approbation? First, he respected Darnand as a comrade-in-arms; he was not a scheming politician like Laval. In 1918 the marshal had decorated the future head of the Milice for his part in the second Battle of the Marne. Second, the two soldiers shared an intense dislike of internal disorder. Although Pétain appreciated that STO and total occupation were driving people to extremes, this was no excuse for indiscipline. As in 1941, and in 1917, mutiny had to be put down. 'Whoever participates in resistance organizations,' he declared solemnly on 28 April 1944, 'compromises the future of the country.'[55] There may also be a third reason why Pétain approved of the Milice. When Laval had originally conceived of the organization, he had envisaged it as a valuable counter-weight against the Paris collaborationists. Although he was moving government in a fascist direction, he remained fearful that the Germans might dispense with Vichy altogether and establish a pro-Nazi regime in Paris. Indeed, the capital was awash with intrigue as various fascists sought favour with Abetz. Pétain was also conscious of Vichy's vulnerability, and shared his leading minister's disdain for the ultras. Perhaps he too believed that the Milice could be used to ward off a collaborationist take-over, just as the Légion in 1940 had been a tool to offset Déat's plans for a *parti unique*.

Whether Pétain would have used the Milice to dismiss Laval remains debatable, yet it is known that in April and November of 1943 he was thinking of repeating the coup of 13 December. What rekindled this desire for power and how successful was Pétain in rebuilding his authority?

. . . .

Even though circumstances in 1943 were different from those of 1940, Pétain's reasons for wanting rid of Laval had changed little. His intense personal dislike of the minister had not abated with time. Nor had the marshal relinquished his suspicions about Laval's methods of working. Having surrendered many of his constitutional powers, Pétain found it even more difficult to call the Auvergnat to book. He was rarely informed of government plans and was not always invited to cabinet meetings. Kept in the dark, he was particularly anxious about Laval's rumoured projects for the remodelling of the French army; after all, it was not the job of a politician to involve himself in military affairs. Laval's domestic policies were also a cause for concern. These had swelled the ranks of the Resistance and had destroyed what was left of Vichy's credibility. The marshal was only too aware that his own popularity was beginning to suffer. In order to recover his lost authority, the old soldier believed a return to the values of the National Revolution was essential. Laval, of course, had no patience with this project and, in a cabinet reshuffle of March 1943, removed the remaining traditionalists, notably Barthélemy, from office. Finally, the *chef de l'état* was unhappy at his Prime Minister's diplomatic initiatives. These had not saved the navy and the empire, and had not prevented the total occupation of France. Always confident of his own abilities, Pétain felt he could do better. In this respect, he might have been influenced by a representative of the Portuguese dictator, Salazar. On a recent trip to Vichy, the emissary had suggested that Vichy could play a mediating role in bringing the United States and Germany together in a compromise peace designed to contain the common enemy, communism.[56] Pétain immediately appreciated the prestige to be had in fulfilling such a mission, but recognized that he would have to recover many of his old powers if he were to act the part of world statesman.

Convinced that glory was still at hand and egged on by his close advisers, the marshal began a series of behind-the-scenes manoeuvres to free himself of Laval. In late April 1943 he sent

Fonck to Paris to quiz German intelligence about a possible change of government. The present cabinet, it was argued, no longer met the needs of the situation either internally or externally. The marshal, Fonck continued, had no desire to bear the responsibility for this government and wanted it to be understood that he would quit his post if Germany did not get rid of Laval. Not surprisingly, Hitler would have none of this. He still interpreted Laval's earlier dismissal as a personal affront to himself and, in a letter to Pétain of 29 April 1943, announced that he would not tolerate another 13 December.[57] Laval, he continued, was the only Vichy minister capable of assuring France the place it deserved in the New Europe. In truth, the Führer continued to despise Laval. The two men had only recently met, on 19 April, when they had discussed the future of collaboration. Here Laval had trotted out his familiar arguments for Franco-German reconciliation, merely reconfirming Hitler's prejudices. Yet, as Ribbentrop acknowledged, it was important to keep the Frenchman in place. Despite being untrustworthy, he had at least nailed his colours to the Axis mast and would not change sides in a hurry.[58]

This rebuff did not deter the marshal from his plans to sack Laval. Events in the summer of 1943 only hardened his determination. From Rome came news of Mussolini's overthrow. The fall of fascist Italy cast fresh doubts in Pétain's mind about an overall German victory and strengthened his conviction that the moment was ripe for a compromise peace. From Paris came disturbing rumours of collaborationist plots to overthrow Laval. Pétain knew only too well that his own head would roll if such intrigues were successful. And from Algiers came the announcement that the CFLN was planning to try all members of the Vichy government. To Pétain, this was a further affront to his dwindling authority and added to his worries about the growth of internal resistance. France needed strong leadership, something which Laval was not providing.

Although Pétain remained convinced of the need to dismiss his minister, he was still uncertain how best to proceed. As befitted an arch-schemer, he explored all options. On 31 August he dispatched a secret message to Giraud and de Gaulle in Algiers. This made known that the *chef de l'état* was willing to hand over power to the two generals at the Liberation so long as they, in the meantime, pledged their loyalty to him. In this way, the legitimacy of succession would be guaranteed and the internal order of France maintained.[59] As Pétain knew that this initiative had little chance of success, he also instructed Auphan, out of government since November 1942, to draw up a plan to meet the new political situation. This document was produced on 13 September.[60] Among other recommendations, it called for the removal of Laval, the suspension of STO, the remodelling of the anti-Jewish laws along Christian lines, the abolition of the Milice, the dissolution of the LVF, the suppression of the Ministry of Information and the outlawing of the collaborationist groups in Paris. In addition, the report sketched out a proposal for the restructuring of government and even contained a draft letter to Hitler announcing Laval's dismissal. Auphan recognized that these proposals would be resisted by the Germans, who were likely to appoint a Gauleiter for France and arrest all concerned in the scheme. Yet he concluded that such reprisals would not be a problem so long as Pétain rode out the crisis and appointed a 'regency council' should he be unable to exercise his powers. This body would thus retain the dignity of government and prevent France from drifting into civil war.

The ingenuity of Auphan's ideas impressed Pétain, who was quick to take up the suggestion for a remodelling of government. On 27 September a revised draft of the constitutional act no. 4 was prepared. It will be recalled that this law dealt with the succession and currently named Laval as dauphin, albeit for a period of one month after which a definitive successor would be appointed. According to the new draft, a seven-man 'regency council' would be set up should Pétain be unable to exercise his functions. Significantly, this council would comprise public servants, not politicians. Auphan, of course, was to be a member. So too were Bouthillier, the former Minister of Finance, Professor Gidel, rector of the Sorbonne, François Porché, vice-president of the *conseil d'état*, and président Caous, a legal dignitary. Two curious nominees were General Weygand, a prisoner in Germany since November 1942, and Léon Noël, the former ambassador to Poland, who had repeatedly advised Pétain to stand down in favour of de Gaulle. Like Weygand, the diplomat did not hear of his nomination until after the war.[61] This was hardly surprising. Given the explosive nature of the proposed law, care was taken to keep the scheme secret. The powers of the 'regency council' were also kept quiet. Should the marshal's incapacity prove permanent, the body would hand over power to the National Assembly. This recommendation should not be taken to mean that Pétain was a sudden convert to parliamentarianism. It was instead a tactical ploy designed to stress Vichy's constitutionality, important given that a Consultative Assembly was in the process of being formed at Algiers.

Having settled on a plan of action, Pétain explored possible German reactions to a change of government. On 12 October he told General Neubronn, the German military representative at Vichy, that Laval had to go otherwise anarchy would break out throughout all of France. On the same day, General Brécard in Paris, acting on the marshal's behalf, asked Knochen whether Hitler was still committed to Laval.[62] It was, however, not until 26 October that Pétain dared speak to Laval himself. In a tense interview, he informed his minister that the country was in a state of upheaval; new men were required to lead government if internal order was to be retained. Laval, who had long been planning a reshuffle of his own which would remove the last remaining members of the marshal's entourage, immediately knew something was afoot but, accustomed to living with intrigue, remained confident that, for the moment at least, his position was secure.

The crisis broke on 12 November when Pétain presented Laval with two texts. The first was yet another version of constitutional act no. 4. On reflection, it had been decided that the draft reached on 27 September was too dangerous as the Germans would arrest all those named in it.[63] Thus the revised version omitted the idea of a 'regency council'. Instead it merely stated that the marshal's constituent powers would revert to the National Assembly should he die before a new constitution had been ratified. The second text was a speech (written by one of the marshal's close confidants, Lucien Romier) which Pétain intended to broadcast on the radio the following day. Betraying a concern for the maintenance of order, this announced,

Today I incarnate French legitimacy. I intend to preserve it as a sacred trust and to return it, upon my death, to the National Assembly whence I received it, if the new constitution is not ratified . . . I do not want my death to inaugurate an era of disorders which would imperil the unity of France. This is the purpose of the constitutional act which will be promulgated in the *Journal Officiel.*[64]

Unlike some earlier encounters between the two men, the meeting did not degenerate into a squall. Laval even managed a joke, pointing out to Pétain the irony of an anti-parliamentarian marshal recalling the National Assembly.[65] There is much speculation as to why Laval was good-humoured. Aware that there was a plot brewing against him, he might well have been anticipating a manoeuvre of this kind. It is also possible that he welcomed the return of the chambers, confident that he would be able to sway the deputies and senators. It is most likely that Laval's apparent friendliness derived from the belief that he could ultimately outfox the marshal. Although he did not oppose Pétain's plans in their entirety, it is significant that he asked for a delay in which to prepare public opinion and obtain German support. The head of state, however, was unwilling to brook any hold-ups. While he agreed to inform the Germans as a matter of courtesy, he claimed it was pointlesss to request their authorization.

On learning of Pétain's intentions, German representatives at Vichy were troubled but, on Laval's recommendation, were prepared to let the speech go ahead. Berlin was not so magnanimous. At 6 p. m. on 13 November came news that the Germans forbade the broadcast of the speech, which had been recorded some six hours earlier and was due to be transmitted at 7.30 p.m. Deeply offended by this ban, Pétain was moved to one of his bravest acts of the Occupution.[66] That evening he summoned Krugg and informed him that, until the speech was released, he was unable to fulfil his duties. As Ménétrel observed, the marshal had gone on strike.

Government at Vichy had come to a standstill, but behind the scenes there was much manoeuvring. For his part, Laval rued his earlier decision to be so indulgent towards the marshal and now spent much of his energy trying to persuade his superior to change his mind. For their part, the Germans were also deciding their next move. Initially, Krugg had promised Pétain that the ban on his broadcast was temporary, and told him that the German government would make its full position clear in 48 hours. In the event, it took three weeks. The reasons for this lengthy delay were twofold: first, the Germans were busy preparing a lengthy ultimatum to be presented to Vichy; second, they needed time to put troops into position should there be any untoward reaction to this document.

The ultimatum, dated 29 November, took the form of a letter from Ribbentrop to Pétain. It began with a justification of the German refusal to agree to Pétain's proposed constitutional changes. It then criticized the broad lines of Vichy policy before outlining three demands. To begin with, Ribbentrop insisted that any proposed changes to laws should be submitted to the German government for approval. Next, he insisted that Laval be allowed to remodel the French cabinet in a way that was acceptable to Berlin. Finally, Vichy was instructed to remove from its administration all those who had hampered the work of reconstruction. Typically, the letter closed with a veiled threat. The German Foreign Minister expressed confidence in Pétain and expected him to comply with German wishes. If he did not, the Führer left it to the marshal to draw his own conclusions as to what might happen.[67]

The letter was delivered to Vichy on 4 December by Abetz, now back in favour with Berlin. As planned, the ultimatum was accompanied by an impressive show of force on the part of German security forces, who surrounded the Vichy capital. Aware that he was in an impossible situation, Pétain knew that he would have to capitulate. Yet he was determined to be as awkward as possible and dragged his heels accordingly. On 5 December he informed Abetz that he would resume his duties forthwith and promised to explain his position in a subsequent letter. This was not enough for Ribbentrop, as the marshal had not complied with the original ultimatum. Thus Abetz was instructed to repeat the demands. Still playing for time, on 11 December Pétain drafted another vague letter to Hitler. Only on 19 December did he give a written pledge that he would submit all legislative amendments for German approval. On 29 December he agreed not to blackball any new appointments in his government or stand in the way of any dismissals the Germans thought necessary. The same day Hitler appointed a Gauleiter, Renthe-Fink, to keep a watch on Vichy. Capitulation was complete. The next day the first collaborationists entered the regime. Among the most notable of these were Darnand, who became Secretary General for the Maintenance of Order, and Philippe Henriot, who was appointed Secretary of State for Information and Propaganda. For the moment, Déat and Doriot remained outside of government. Conveniently, Doriot was on the eastern front; Déat was outmanoeuvred by Laval, who offered the RNP leader a series of minor portfolios. Only in March 1944 did Nazi pressure ensure Déat's inclusion as Minister of Labour and National Solidarity. Ultimately, Pétain's opposition in November and December 1943 had been futile. By going on strike, he had attempted to make the French government a purely administrative regime. This should have been his solution in 1940. In 1943 it was too late to turn the clock back: 'Having grasped for sovereignty in 1940 . . . Pétain was condemned to exercise that wisp of sovereignty under German surveillance to the bitter end.'[68] It was to prove an uncomfortable experience.

. . .

NOTES AND REFERENCES

1. H.R. Lottman, *Pétain* (Paris: Seuil, 1984), p. 281.
2. R. Griffiths, *Marshal Pétain* (London: Constable, 1970), p. 300.
3. P. Boegner (ed.), *Carnets du Pasteur Boegner* (Paris: Fayard, 1992), p. 218.
4. J. Carcopino, *Souvenirs de sept ans, 1937–1944* (Paris: Flammarion, 1953), p. 580.
5. J.-P. Cointet, *Pierre Laval* (Paris: Fayard, 1993), p. 374.
6. B. Serrigny, *Trente ans avec Pétain* (Paris: Plon, 1959), p. 213.
7. R.O. Paxton, *Vichy France. Old Guard and New Order, 1940–1944* (New York: Alfred A. Knopf, 1972), p. 267.
8. J. Jardin, *Vichy Boyhood. An Insider's View of the Pétain Regime* (London: Faber & Faber, 1975), p. 58.
9. Paxton, *Vichy France*, p. 312.
10. Laval's speech published in D. Veillon, *La Collaboration. Textes et débats* (Paris: Le Livre de Poche, 1984), pp. 154–5.
11. H.R. Kedward, *Occupied France. Collaboration and Resistance, 1940–1944* (Oxford: Basil Blackwell, 1985), p. 61.
12. Cointet, *Pierre Laval*, p. 379.
13. Testimony of Laval, 3 August 1945, in *Procès du maréchal Pétain. Compte rendu officiel in extenso des audiences de la Haute Cour de Justice* (Paris: Louis Paliente, 1976), p. 254.
14. G. Warner, *Pierre Laval and the Eclipse of France* (London: Eyre & Spottiswoode, 1968), p. 302.
15. Testimony of Laval, 3 August 1945, in *Procès du maréchal Pétain*, p. 254.
16. Interjection of Pétain, 3 August 1945, in ibid., pp. 255–6.
17. Warner, *Pierre Laval*, p. 302.
18. M. Marrus and R.O. Paxton, *Vichy and the Jews* (New York: Basic Books, 1981), pp. 234–49.
19. Paxton, *Vichy France*, p. 182.
20. Boegner, *Carnets*, p. 158 and p. 185.

21. Kedward, *Occupied France*, p. 62.
22. Paxton, *Vichy France*, pp. 304–5 discusses these letters.
23. M. Ferro, *Pétain* (Paris: Fayard, 1987), pp. 431–2.
24. Warner, *Pierre Laval*, p. 323.
25. Griffiths, *Pétain*, p. 309 gives a good summary of events on 8 November.
26. Ibid.
27. This telegram is in H. Noguères, *Le veritable procès du maréchal Pétain* (Paris: Fayard, 1955), p. 419.
28. The origins of the 'secret telegrams' story may be found in Ménétrel's notes, written after the events of November 1942, in ibid., pp. 446–8.
29. Warner, *Pierre Laval*, pp. 331–2, who casts serious doubts on the 'secret telegrams' story.
30. Ferro, *Pétain*, pp. 429–30.
31. Warner, *Pierre Laval*, p. 335.
32. Ibid., pp. 331–2.
33. Ibid., p. 337.
34. Ibid., p. 338.
35. Messages of 11 November 1942 in J.-C. Barbas (ed.), *Philippe Pétain. Discours aux francais, 17 juin–20 août 1944* (Paris: Albin Michel, 1989), p. 365 and Ferro, *Pétain*, pp. 442–3.
36. Ferro, *Pétain*, p. 466.
37. Ibid. and Kedward, *Occupied France*, pp. 64–5.
38. Griffiths, *Pétain*, p. 313.
39. Ibid.
40. H. Coutau-Bégarie and C. Huan, *Darlan* (Paris: Fayard, 1989), p. 619. Controversy still surrounds whether Auphan sent this third 'secret telegram' on his own initiative, or with the knowledge of Pétain.
41. R.O. Paxton, 'Darlan, un amiral entre deux blocs. Réflexions sur une biographie récente', in *Vingtième Siècle*, (36) 1992, p. 15.
42. This telegram is in Noguères, *Le veritable procès*, pp. 496–8.
43. Griffiths, *Pétain*, p. 314.
44. Ibid., p. 315.
45. J.-B. Duroselle, *L'abîme. Politique étrangère de la France, 1939–1944* (Paris: Imprimerie Nationale, 1982), p. 413.
46. Paxton, *Vichy France*, p. 325.
47. Marrus and Paxton, *Vichy France and the Jews*, p. 302.
48. Ibid., pp. 302–29.
49. H.R. Kedward, *In Search of the Maquis. Rural Resistance in Southern France, 1942–1944* (Oxford: Oxford University Press, 1993), p. 7.
50. Kedward, *Occupied France*, p. 67.
51. M.R.D. Foot, *SOE in France. An Account of the Work of the British Special Operations Executive in France, 1940–1944* (London: HMSO, 1966), p. 120.

52. Kedward, *In Search of the Maquis*, pp. 55–6.
53. This letter is cited in Ferro, *Pétain*, p. 568.
54. Message of 29 April 1943 in Barbas (ed.), *Discours*, pp. 303–5.
55. Speech of 28 April 1944 in ibid., pp. 324–6.
56. Paxton, *Vichy France*, p. 323.
57. Ibid.
58. Warner, *Pierre Laval*, p. 368.
59. Griffiths, Pétain, p. 322.
60. *Plan de redressement de la politique française* in G. Jeantet, *Pétain contre Hitler* (Paris: La Table Ronde, 1966), pp. 269–79.
61. Ibid., pp. 11–13.
62. Warner, *Pierre Laval*, p. 381.
63. Griffiths, *Pétain*, p. 324.
64. Quoted in Noguères, *Le veritable procès*, pp. 567–8 and Warner, *Pierre Laval*, p. 382 from where this translation has been taken.
65. Warner, *Pierre Laval*, p. 381.
66. Griffiths, *Pétain*, p. 325.
67. Ultimatum quoted in Warner, *Pierre Laval*, pp. 383–4.
68. Paxton, *Vichy France*, p. 325.

Chapter 8

THE EXILE, 1944 . . .

In March 1944 the author Galtier-Boissière recorded the latest news from Vichy: 'Did you know that the Marshal is dead?' 'No, since when?' 'It happened three months ago, but his entourage kept it from him.'[1] It was a cruel joke, yet a telling one. Although in April Pétain visited Paris, where he was enthusiastically greeted, it was clear that he presided over a shadow regime. With the impending allied invasion of France, eventually launched on 6 June, German guards moved him around the country from one 'safe house' to another. On 8 September he was transferred to the old Hohenzollern castle of Sigmaringen where he lived alongside some of the most rabid collaborators. He did not return to France until April the following year. In August the High Court sentenced him to death, a sentence quickly commuted to life imprisonment. He lived out the remainder of his days exiled on the Île d'Yeu. Death, when it came on 23 July 1951, would refuel the Pétain myth. The shoddy way in which he had been treated in his final days turned him into a martyr and only served the cause of those who sought to rehabilitate his reputation.

· · ·

The Pétain of 1944 cuts a sorry figure. Increasingly morose and lacking in energy, he went through the motions of governing, receiving diplomats and discussing policy with his advisers, notably two new appointees, Jean Tracou and Louis-Dominique Girard, but he was excluded from what little power there remained at Vichy. It was Laval who signed decrees and who procrastinated over Sauckel's demands for further French workers. In March Pétain could do nothing to prevent the arrival of Déat into his government. Although Tracou would

have us believe that the marshal kicked up a fuss over the
RNP leader's appointment, even threatening to resign,[2] in truth
Pétain's protest to Renthe-Fink was half-hearted, an acknowledgement that there was nothing he could do to thwart German wishes.

Pétain's trip to Paris the following month, the only visit he
made there during the Occupation, was a further indication of
his hollow authority. Since the beginning of the year the Allies
had intensified their bombing of French towns and cities. One
particularly heavy raid over Paris on 20 April 1944 left 651
dead and 461 wounded. To honour the victims, General Brécard
organized a special religious ceremony and suggested Pétain
should attend. Despite German demands that this should be
a private affair, the press soon got wind of what was happening, and when the Vichy leader arrived in the capital on 26
April he was mobbed by enthusiastic crowds shouting 'Vive
le maréchal'. Emboldened by this reception, he made an
impromptu speech which referred to the Germans as his 'captors'.[3] Although it was a brave gesture, it accomplished little as
the words ultimately fell prey to censorship. It also seems that
the men and women who lined the streets to welcome Pétain
did not celebrate him as the *chef de l'état français*; Pétainism,
of course, had never been that strong in the occupied zone.
Rather, with expectations high of an allied invasion, he was
perceived as a symbol of enduring France, a sign that the
country would soon be rid of the enemy. A similar symbolism
would surround de Gaulle when he visited Paris four months
later, ensuring that the general was saluted by the same people
that had cheered the marshal.[4]

The only way in which the Pétain of 1944 could influence
events was in overseeing the smooth passage of power to a
post-war regime. This was acknowledged by the Germans, who
in May placed the marshal under close guard, moving him
from one part of the country to another; they did, however,
permit him to tour the towns of eastern France. It was during
one of these visits that he learned of the allied landings in
Normandy. Disorder had always been one of his phobias, and
he now believed it was his duty to prevent France from plung-
ing into chaos. On 6 June he spoke on the radio, ordering
officials to stay in place; he wanted no repetition of the disarray that accompanied the *exode*.[5] On 14 June he informed
members of the Légion that it was their duty to maintain a

strict neutrality.[6] Alongside public denunciations of the Resistance, Pétain also made private condemnations of German behaviour. When on 10 June the Waffen-SS butchered the villagers of Oradour-sur-Glane, he was moved to rage. Tracou records that the marshal summoned Renthe-Fink to his office and described Germany as 'a nation of savages'.[7] In early August, Pétain would write to Laval complaining of the excesses of the Milice. Superficially, there appears to be an even-handedness in Pétain's attitude to the events of summer 1944. Yet, as will be recalled from Chapter 7, the marshal retained more than a grudging respect for Darnand. In Pétain's mind, it was the communists, Gaullists and Allies, not the *miliciens*, collaborationists and Germans, who posed the greater threat to internal stability.

Before discussing Pétain's plans for the transition of power, it is worth remembering that others too wished to see an orderly handover of authority. In Algiers, de Gaulle, anxious to prevent either communist resisters or American military personnel stepping into the shoes of Vichy officials, devised a scheme whereby Gaullist super prefects, known as *commissaires de la république*, would move into key administrative posts.[8] In Spain, Giraud's supporters, always on the look-out for an opportunity to thwart de Gaulle's ambition, established contact with François Piétri, Vichy's ambassador at Madrid, and made it known that the Americans wanted the marshal to hand over his authority to parliament.[9] This was the only way to forestall a Gaullist dictatorship. Jacques Lemaigre-Dubreuil, the head of the Giraud faction, even claimed that the USA, desirous to prevent Soviet domination of Europe, was prepared to contemplate a compromise peace between Germany and the USSR. Such claims should be treated with caution. Although Washington undoubtedly had its suspicions of de Gaulle, it is doubtful whether the Lemaigre-Dubreuil mission was ever genuine. Perhaps aware of this, on 14 June Ribbentrop ordered the Madrid negotiations to be broken off.[10]

Never one to be surpassed when there was scheming to be done, Laval too was seeking to play a part in any Liberation negotiations, and was disappointed by the failure of the Madrid discussions. Additionally, he was on the look-out for an opportunity to thwart the ultra-collaborationists who, following the assassination of Henriot on 28 June, were again busy plotting a *coup d'état*. It was with these objectives in mind that, on

12 August, Laval surfaced in Nancy where Herriot was being held in forced residence.[11] Here, Laval asked the former president of the Chamber of Deputies to reconvene parliament, yet he received a suitably non-commital response. It mattered little. On 16 August the Germans rearrested Herriot, and the idea was dropped.

Although the proposal to reconvene the National Assembly was similar to the plan floated by Pétain the previous November, the marshal had little enthusiasm for Laval's schemes. Between 12 and 16 August urgent telephone calls from Laval urged the *chef de l'état* to make his way to Paris in order to confer legitimacy on the Herriot operation. Pétain, now back in Vichy, did nothing. As in December 1940, he feared that, once in Paris, the Germans would take him prisoner and remove him from France. Nor had he any desire to be seen soliciting favours from Herriot. His contempt for parliamentarianism remained intact. Reflecting on the institutions of the old Republic, he remarked, 'They did nothing for the people. They gave them words and apéritifs.'[12] Most importantly, Pétain had ideas of his own. By summer 1944, he had come to the reluctant conclusion that he had little alternative but to hand over power to de Gaulle; this would at least prevent a communist take-over.

To this end, in early July Pétain's office tried, via the Vatican, to open a line of dialogue with Gaullist officials. When this failed, on 11 August Pétain instructed Auphan to make contact with de Gaulle in order to negotiate whatever 'political solution' would avert civil war and safeguard the principle of legitimacy. In case Pétain was prevented from exercising office, Auphan was instructed to summon the 'regency council' which had been mooted in the proposals of November 1943. By choosing Auphan, who had resigned from government at the time of 'Operation Torch' without joining the Resistance, Pétain believed that he had found a negotiator who would be acceptable to all. The old man did not understand that de Gaulle, whose claims to legitimacy rested on very different grounds, had no intention of being anointed king by anyone acting in Pétain's name.[13]

Although there is evidence to show that members of Pétain's entourage were involved in yet further attempts to contact both the Resistance and the Americans, by mid-August the overriding question was what would happen to the marshal. While he wished to remain on French soil, Hitler had other ideas. On 17 August Vichy ministers were ordered to Belfort in the east of France, in preparation for their removal to Germany.[14] Laval, in Paris, refused and tendered his resignation, only to be driven by the Germans to Belfort that evening. Likewise Pétain refused, but on 20 August he too was escorted to Belfort. He left behind two texts, the first a formal protest to Hitler, the second a message to the French people. Drafted in collaboration with Henri Massis, this latter document was distributed in poster form throughout France, and was clearly written with half an eye on the trial that might await the marshal.[15] Emphasizing the sacrifices that he had made by remaining in France during the Occupation, Pétain appealed for order and reassured his people that through his actions they would rediscover the path to 'sacred union' and the 'renaissance de la patrie', an indication that even in these desperate hours he retained a faith in the values of the National Revolution.

With his departure, Pétain ceased to be head of the Vichy state. On 25 August he declared that henceforth he would only accept his wages as a marshal of France. It served German purposes, however, to keep up the fiction of the Vichy government, and on 8 September Pétain was transferred to Sigmaringen. There he lived an uncomfortable existence among ex-*miliciens* and arch-collaborationists such as Doriot, Déat, Darnand, Marion and de Brinon.[16] Under de Brinon's stewardship, these men claimed to embody the French state, which was now titled the French Commission for the Defence of National Interests. Their infighting need not detain us for long. It was appropriate that the squabbling which had characterized the Vichy cabinets should have degenerated into political parlour games played out in a picture-postcard castle overlooking the Danube. Pétain himself, in common with Laval, took no part in these charades, refusing de Brinon the right to invoke his name. When on 5 April 1945 the marshal heard that the whole of the Vichy regime was to be tried in France *in absentia*, he wrote to Hitler requesting that he should be allowed to travel to Paris. Convinced that history, if not a Gaullist tribunal, would vindicate his actions since the armistice, he felt that he had no other option other than to return. No reply came. Two weeks later, with allied troops deep inside of Germany, Pétain was moved again, this time to Schloss Zeil, north of Wangen. On 22 April his captors, uncertain what to do with their prisoner, escorted him to Switzerland. Two days later Pétain re-entered France where he was formally received by General Koenig acting on behalf of the French government. Standing stiffly to attention, Koenig refused to salute or shake the hand of the former *chef de l'état français.*

. . .

Despite Pétain's fears, the Liberation did not degenerate into a civil war. This was largely because Vichy officials generally cooperated in the handover of power. Nor did the Communist-led Front National, as de Gaulle later claimed, attempt to use the Liberation as a vehicle by which to launch a revolution. None the less, some resisters did take justice into their own hands. According to former Vichyites there were over 100,000 summary executions; in truth, there were fewer than 8,000 unofficial killings.[17] The established courts, which remained in being until 1951, sentenced 2,853 to death and a further 3,910 *in absentia*, yet only 767 executions took place. A further 38,266 people received jail terms, but most had been released by October 1952. In addition, 49,723 people were sentenced to national degradation, but in 1952 only a quarter of these remained under sanction. Of 50,0000 government employees investigated at the Liberation, 11,343 were sacked or subjected to lesser punishments. Subsequent amnesty laws of January 1951 and August 1953 permitted many civil servants and Vichy ministers to re-enter public life. Overall, the *épuration* was a modest affair, especially compared to what went on in Belgium, Denmark and Holland, and in comparison to Vichy's own purge of Republican officials.

The main show trials began in Paris in late 1944. Preparations for these had long been under way. On 3 September 1943 the CFLN had declared that, through the signing of the armistice and pursuit of collaboration, Pétain and his ministers were guilty of treason. On 18 November 1944 the Provisional Government established a High Court of Justice to try all members of the 'governments or pseudo-governments which had their seat on metropolitan territory' between June 1940 and August 1944 'for crimes or offences committed in the exercise of or connected with their functions'.[18] Darnand, de Brinon and Laval all appeared before this body and were sentenced to death. Others, such as Vallat and Chevalier, were given jail terms. Those, for example Carcopino, who had later aided the Resistance were released. Some managed to escape the full rigours of French justice. Déat, Bonnard and Darquier took refuge in Spain and were tried *in absentia*. Doriot was not so lucky; he fell victim to an air-attack in Germany.[19]

Although the CFLN made great play of wanting to try Pétain, de Gaulle had hoped that the trial would never take place with the marshal present. In conversation with Georges Duhamel, the secretary of the Académie Française, the general quipped, 'Let him go down to the Côte d'Azur and be forgotten.'[20] Such sentiment derived not so much from a sense of mercy but from a wish to avoid recriminations at a time when France needed to build for the future. No doubt de Gaulle was struck by the findings of a *sondage* conducted in October 1944 by the French Institute for Public Opinion. Asked whether Pétain should be punished, 32 per cent said 'yes', 58 per cent replied 'no', and 10 per cent admitted they 'didn't know'.[21] It was, then, with some disappointment that de Gaulle learned in April 1945 that Pétain had surrendered himself to the French authorities.

After several preliminary hearings, Pétain's trial took place between 23 July and 15 August 1945 at the Palais de Justice in Paris. Overseeing the events was the chief judge, Paul Mongibeaux, who had earlier sworn an oath of loyalty to the marshal. The prosecution was represented by André Mornet who, in 1942, had acted as one of the prosecutors at Riom. He had also sat on one of Vichy's naturalizations committees. For his defence, Pétain called on the services of another Riom advocate, Fernand Payen. It soon became clear that Pétain's ablest lawyer was Jacques Isorni, a 34-year-old barrister, who had recently put up a vigorous defence of Robert Brasillach, although this had not saved the collaborationist writer from the firing squad. Given that the jury for the Pétain trial was made up of resisters and former parliamentarians who had voted against Pétain on 10 July 1940, Isorni had every right to fear that the verdict in his new case would be a foregone conclusion.

As has been observed, the marshal's trial 'was more remarkable for the events which it had to deal with rather than the way in which they were treated'.[22] Even then, certain issues remained taboo. Although in the preliminary hearings Pétain was tackled on the origins of Vichy's racial laws, the question of Jewish persecution did not feature prominently in the proceedings, an indication that in the *après-guerre* few were prepared to admit or come to terms with the part played by Vichy in the Holocaust. Rather most of the arguments centred on the armistice and foreign policy. Given that the hearing was conducted at the hottest time of the year, the proceedings often took on a lugubrious air, yet there remained plenty of court-room drama. Laval, appearing as a defence witness, revived his old skills as a barrister to put on a brilliant performance, rehearsing the arguments he would later use at his own trial. None of the other 64 witnesses – among them Blum, Daladier, Jeanneney, Lebrun and Reynaud appearing for the prosecution, and Chevalier, Loustanau-Lacau, du Moulin de Labarthète and Weygand acting for the defence – generated such passion. Isorni, in his summing up, also gave a star turn, stressing the ways in which his client had acted to save the French from further punishment, and evoking the scene of Pétain's execu-tion should the death penalty be exacted.[23]

A further moment of drama had come on the opening day of the trial when Pétain read out a lengthy statement, drafted in consultation with Isorni. This began by denying the court the right to try him: 'It is the French people who by its repre-sentatives gathered in the National Assembly on 10 July 1940, entrusted me with power. It is to the French people that I have come to make my account. The High Court, as constituted, does not represent the French people, and it is to them alone that the marshal of France, head of state, will address himself.'[24] Thereafter Pétain recited an *apologia* for his wartime actions beginning with the armistice which, he disingenuously claimed, had aided the allied victory by ensuring a free Mediterranean and the integrity of the French empire. It was not long before he returned to familiar themes. Through his policy of collabo-ration, he had hoodwinked the Germans. By remaining on metropolitan soil, he had saved his people from further suffer-ing. Meanwhile, de Gaulle had led the struggle from overseas. In this manner, as Isorni claimed, the marshal had served as the 'shield' of France and the general the 'sword'. At no point did Pétain acknowledge that his actions might have intensified the punishments inflicted on his country. Nor, of course, did he accept that the policy of collaboration had been designed to enhance his own standing. He did, however, remain con-vinced that he was the incarnation of France. Thus in his closing paragraphs he invoked his authority as a marshal and recalled 'the gift of his person'.[25] After concluding his statement, Pétain retreated into a dignified silence. Sitting in the middle of the courtroom, dressed in a military uniform and bearing one single decoration, the Médaille Militaire, his interjections during the later proceedings were few and far between. Although his silence was partly due to his deafness, it also reflected his contempt for the whole proceedings.

Together Pétain and Isorni had devised a skilful defence, far more effective than that originally suggested by Payen who had wanted to claim diminished responsibility on the grounds of old age.[26] It did not, however, sway the verdict. On 15 August the jury returned to pronounce the death penalty. Two days later de Gaulle intervened to commute the sentence to life imprisonment, and arranged for the condemned man to be taken away from Paris to the Fort du Portulet in the remote south-west. An opinion poll conducted that month indicated support for the jury's decision and showed that public attitudes had shifted since the previous autumn.[27] Among the respondents, 37 per cent considered a life sentence justified; a further 37 per cent believed that a lesser sentence would have been more appropriate; only 17 per cent believed that the marshal should not have been tried. This turnaround in opinion has been put down to the short-lived euphoria of the Liberation and to the public's anger at the pitiful condition of deportees who had recently returned from Germany and the east.[28]

De Gaulle later claimed that it was his intention for Pétain to stay at the Fort du Portulet for two years, before being allowed to finish his life at Villeneuve-Loubet. Instead, in November 1945 the prisoner was transferred to the Île d'Yeu, an island south of the Brittany peninsula, and known today for its water-sports facilities. Sliding into senility and haunted by frequent hallucinations, including one of a roomful of naked women,[29] it was in this remote spot that he died on 23 July 1951. It was here, too, that he was buried, despite his wish to lie alongside his troops at Douaumont. Pétain's supporters, notably Isorni,[30] have repeatedly demanded that this wish be recognized. In 1973, a band of right-wing fanatics took matters into their own hands, digging up the body and heading off for Verdun. The marshal's remains were eventually discovered in a garage outside Paris, and returned to their island resting-place, where they remain to this day.

. . .

The skilful nature of Isorni's defence, the cruel way in which an old man was left to die and the banishment of his corpse from Douaumont refuelled the Pétain myth, turning a marshal into a martyr. The late 1940s and early 1950s were awash with moving accounts[31] of Pétain's last days in exile. At the same time, former Vichyites, among them Tracou, Girard, Bouthillier and Baudouin, all eager to rehabilitate their reputations, published memoirs of the Occupation.[32] It was their claim that, by signing the armistice and by remaining in France, the marshal had diluted German demands and had rescued France from the fate of Polonization. Inevitably, such an interpretation found its way into the history books. In 1954 Robert Aron, one of the so-called intellectual 'non-conformists' of the 1930s, wrote the first scholarly account of the Vichy regime.[33] Given privileged access to trial records and drawing heavily on the memoirs and oral testimonies of former *maréchalistes*, Aron argued, in Sellar and Yeatman fashion, that there had been two Vichys: a 'bad' Vichy of Laval, all too ready to collaborate, and a 'good' Vichy of Pétain, which had struggled to fend off German demands.

The Pétain myth was also perpetuated by a hard core of Vichyites who gravitated to the Association pour Défendre la Mémoire du Maréchal Pétain (ADMP). This was founded on 6 November 1951 by Isorni, and until 1965 boasted Weygand as its honorary chairman. Although by its own admission it has never become a popular movement, between 1951 and 1971 its board of directors included 36 high-ranking officers, 22 former ministers, 12 members of the Académie Française, and a number of prefects and other top civil servants.[34] It even drew support from former resisters, most notably Colonel Rémy, the pseudonym of Gilbert Renaud, one of the founders of the Gaullist Rassemblement du Peuple Français (RPF), who came to believe that France in 1940 had needed both Pétain and de Gaulle. Essentially, the objectives of the ADMP were, and remain, threefold: to secure a judicial review of the Pétain case; to ensure the transfer of the marshal's remains to Douaumont; and to rehabilitate the values of the National Revolution.

On the political front, it was the Algerian crisis of 1960–2 that offered the Pétainists their greatest opportunity. Following de Gaulle's granting of independence to the former colony, there was an outcry on the part of army officers and French Algerian settlers, who felt betrayed by metropolitan government. As has been observed, the military and Algeria had always been fertile breeding-grounds for Pétainism,[35] and it was no surprise that *maréchalistes* should have exploited the crisis for their own ends. It is also significant that the Organisation de l'Armée Secrète (OAS), a terrorist movement of renegade soldiers and dissident politicians united in their hatred of de Gaulle and their desire to keep Algeria French, came to espouse a political philosophy similar to Pétainism.[36] Milking the colonial crisis for all that it was worth, in 1965 the former Vichy minister Jean-Louis Tixier-Vignancours stood against de Gaulle in the presidential elections.[37] Adopting a Pétainist manifesto, his failure to secure more than 5 per cent of the vote was a sure-fire indication that only a small proportion of the population remained loyal to the marshal's precepts.

Certainly the task of the 'keepers of the flame' has not been an easy one. Since 1945 the Pétain myth has taken several knocks. For much of the Fourth Republic and the Gaullist phase of the Fifth, it had to compete with a counter-myth, that of 'a nation of resisters'.[38] It was not only de Gaulle who articulated this concept. The political classes of post-war France, left and right, that emerged from the Resistance saw their task as rebuilding French institutions and society, and had no desire to reflect on their country's past failings. Then, in the aftermath of the *événements* of May 1968, the 'mirror cracked' as both Pétainist and 'resistancialist' mythology was questioned. First came Marcel Ophuls' film, *The Sorrow and the Pity* of 1969.[39] This documentary of daily life in occupied Clermont-Ferrand, a town held typical of France during the war years, suggested that the population had been all too willing to collaborate. The film caused a scandal and, until 1981, was banned on French television and could only be seen on the cinema-screen. Next came Robert Paxton's *Vichy France. Old Guard and New Order*, published in 1972. Drawing largely on Nazi archives, this painted a very different picture to that of Aron, and corroborated the earlier findings of the German author, Eberhard Jäckel.[40] According to Paxton and Jäckel, the initiative for collaboration had stemmed largely from the French themselves.

By the 1980s the Occupation had become an 'obsession' as a new generation of scholars, spurred on by Paxton's conclusions, exposed the autonomy enjoyed by the Pétain government, highlighting the xenophobic and repressive nature of the National Revolution. Although in the 1990s there are signs that the historical profession is prepared to moderate some the harsher verdicts which appeared in the wake of Paxton,[41] the issue of Vichy's racism has remained central to the recollection of the war years. With the emergence of a rejuvenated anti-semitic right fronted by Jean-Marie Le Pen's Front National, a number of prominent Jewish individuals, among them Serge Klarsfeld and Bernard-Henri Lévy, have worked hard to establish Vichy's role in the Holocaust.[42] As a result, in the past 15 years France has witnessed a series of trials concerned with crimes against humanity. Those in the dock have included the SS man, Klaus Barbie, and several Vichy functionaries, among them Bousquet, Jean Leguay, Maurice Papon, Maurice Sabatier and Paul Touvier. Even mainstream politicians have come under scrutiny. In the 1980s, it was established that the socialist President François Mitterrand, despite his Resistance credentials, had been an early supporter of Pétain and had received the Francisque in recognition for his work for the Centre d'Entraide, a Vichy welfare agency that looked after prisoners-of-war.[43] In 1994 a terminally ill Mitterrand, perhaps in an act of catharsis, acknowledged that he had indeed been a devoted Pétainist and revealed that he had enjoyed a post-war friendship with Bousquet.[44] Coming at the time of the fiftieth anniversary of the Liberation, such revelations troubled public opinion, yet at least went some way to explain why earlier in his presidency Mitterrand had been willing to lay a wreath on Pétain's tomb and had been reluctant for the French state to accept full responsibility for the persecution of Jews.[45]

Ultimately, the Pétain legacy remains an ambiguous and divisive one, something borne out by successive opinion polls. In two *sondages* conducted in 1971 and 1983, interviewees were questioned about the appropriateness of the marshal's sentence.[46] On both occasions, three broad categories of opinion were discovered: the undecided, whose numbers have grown; a second group favouring leniency, whose numbers have never been more than a third; and a majority who always insisted on some form of penalty, even if it was merely symbolic.[47] Only a minority, drawn largely from the extreme left, have ever insisted on the death penalty. While the findings of such polls are open to differing interpretations, it appears that attitudes towards Pétain have not been constant; there have instead been cycles of hostility and leniency.[48] The polls also underscore the weakness of the hard-core Pétainists; those favouring a total acquittal have consistently been in the minority. Finally, these enquiries suggest generational differences in attitudes towards the marshal. Those who lived through the war years were initially against Pétain so long as events were fresh in their minds; as time passed they moderated their views.[49] In 1971, 58 per cent of the 50–64 age group and 62 per cent of over-65s demanded some form of penalty. In 1983, 50 per cent of the over-65s favoured acquittal. Meanwhile, a younger generation, who had not experienced the Occupation first-hand, developed anti-Pétain feelings of its own. In 1971, 55 per cent of the under-35s favoured some type of punishment; in 1983, 51 per cent of the 18–24 age group and 41 per cent of the 25–34 age range supported a sanction.

Whether such anti-Pétain sentiments will be passed on to further generations has yet to be seen. Observing the reactions of Parisian cinema-goers who, in 1993, went to see the film *Pétain* by Jean Marboeuf, the *Guardian* correspondent Paul Webster commented that it was the older members of the audience, those able to remember the *années noires*, that appeared most agitated by the issues raised in the film.[50] Viewers in their early twenties seemed unaware of what all the fuss was about. With the passing of time, the wounds opened by the Occupation will undoubtedly close over, but given the way in which the past weighs heavily on the present in French politics it is unlikely they will ever heal completely, ensuring that Pétain will remain a fundamental part of the Vichy 'syndrome'.

. . .

NOTES AND REFERENCES

1. J. Galtier-Boissière, *Journal, 1940–1950* (Paris: Quai Voltaire, 1992), p. 174.
2. J. Tracou, *Le maréchal aux liens. Le temps du sacrifice* (Paris: Editions André Bonne, 1948), p. 266.
3. Speech of 26 April 1944 in J.-C. Barbas (ed.), *Philippe Pétain. Discours aux français, 17 juin 1940–20 août 1994* (Paris: Albin Michel, 1989), p. 323.
4. M. Ferro, *Pétain* (Paris: Fayard, 1987), p. 545.
5. Message of 6 June 1944 in Barbas (ed.), *Discours*, p. 336.
6. Message of 14 June 1944 in ibid., p. 338.
7. Tracou, *Le maréchal*, pp. 309–10.
8. R.O. Paxton, *Vichy France. Old Guard and New Order, 1940–1944* (New York: Alfred A. Knopf, 1972), p. 327.
9. Ibid., p. 328.
10. G. Warner, *Pierre Laval and the Eclipse of France* (London: Eyre & Spottiswoode, 1968), pp. 393–6.

11. P. Laval, *Laval parle. Notes et mémoires rédigés par Pierre Laval dans sa cellule, avec une préface de sa fille et de nombreux documents inédits* (Geneva: Editions du Cheval Ailé, 1947), p. 157.
12. Pétain quoted in H.R. Lottman, *Pétain* (Paris: Seuil, 1984), p. 507.
13. Paxton, *Vichy France*, p. 329.
14. J. Isorni, *Mémoires*, vol. 3 (Paris: Robert Laffont, 1988), p. 384.
15. Message of 20 August 1944 in Barbas (ed.), *Discours*, pp. 340–2.
16. The atmosphere at Sigmaringen is conveyed in L.-F. Céline, *D'un château à l'autre* (Paris: Gallimard, 1957).
17. All figures from M. Larkin, *France Since the Popular Front* (Oxford: Clarendon Press, 1986), pp. 124–5.
18. Ordinance of 18 November 1944 cited in Warner, *Pierre Laval*, p. 408 and quoted in full in C. de Gaulle, *Mémoires de guerre*, vol. 3 (Paris: Plon, 1954), pp. 408–9.
19. A full list of sentences may be found in P. Novick, *The Resistance Versus Vichy. The Purge of Collaborators in Liberated France* (London: Chatto & Windus, 1968), pp. 222–3.
20. De Gaulle quoted in Lottman, *Pétain*, p. 536.
21. This poll is discussed in ibid., p. 538.
22. R. Griffiths, *Marshal Pétain* (London: Constable, 1970), p. 335.
23. *Plaidoirie* of Isorni, 14 August 1945, in *Procès du maréchal Pétain. Compte rendu officiel in extenso des audiences de la Haute Cour de Justice* (Paris: Louis Paliente, 1976), p. 472.
24. Pétain's statement, 23 July 1945, in ibid., p. 15.
25. Pétain's statement, 23 July 1945, in ibid.
26. J. Roy, *The Trial of Marshal Pétain* (London: Faber & Faber, 1968), pp. 19–20.
27. This poll is discussed in H. Rousso, *Le syndrome de Vichy, 1944 . . .* (Paris: Seuil, 1987), p. 304.
28. Ibid., p. 305.
29. J. Simon, *Pétain, mon prisonnier. Présentation, notes et commentaires de Pierre Bourget* (Paris: Plon, 1978), p. 141.
30. See, for example, J. Isorni, *La correspondance de l'île d'Yeu* (Paris: Flammarion, 1966).
31. Notably J. Isorni, *Souffrance et mort du maréchal Pétain* (Paris: Flammarion, 1951).
32. See bibliographical essay in this volume.
33. R. Aron, *Histoire de Vichy* (Paris: Fayard, 1954).
34. Rousso, *Le syndrome*, p. 54.
35. R. Vinen, 'Vichy: Pétain's Hollow Crown', *History Today*, 40 (1990), p. 19.
36. Griffiths, *Pétain*, p. 343.
37. Vinen, 'Pétain's Hollow Crown', p. 19.
38. The historiography of Vichy is brilliantly outlined in Rousso, *Le syndrome*.

39. The screenplay is published as M. Ophuls, *The Sorrow and the Pity* (London: Paladin, 1972). See J. Sweets, *Choices in Vichy Framce* (New York: Oxford University Press, 1986) for a more measured picture of life in Clermont-Ferrand.
40. E. Jäckel, *Frankreich in Hitlers Europa. Die Deutsche Frankreichpolitik im Zweiten Weltkrieg* (Stuttgart: Deutsche-Anstalt, 1966), and Paxton, *Vichy France.*
41. K. Munholland, 'Wartime France: Remembering Vichy', in *French Historical Studies,* 18 (3) (1994), p. 803. For recent sympathetic portrayals of Vichy, see F. Dreyfus, *Histoire de Vichy* (Paris: Perrin, 1989) and H. Coutau-Bégarie and C. Huan, *Darlan* (Paris: Fayard, 1989).
42. S. Klarsfeld, *Vichy-Auschwitz,* 2 vols (Paris: Fayard, 1982) and B.-H. Lévy, *Archives du procès Klaus Barbie* (Paris: Globe, 1986).
43. C. Nay, *Le noir et le rouge ou l'histoire d'une ambition* (Paris: Grasset, 1984), pp. 96–109.
44. F. Péan, *Une jeunesse française* (Paris: Fayard, 1994).
45. E. Conan and H. Rousso, *Vichy, un passé qui ne passe pas* (Paris: Fayard, 1994) pp. 200–7 and p. 296 and R. Gildea, *France Since 1945* (Oxford: Oxford University Press, 1996), pp. 75–8.
46. Rousso, *Le syndrome,* p. 305 gives the full details of these polls.
47. Ibid., p. 307.
48. Ibid., p. 309.
49. Ibid., p. 309.
50. Paul Webster in the *Guardian,* 6 May 1993. Marboeuf's film was based on Ferro's 1987 biography of Pétain, and starred Jacques Dufilho as the marshal and Jean Yanne in the role of Laval.

Chapter 9

THE MAN AND THE MYTH

Given the continuing importance of the Occupation in the French national consciousness, Pétain remains a symbol some 50 years after his death. Some cling to the 'black legend' of the marshal. For them, he will be recalled not for his triumph at Verdun or his quelling of the mutinies, but as the culprit responsible for the defeat of 1940, a treacherous soldier who conspired to overthrow the Republic and who kowtowed to the enemy, even agreeing to the deportation of Jews and French workers. Others will continue to revere him as a semi-mystical figure, who bequeathed to the nation the supreme sacrifice of 'the gift of his person' in order to save his people from further suffering. No amount of documents displaying his readiness to collaborate with Germany will dispel their faith in Pétain as the 'shield' of France.

By stripping away the mythology surrounding Pétain, the present study has uncovered a man who was never quite the hero or the villain of popular belief. He had begun life as a peasant, choosing the army as a job not because he craved revenge for the defeat of 1870, but because he sought a steady income. The military provided just that. Although he was irritated by his lack of promotion, he was resigned to his fate, being posted from one dreary garrison town to another. The only thing that distinguished his pre-1914 career was his unorthodox military thinking. His views on fire-power were always the most original aspect of his thought. Yet had he been killed during the opening engagements of the First World War, not such an unlikely prospect given his presence at the Marne and his willingness to lead from the front, it is doubtful whether he would be remembered today. His name would be one of the thousands inscribed on the war memorials that dot the towns and villages of provincial France.

Had he died shortly after the First World War, as did several of those generals promoted to the rank of marshal in 1918–19, it is likely that every town in France would boast a *rue du maréchal Pétain*. His body would lie at Douaumont, and he would be recalled as the most humane and effective of the French High Command. Much of this praise would be deserved. Whether he was truly the 'Victor of Verdun' or not, that battle and his handling of the mutinies remain his finest moments, and he was rightly proud of his achievements. He had shown himself a perceptive and flexible soldier whose awareness of trench warfare had averted unnecessary slaughter. He was, however, more of a tactician than a strategist. When he became Commander-in-Chief in 1917, he undoubtedly possessed a wider vision of how to win the war, but was overly cautious in his approach. A seeping pessimism, derived from his natural temperament and disgust at the callous loss of life, also inculcated in him a hesitation that could have proved disastrous. In March 1918, at the time of the German advance, this hesitancy, coupled with his mistrust of the British, placed the whole of the allied war effort in jeopardy. It was fortunate for his reputation that the crisis soon passed, allowing Pétain to recover his equilibrium and play a key role in the eventual defeat of Germany.

Had Pétain died in the early 1920s he would not, of course, feature today in a series entitled 'Profiles in Power'. Regardless of his political meddlings and snubs to Poincaré, the authority he had exercised to that point had largely been confined to the military sphere. None the less, the origins of his power as a symbol may be traced back to the square at Metz where, on 8 December 1918, he received his marshal's baton. Although the left continued to carp over his treatment of working-class mutineers, the public at large, exhausted by the unrelenting demands of four years of fighting, looked on Pétain with gratitude. Through his compassion and defence of Verdun, the most momentous battle of the war, he, more than any other general, had become the symbol of French victory. The fact that Pétain went on to outlive the other marshals only intensified the aura surrounding his position.

Government ministers were no less dazzled by his brilliance than was the public at large, and in the 1920s they entrusted him with a series of military posts, even though these jobs lay beyond his experience. Pétain himself had no doubts about his own worth. Before 1914 he had displayed little appetite for power; afterwards he had ambition aplenty. Enjoying his new-found role as France's military guru, he advanced a predomi-nantly defensive strategy that had proved its value at Verdun, and which triumphed again over the Berber tribes in the Rif. In consequence, France built up its infantry and dug the earth-works for the Maginot Line. New killing machines, such as tanks and planes, only played a limited role, in Pétain's thinking, as appendages to the infantry. Self-belief had thus undermined his abilities as a flexible tactician; ultimately, it endangered the allied armies in May–June 1940. None the less, Pétain cannot shoulder all the blame for the fall of France. The decisions to leave the Ardennes insufficiently guarded, to implement the Breda variant of the Dyle Plan and to relinquish a strategic reserve were taken by others, not by Pétain.

Despite his being the symbol of French victory, political power was a long time coming to Petain, and never fully materi-alized before 1940. This came as a disappointment to many. When in 1934 Pétain accepted a post in the Doumergue cabinet, he was widely regarded as a rock of stability who would rescue France from the disorder that had recently been witnessed on the streets of Paris. The election of the Popular Front and the growth of external tension reinforced the impression that the nation required a firm hand in charge of government. For journalists such as Hervé that man could only be Pétain; vet-eran parliamentarians such as Laval, no longer certain of the system that had served them well, thought the same.

For his part, the marshal agreed that he was the man to rescue France, and welcomed press attention to articulate a simplistic philosophy little different to that of other military men of his generation. Yet he remained reluctant to throw his hat into the political ring. In part, this was due to his soldier's mistrust of parliamentarians. For a man renowned for his sar-castic wit, it was always ironic that he never saw anything incon-gruous in his own propensity for wheeler-dealing. The other route to power was, of course, the illegal one, yet as a loyal soldier he was not prepared to act unconstitutionally, and thus kept his distance from the right-wing leagues and the plots to overturn the Republic. Rather he was more attracted by the constitutional path to power. In that sense he was the 'Repub-lican marshal' of popular belief. Yet there was no disguising his preference for an authoritarian Republic. Nor was there any hiding his distaste for democratic procedures. As a man accustomed to discipline and order, he was unwilling to trust in the electorate by putting himself up for the presidency, a post for which he felt nothing but contempt.

Sure of his own importance, Pétain had to be summoned to power, just as he had been called to defend Verdun and end the mutinies. Waiting patiently in Spain, joking that he was unable to return to France because he had no mistress waiting for him in Paris, the call came in May 1940 with the allied armies already in a state of advanced disarray. Remembering his courage at Verdun and his compassion for the *poilu*, Reynaud had anticipated that the marshal would add backbone to the war effort. That such an intelligent politician as Reynaud could have thought this is testimony to the strength of the Pétain myth. He soon discovered the real Pétain: the surly pessimistic soldier, contemptuous of the British, and all too ready to do down his cabinet colleagues and press for an armistice. The real Pétain also remained hidden from the National Assembly which in July 1940 voted itself out of existence. It is doubtful whether the deputies and senators would have succumbed so readily to Laval's motion suspending the 1875 constitution had it not been for the aura which still surrounded marshalship.

There was, of course, a further group of people who remained ignorant of the Pétain of flesh and blood: the French public. In large measure, this was due to his earlier reluctance to comment on national affairs. Untainted by any close connections with a republican regime discredited by defeat, he emerged in the midst of the *exode* as a ready-made hero. Vichy propaganda, so ineffectual in other spheres, was quick to play on this. To the young, he was presented as a kindly grandfather figure, not a frail old man of 84 who had no children of his own. To the peasantry, he was portrayed as one of their own, not the man who had deserted his birthplace in the Pas-de-Calais for a large house in the south and the sophisticated salons of Paris. To Catholics, he was the product of the *école libre*, the pious marshal; no mention was made of the fact that he rarely attended mass and was married to a divorcée. To the soldiers of France, he was heralded as the great patriot, not a scheming and power-hungry politician. Only a small number of people saw through the myth, notably de Gaulle, who had worked with Pétain at close quarters, and those elements of the extreme right who, in the 1930s, had openly mocked the marshal's traditionalist leanings. It would take the wider developments of the war for others to deconstruct the symbolism surrounding Pétain: the handshake at Montoire; the loss of the colonies; the shooting of hostages; the deportation of Jews; the introduction of STO; and the founding of the Milice. Even then members of the Resistance found it difficult to break down people's loyalties to the old man. The crowds that greeted Pétain at Paris in April 1944 were testimony to his enduring appeal.

Pétain himself sought to reciprocate this trust by protecting his people from further suffering. Although his tactical sense might have deserted him in 1918, his compassion had not. He was heart-broken by the *exode* and the fate of the 1,500,000 prisoners-of-war held in Germany. It was this sense of humanity which kept him in France in 1940 despite the humiliating terms imposed by the Germans. As Serrigny remarked, Pétain cared more for the French than he did for France. This compassion remains one of the most redeeming aspects of Pétain's character, although it should be noted that it did not extend to all sections of the community. Yet should Pétain have died shortly after the armistice, or indeed in 1942, it seems likely that his reputation as a caring leader would have remained intact, regardless of the measures which Vichy took against Jews and other 'undesirables'. As it was, the prolongation of the war exposed the inadequacies of his so-called 'shield policy'. In its attempts to preserve French autonomy, Vichy did more and more of the Germans' dirty work for them, founding the GMR and Milice to hound out resisters and *réfractaires* from STO. In this way, Vichy ran the risk of Polonizing itself.

Whether Pétain ever understood this remains doubtful, otherwise in October 1941 he might well have gone through with his threat to surrender himself to the Germans in protest at the shooting of hostages. His judgement was constantly blurred by his sense of vanity and his appetite for power, and it should be remembered that it was these baser instincts, as much as his compassion, which dictated his decision to stay in France in June 1940 and November 1942. This thirst for power remained unquenched throughout the Occupation. At long last, he had the opportunity to implement the ideas which he had formed during the interwar years. He had little sense that occupation was not the ideal time in which to launch a major overhaul of his country's institutions. People quickly appreciated the yawning gulf between the reality of their own lives and the images of Vichy propaganda. None the less, the National Revolution did leave its impression on France, albeit a different one to that which Pétain had intended. He had visualized a traditionalist, corporatist France, infused with a strong religious sense, and divided into medieval provinces. By 1941 this project was already being supplanted by that of the technocrats. In the event, it was their reforms, not Pétain's, which proved the longer lasting, largely because they caught the mood of the age, closely mirroring the schemes for renewal that were later developed by the Consultative Assembly at Algiers.

Alongside these plans for progressive reform, the National Revolution possessed a vicious streak. Pétain always intended that those he dubbed the 'anti France' would have no part to play in their country's revival. By 1941, with an 'ill wind' sweeping through the country, these elements were coming to resemble the mutineers he had encountered in 1917. Prominent among this list of subversives were the politicians of the Third Republic. He was thus eager to rid his cabinets of former parliamentarians, and took satisfaction in seeing Daladier, Blum and others in the dock at Riom. Then there were the freemasons, a traditional bugbear of the French right. As the marshal himself remarked, to be a Jew was a matter of accident; to be a freemason was a matter of choice. The most dangerous subversives were, however, the communists. Pétain had done battle with communism on a number of occasions. In 1940 he was ready to do combat once again, and he conveniently blamed the emergence of internal resistance on the left. As the Occupation dragged on, anti-communism came to play a bigger part in Pétain's thinking. The invasion of the Soviet Union was like a rush of adrenalin through his veins, far more vitalizing than the shots of amphetamine he regularly received from Ménétrel. Not only did this event give a renewed purpose to the National Revolution, it also gave an added dimension to Pétain's policy of collaboration. Through cooperation with Germany, France would indirectly be helping to rid Europe of Bolshevism. Accordingly he possessed more than a sneaking admiration for the LVF. Even in 1943 he hoped that France could play a role in bringing Germany and the USA together in a compromise peace designed to combat the influence of the USSR.

By contrast, Jews came fairly low down on Pétain's list of 'undesirables'. In the 1890s his name would not appear among the list of subscribers to the fiercely antisemitic newspaper, *La Libre Parole*, which organized a collection for the widow of Colonel Henry, the officer involved in fabricating evidence against Dreyfus. Nor, during the Occupation, did Jews figure in Pétain's speeches; he even included Jews and blacks among his friends. None the less, behind his impassive façade, he possessed an unthinking xenophobia, typical of many conservatives of his generation. It was a racism that proved tragic. In 1940 there was no public outcry for an antisemitic programme. Nor was Germany pressing Vichy to undertake anti-Jewish measures. Rather the moves towards the *Statuts des Juifs* came from within Vichy itself, and Pétain did nothing to stop these. While he displayed some concern for those Jews, notably former servicemen, who had assimilated something of French culture, he approved of Vallat's attempts to free France of alien influences. Later, in 1942, when church representatives apprised him of the full horrors of the Holocaust in France, he still refused to act. The surrender of foreign Jews in exchange for the lives of French ones bore all the hallmarks of Laval's cynical thinking, and Pétain clearly had little liking for this policy. None the less, the marshal saw no alternative. If the lives of French nationals could be saved by sacrificing foreigners, then so be it.

Pétain's name will be for ever associated with the fate of the Jews, and rightly so. Although the numbers deported from France were not as great as those from other countries, the tragedy was no less for that. Pétain himself would have been disappointed that he should be remembered in this way, and it was perhaps fortunate for his peace of mind that in 1945 his prosecutors were reluctant to bring up the question of Jews for fear of highlighting France's more general complicity in the Holocaust. Instead, Pétain had hoped that he would be remembered for other things: for reducing the demands of the armistice; for the National Revolution; and for the rescuing of France from the worst defeat in its history, a 'diplomatic Verdun'. In his mind these objectives could only be achieved through a policy of collaboration with the enemy. Contemptuous of Britain, his behaviour remained free of any double-dealing, even after December 1941 when the USA entered the war. By that stage in the conflict, the marshal's foreign policy had already degenerated into a desperate struggle to justify the decisions he had made in 1940. While Pétain was not alone in under-estimating the uncompromising nature of Hitler's position – Laval and Darlan were just as guilty – his naive belief that the Nazis were comrades-in-arms and open to persuasion was breath-taking. In 1944, with the allied armies already in France, he still hoped that he could salvage something from the wreckage.

Ultimately, the circumstances of the Occupation conspired to rob Pétain of his powers, leaving him a pathetic figure, con-fined at Sigmaringen, exercising the last vestiges of his constitu-tional authority over a puppet government. In 1940 his position had seemed unassailable. The cult of marshal was everywhere; Pétainist *notables* were in office; the Légion reigned supreme; and the collaborationists at Paris were held in check. By the close of that year, through a process of ministerial reshuffles, Pétain had also fashioned a cabinet largely to his own liking. Yet already he was losing control. The failure of government policies, the inter-ministerial rivalries, the challenge of the Free French, the loss of the colonies and the growth of internal dissidence posed a series of challenges to his authority. His quest for a breakthrough in Franco-German relations also threatened his position. It was largely thanks to this desire for a foreign policy success, more concrete than the one achieved at Montoire, that he relinquished an ever-increasing amount of power first to Laval, next to Darlan, then to Laval again. Meanwhile, the emergence of a truly global conflict in 1941 forced Hitler to take an even tougher line with France, further constraining Pétain's freedom of action. By the time German armour rolled over the demarcation line in November 1942, the marshal's transformation into a figurehead was almost complete. While the constitutional crisis of November 1943 displayed that he was not completely lacking in influence, his government could now do little without Nazi permission.

Whatever one's own viewpoint, it is difficult not to feel a smidgen of pity for Pétain. He remains truly a figure of pathos. Until 1918 he had been a brave and humane soldier seemingly in charge of his own destiny; thereafter he became a prisoner. To begin with, he was ensnared by the cult of marshalship that was born out of the First World War. If he had possessed anything of the qualities which were accredited to him, he would have recognized the dangers inherent in his position. As it was, he believed in the Pétain myth as much as the public did, and readily accepted power in 1940, not recognizing that he would be trapped by the circumstances of the defeat and Occupation. Afterwards, he was literally a prisoner, first at Sigmaringen, then on the Île d'Yeu where he eventually succumbed to senile dementia. Even in death he remains a prisoner, his body banished from the graveyard at Douaumont, and his legacy inextricably caught up with that of the Occupation.

BIBLIOGRAPHICAL ESSAY

Pétain himself left no memoirs, once remarking that 'history would be his judge'. In truth, he disliked writing and, as was the practice for high-ranking French soldiers, employed junior officers to draft articles and books for him. This does not mean that the views expressed in these works were not Pétain's own. He took a schoolmasterly pleasure in correcting the proofs submitted by his ghost writers, deleting adjectives and expunging the semi-colon, that 'bastard of punctuation'. This clear and clipped style is evident in his *La bataille de Verdun* (Paris: Payot, 1929), composed in fact by General Laure. More revealing is Pétain's own account of the mutinies printed in Edward Spears, *Two Men who Saved France* (London: Eyre & Spottiswoode, 1955), and his letters printed in M.A. Pardee, *Le maréchal que j'ai connu* (Paris: Editions André Bonne, 1952).

Pétain's political philosophy is best observed through his many articles published in *La Revue des Deux Mondes* during the 1930s. These were largely written by Loustanau-Lacau. The marshal's wartime speeches are also revealing. There are several collections of these, the most comprehensive and best documented being that compiled by Jean-Claude Barbas, *Philippe Pétain. Discours aux français, 17 juin 1940–20 août 1940* (Paris: Albin Michel, 1989). The useful appendices provide a detailed breakdown of the language deployed by the marshal's speechwriters. Transcripts of his principal broadcasts, together with the notes Pétain compiled in answer to questions posed by prosecution lawyers preparing his trial, are included in *Quatre ans au pouvoir* (Paris: La Couronne Littéraire, 1949).

Although Pétain himself left no memoirs, he frequently appears in those of others. His experiences during the First

World War are observed in Marshal Fayolle, *Cahiers secrets de la grande guerre* (Paris: Plon, 1964); Abel Ferry, *Les carnets secrets d'Abel Ferry* (Paris: Grasset, 1957); Paul Painlevé, *Comment j'ai nommé Foch et Pétain* (Paris: Félix Alcan, 1932); Jean de Pierrefeu, *GQG. Secteur 1. Edition définitive revue et augmentée*, 2 vols (Paris: Les Editions G. Crès et Cie, 1922); General Serrigny, *Trente ans avec Pétain* (Paris: Plon, 1959); and Alexandre Ribot, *Journal d'Alexandre Ribot* (Paris: Plon, 1936). The defeatist marshal of 1939–40 is convincingly portrayed in Edward Spears, *Assignment to Catastrophe*, 2 vols (London: Heinemann, 1954) and less objectively in Charles de Gaulle, *Mémoires de guerre*, 3 vols (Paris: Plon, 1954–9). The senile old man on the Île d'Yeu is sympathetically observed in Joseph Simon, *Pétain, mon prisonier. Présentation, notes et commentaires de Pierre Bourget* (Paris: Plon, 1978). Attempts to rehabilitate Pétain are recounted by Jacques Isorni, notably in his *La correspondance de l'île d'Yeu* (Paris: Flammarion, 1966). See, too, Isorni's *Mémoires*, 3 vols (Paris: Robert Laffont, 1984–8).

It would be myopic to cite all of the many memoirs by Vichy ministers and officials. Arguably the most intimate portraits of Pétain are contained in Joseph Barthélemy, *Le ministre de la justice. Mémoires, Vichy 1941–1943* (Paris: Pygmalion, 1989); Paul Baudouin, *Neuf mois au gouvernement, avril–décembre 1940* (Paris: La Table Ronde, 1948); Jacques Bénoist-Méchin, *De la défaite au désastre*, 2 vols (Paris: Albin Michel, 1984); Yves Bouthillier, *Le drame de Vichy*, 2 vols (Paris: Plon, 1951–2); Jérôme Carcopino, *Souvenirs de sept ans, 1937–1944* (Paris: Flammarion, 1953); René Gillouin, *J'étais l'ami du maréchal Pétain* (Paris: Plon, 1946); Henri du Moulin de Labarthète, *Le temps des illusions. Souvenirs juillet 1940 – avril 1942* (Geneva: Le Cheval Ailé, 1946); and Jean Tracou, *Le maréchal aux liens. Le temps du sacrifice* (Paris: Editions André Bonne, 1946).

Studies on Pétain abound, and show no sign of abating. Unsurprisingly, most of these have been highly partisan in nature, often reopening the issues of his trial. A good overview of this historiography is provided by Bernard Laguerre, 'Les biographies du maréchal Pétain', in Jean-Pierre Azéma and François Bédarida (eds), *Vichy et les français* (Paris: Fayard, 1992), pp. 45–56. As Laguerre observes, the model for those authors wishing to portray Pétain as a traitor is provided by Albert Bayet, *Pétain et la cinquième colonne* (Paris: Editions du Franc-Tireur, 1944), written while the author was in the USA. The same themes are pursued in Charlereine, *Le maréchal défaite* (Paris: Gallimard, 1945) and Jean Galtier-Boissière, *Tradition de la trahison chez les maréchaux* (Paris: P.Trémois, 1945) both composed in the heat of the *après-guerre*.

Pétain's supporters were not slow to hit back, building on the hagiographical portrait drawn by General Laure, *Pétain* (Paris: Berger Levrault, 1942) and developing themes articulated by the marshal's defence team. For example, the double-game argument is disingenuously deployed in Louis Rougier, *Mission secrète à Londres. Les accords Pétain–Churchill* (Paris: La Diffusion du Livre, 1946) and Louis-Dominique Girard, *Montoire. Verdun-Diplomatique* (Paris: Editions André Bonne, 1948). The Girard volume so incensed the Ministry of Interior that it was classified alongside works of pornography, and thus banned from public display. Had it been erotica, it is tempting to believe that Pétain himself might have shown more interest in it. Apparently when his wife presented him with a copy he complained it was too long and put it to one side; only later did he bother to read the book. Further sympathetic portrayals were prompted by the marshal's death in 1951. See especially Jacques Isorni, *Souffrance et mort du maréchal Pétain* (Paris: Flammarion, 1951) and General Héring, *La vie exemplaire de Philippe Pétain* (Paris: Paris-Livres, 1956).

The first 'objective' biographies of Pétain appeared in the 1960s: Jean Plumyène's brief *Pétain* (Paris: Seuil, 1964); Georges Blond's *Pétain, 1856–1951* (Paris: Presses de la Cité, 1966); and Pierre Bourget's *Un certain Philippe Pétain* (Paris: Casterman, 1966). On closer inspection, it may be seen that the latter two titles constitute a plea for an acquittal, playing down the marshal's role in such things as the deportation of Jews and French workers. Less ambiguity surrounds Isorni's unashamedly apologetic *Philippe Pétain*, 2 vols (Paris: La Table Ronde, 1972) which, despite its partisan nature, remains a useful study containing much important documentation. See also his *Le condamné de la citadelle* (Paris: Flammarion, 1982). Several other authors have tried to rehabilitate Pétain, yet it is doubtful whether anyone will better the case first put forward, ironically enough, by an Englishman, Sisley Huddlestone, in his *Pétain. Patriot or Traitor?* (London: Andrew Dakars Ltd, 1951). Indeed, a number of anglophone authors have adopted a sympathetic line, notably Philip Guedella, *The Two Marshals* (London: Hodder & Stoughton,

1943) and Glorney Bolton, *Pétain* (London: George Allen & Unwin, 1957).

It has only been with the passing of time that truly dispassionate studies have become more plentiful. These include Pierre Pelissier's rather mundane *Philippe Pétain* (Paris: Hachette, 1980); Raymond Tournoux's *Pétain et la France* (Paris: Plon, 1980); Herbert R. Lottman's *Pétain* (Paris: Seuil, 1984) which is far superior to the abridged English translation, *Pétain. Hero or Traitor?* (New York: Viking, 1985); and Philippe Alméras' *Un français nommé Pétain* (Paris: Robert Laffont, 1995). This last-named study makes scant use of recent research, and adds little to our knowledge of the marshal. Guy Pedroncini is currently writing a three-volume biography, and has already completed the first two instalments: *Pétain. Le soldat et la gloire, 1856–1918* (Paris: Perrin, 1989) and *Pétain. La victoire perdue, novembre 1918 –juin 1940* (Paris: Perrin, 1995). Both of these dwell largely on military matters, and the author has yet to confront the sensitive issues posed by the Occupation.

Without doubt, the best biographies remain Richard Griffiths' *Marshal Pétain* (London: Constable, 1970), reissued in 1995 with a new preface, and Marc Ferro's *Pétain* (Paris: Fayard, 1987). Although Griffiths' chapters on the Vichy years should be read in tandem with recent research into the Occupation, he draws the most convincing portrait of Pétain before 1940. Ferro provides a virtual day-by-day commentary on the marshal's time at Vichy, although he does look back to Verdun. His book also constitutes the basis of the 1993 film *Pétain* by Jean Marboeuf.

Biographies of leading French politicians contain further valuable material on Pétain. The most helpful include: Pierre Assouline, *Jean Jardin, 1904–1976, une éminence grise* (Paris: Balland, 1986); J.-P. Brunet, *Doriot* (Paris: Balland, 1986); Jean-Paul Cointet, *Pierre Laval* (Paris: Fayard, 1993); Hervé Coutau-Bégarie and Claude Huan, *Darlan* (Paris: Fayard, 1989); Bernard Destrumeau, *Weygand* (Paris, Perrin, 1989); Fred Kupferman, *Laval* (Paris: Balland, 1987); Jean Lacouture, *De Gaulle*, 3 vols (Paris: Seuil, 1983–6); and Geoffrey Warner, *Pierre Laval and the Eclipse of France* (London: Eyre & Spottiswoode, 1968).

There exist several non-biographical studies that say much about Pétain. A solid account of his military philosophy is presented in Stephen Ryan, *Pétain the Soldier* (South Brunswick and New York: A.S. Barnes & Co., 1969). On Verdun, see the proceedings of two conferences contained in Maurice Genevoix (ed.), *Verdun 1916* (Nancy: Presses Universitaires de Nancy, 1975) and Gérard Canini (ed.), *Mémoires de la Grande Guerre. Témoins et témoignages* (Nancy: Presses Universitaires de Nancy, 1989). Number 182, 1996, of *Guerres Mondiales et Conflits Contemporains* commemorates the eightieth anniversary of Verdun with some important articles. Alistair Horne, *The Price of Glory. Verdun 1916* (London: Macmillan, 1962) provides an excellent guide to the battle, and is better than Georges Blond, *Verdun* (London: André Deutsch, 1965). Among the numerous studies on the mutinies, the most comprehensive remains Guy Pedroncini, *Les mutineries de 1917* (Paris: Presses Universitaires de France, 1967). The same author has also provided a rounded portrait of Pétain in 1918: *Pétain. Général en chef, 1917–1918* (Paris: Presses Universitaires de France, 1974). The wider issues of the war are best approached through Jean-Baptiste Duroselle, *La France et les français, 1914–1920* (Paris: Editions Richelieu, 1972).

Pétain's private life and plans for retirement after 1918 are well handled by Henri Amouroux, *Pétain avant Vichy. La guerre et l'amour* (Paris: Fayard, 1967) which is more reliable than Louis-Dominique Girard's *Mazinghem ou la vie secrète du maréchal Pétain, 1856–1951* (Paris: privately published, 1971). Raymond Tournoux's *Pétain and de Gaulle* (London: Heinemann, 1966) also sheds light on the 'private' Pétain. In addition, see the documents edited by Pierre Bourget, *Témoignages inédits sur le Maréchal Pétain* (Paris: Fayard, 1960). Something of the marshal's day-to-day existence at the Hôtel du Parc is glimpsed in Michèle Cointet-Labrousse, *Vichy Capitale* (Paris: Perrin, 1993).

The Rif war indicated that Pétain still possessed an appetite for power, and a glowing account of his Moroccan exploits is contained in General Laure, *La victoire franco-espagnole dans le Rif* (Paris: Plon, 1927). More objective analyses are provided by D.S. Woolman, *Rebels in the Rif. Abd el-Krim and the Rif Rebellion* (Stanford: Stanford University Press, 1968) and the essays in *Abd el-Krim et la République du Rif* (Paris: Masparo, 1976).

The second volume of Pedroncini's biography, *La victoire perdue*, constitutes the most up-to-date account of Pétain's influence on military thinking between the wars, and is better than Jacques Nobécourt, *Une histoire politique de l'armée. De Pétain à Pétain, 1919–1942*, 2 vols (Paris: Seuil, 1967), although both titles are too indulgent towards the marshal. A good guide to the vast array of books and articles on French preparations for war and the defeat of 1940 is provided by Martyn Cornick, 'The Fall of France 1940: Bibliographical Essay', in *Modern and Contemporary France*, (42) 1990, pp. 37–44. See also the exhaustive bibliography in Martin Alexander, *The Republic in Danger. General Gamelin and the Politics of French Defence, 1933–1944* (Cambridge: Cambridge University Press, 1992). Among the works cited by Alexander and Cornick, the following put Pétain's military contribution into perspective: P.C.F. Bankwitz, *Maxime Weygand and Civil–Military Relations in Modern France* (Cambridge, Mass.: Harvard University Press, 1967); J.-L. Crémieux-Brilhac, *Les français de l'an 40*, 2 vols (Paris: Gallimard, 1990); Robert Allan Doughty, *The Breaking Point. Sedan and the Fall of France, 1940* (Hamden: Archon, 1990); J.A. Gunsberg, *Divided and Conquered. The French High Command and the Defeat of the West* (Westport, Conn.: Greenwood Press, 1979); Alistair Horne, *To Lose a Battle. France 1940* (London: Macmillan, 1969); J.M. Hughes, *To the Maginot Line. The Politics of French Military Preparation in the 1920s* (Cambridge, Mass.: Harvard University Press, 1971); and Robert Young, *In Command of France. French Foreign Policy and Military Planning, 1933–1940* (Cambridge, Mass.: Harvard University Press, 1978).

The origins and evolution of the Pétain myth are expertly handled in Griffiths, cited above, but the most illuminating account is Pierre Servent, *Le mythe Pétain. Verdun ou les tranchées de la mémoire* (Paris: Editions Payot, 1992). The following essays are also of interest: H.R. Kedward, 'Patriots and Patriotism in Vichy France', in *Transactions of the Royal Historical Society*, 5th series, 32 (1982), pp. 175–92; Philip Thody, 'Philippe Pétain: The Victim', in his *French Caesarism. From Napoleon I to Charles de Gaulle* (London: Macmillan, 1989) pp. 75–99; and Richard Vinen, 'Vichy: Pétain's Hollow Crown', in *History Today*, 40 (1990), pp. 13–19. The second volume of Henri Amouroux's *La grande histoire des français sous l'occupation*, 10 vols (Paris: Robert Laffont, 1976–93) sheds important light on the marshal's popularity in the summer of 1940. An evaluation of how the cult of marshalship fared at a local level is provided in Pierre Laborie, *L'opinion française sous Vichy* (Paris: Seuil, 1990), John Sweets, *Choices in Vichy France* (New York: Oxford University Press, 1986) and Dominique Veillon, *Vivre et survivre en France, 1939–1949* (Paris: Editions Payot, 1995). The language of Pétainism is analysed in Gérard Miller, *Les pousse-au-jouir du maréchal Pétain* (Paris: Seuil 1975), and mocked in Marc-Pierre D'Argenson's cleverly titled *Pétain et le pétinisme* (Paris: Editions Créator, 1953). To savour something of the Pétain myth, it is worth reading Gustave Hervé's *C'est Pétain qu'il nous faut* (Paris: Editions de la Victoire, 1935) and René Benjamin's *Le maréchal et son peuple* (Paris: Plon, 1941). The full gamut of Pétainist propaganda is covered by Laurent Gervereau and Denis Peschanski (eds), *La propagande de Vichy, 1940–1944* (Paris: Collection des Publications de la BDIC, 1990).

Pétain's time at Vichy is best handled by Ferro, yet this should be read alongside Jean-Pierre Azéma's *De Munich à la Libération* (Paris: Seuil, 1979), H.R. Kedward's *Occupied France. Collaboration and Resistance* (Oxford: Basil Blackwell, 1985), and Robert Paxton's *Vichy France. Old Guard and New Order, 1940–1944* (New York: Alfred A. Knopf, 1972). While showing signs of age, Paxton remains the key study on the Occupation; Julian Jackson's forthcoming survey on wartime France will also be very welcome. Reasons of space preclude a full listing of the many titles on the *années noires*. From being a taboo subject in the 1950s and 1960s, by the early 1980s Vichy had become an 'obsession' on the part of historians. An insight into the evolution of the historiography – how this has moved on from Robert Aron's *Histoire de Vichy* (Paris: Fayard, 1954) to Philippe Burrin's *La France à l'heure allemande, 1940–1944* (Paris: Seuil, 1995) – is provided in Kim Munholland, 'Wartime France: Remembering Vichy', in *French Historical Studies*, 18 (3) 1994, pp. 801–20. A further guide to this literature and the present state of research may be gleaned from Azéma and Bédarida (eds), *Vichy et les français*, cited above, and their other edited collection, *La France des années noires*, 2 vols (Paris: Seuil, 1993) See also Donna Evleth, *France under the German Occupation, 1940–1944. An Annotated Bibliography* (Westport, Conn.: Greenwood Press, 1991) although this is already out of date and contains some curious omissions.

Mention is made of the following Vichy titles as they all throw invaluable light on particular aspects of Pétain's role as *chef de l'état* and constitute guides to further reading. A good introduction to the ideology of the National Revolution is contained in Michèle Cointet-Labrousse, *Vichy et le fascisme* (Brussels: Editions Complexe, 1987) which is broader than its title suggests. See, too, the essays in the volume published under the auspices of the Fondation Nationale des Sciences Politiques,

Le gouvernement de Vichy (Paris: Armand Colin, 1972), although these have not aged well and are limited in their coverage. The marshal's educational ideas are best approached through W.D. Halls, *The Youth of Vichy France* (Oxford: Clarendon Press, 1981). On his religious convictions, see Nicholas Atkin, *Church and Schools in Vichy France, 1940–1944* (New York: Garland, 1991), Jacques Duquesne, *Les catholiques français sous l'occupation* (Paris: Grasset, 1966) and W.D. Halls, *Politics, Society and Christianity in Vichy France* (Oxford: Berg, 1995). His economic philosophy is tackled by Isabel Boussard, *Vichy et la Corporation Paysanne* (Paris: FNSP, 1990), Richard Kuisel, *Capitalism and the State in Modern France* (Cambridge: Cambridge University Press, 1980) and Richard Vinen, *The Politics of French Business, 1936–1945* (Cambridge: Cambridge University Press, 1991). For the role of women during the Occupation, a subject on which Pétain held decidedly male-chauvinist views, see Francine Muel-Dreyfus, *Vichy et l'éternel féminin* (Paris: Seuil, 1996) and the forthcoming study by Miranda Pollard.

On Pétain's plans for France in the 'new' Europe, see Jean-Baptiste Duroselle, *L'abîme. Politique étrangère de la France, 1939–1944* (Paris: Imprimerie Nationale, 1982), Julian Hurstfield, *America and the French Nation, 1939–1943* (Chapel Hill: University of North Carolina, 1986), Eberhard Jäckel, *Frankreich in Hitlers Europa. Die Deutsche Frankreichpolitik im Zweiten Weltkrieg* (Stuttgart: Deutsche-Anstalt, 1966) and R.T. Thomas, *Britain and Vichy* (London: Macmillan, 1978). For the marshal's relationship with the Paris fascists, see Bertram Gordon, *Collaborationism in France during the Second World War* (Ithaca, NY: Cornell University Press, 1980) and Pascal Ory, *Les collaborateurs* (Paris: Seuil, 1977). Tournoux, *Pétain and de Gaulle,* cited above, handles the relationship between Pétain and the Free French, and is more helpful than Guy Raïssac, *Un combat sans merci. L'affaire Pétain–de Gaulle* (Paris: Albin Michel, 1966). Naturally enough, two stimulating books by H.R. Kedward on resistance – *Resistance in Vichy France* (Oxford: Oxford University Press, 1978) and his *In Search of the Maquis. Rural Resistance in Southern France, 1942–1944* (Oxford: Oxford University Press, 1993) – say more about how resisters saw Pétain rather than how the marshal viewed internal dissidence.

Given its importance, the Holocaust in France is now the key feature of Vichy historiogragphy. The following offer a good introduction to Pétain's role in the persecution of Jews: A.

Cohen, *Persécutions et sauvetages. Juifs et français sous l'occupation et sous Vichy* (Paris: Cerf, 1993); Serge Klarsfeld, *Vichy-Auschwitz*, 2 vols (Paris: Fayard, 1982); Michael Marrus and Robert Paxton, *Vichy and the Jews* (New York: Basic Books, 1981); and Paul Webster, *Pétain's Crime* (London: Papermac, 1991). The wider aspects of Vichy repression are covered in Jean-Pierre Azéma, 'La Milice', in *Vingtième Siècle*, 28 (1990), pp. 83–105, Jean Delperrie de Bayac, *La Milice, 1918–45* (Paris: Fayard, 1969) and Dominique Rossignol, *Vichy et les francs-maçons* (Paris: Jean-Claude Lattès, 1981). Henri Michel, *Le procès de Riom* (Paris: Albin Michel, 1979) shows just how ready Pétain was to prosecute those supposedly responsible for the defeat of 1940.

The Pétain of 1944 is observed in Henry Rousso, *Un château en Allemagne, Sigmaringen* (Paris: Ramsay, 1980), whereas his trial is examined in Jean-Marc Varaut, *Le procès Pétain* (Paris: Perrin, 1995). Varaut also looks ahead to the attempts at rehabilitation. There are several eye-witness accounts to the trial, the majority being sympathetic to the defendant. See, in particular, Jules Roy, *Le Grand Naufrage* (Paris: Julliard, 1966), translated unimaginatively into English as *The Trial of Marshal Pétain* (London: Faber & Faber, 1968). Of further interest are the collection of documents published by Louis Noguères, *Le véritable procès du maréchal Pétain* (Paris: Fayard, 1955), although these were selected to portray Pétain in the most favourable light. Full transcripts of the trial are available, the most recent being *Procès du maréchal Pétain. Compte rendu officiel in extenso des audiences de la Haute Cour de Justice* (Paris: Editions Louis Pariente, 1976). A truncated version of the proceedings may be found in Frédéric Pottecher, *Le procès Pétain* (Paris: Jean-Claude Lattès, 1980). General studies on the *épuration* also include material on the trial. See Herbert R. Lottmann, *The People's Anger. Justice and Revenge in Post-Liberation France* (London: Hutchinson, 1985) and Peter Novick, *The Resistance versus Vichy. The Purge of Collaborators in Liberated France* (London: Chatto & Windus, 1968).

For the subsequent efforts to rehabilitate Pétain, see the sympathetic biographies cited above and the many works by Isorni. The way in which the French have remembered both Pétain and the Occupation is tackled by Henry Rousso, *Le syndrome de Vichy, 1944...* (Paris: Seuil, 1987). See, also, his *Vichy: un passé qui ne passe pas* (Paris: Fayard, 1994), written with Eric Conan. Such is the interest now taken in the *années noires* that the 'Vichy syndrome' has itself become a matter of dispute: see the essays in *French Historical Studies*, 19 (2) (1995). Whether Pétain himself would ever have understood the deep divisions prompted by his actions as *chef de l'état* remains doubtful. As a man obsessed with how he would be viewed by posterity, it was perhaps fortunate for his peace of mind that he died before the debates over his legacy had properly got under way.

MAPS

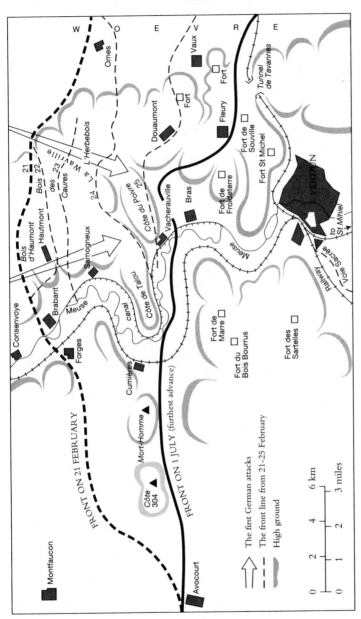

1. The Battle of Verdun
Source: Marc Ferro, *The Great War* (Routledge and Kegan Paul, 1973)

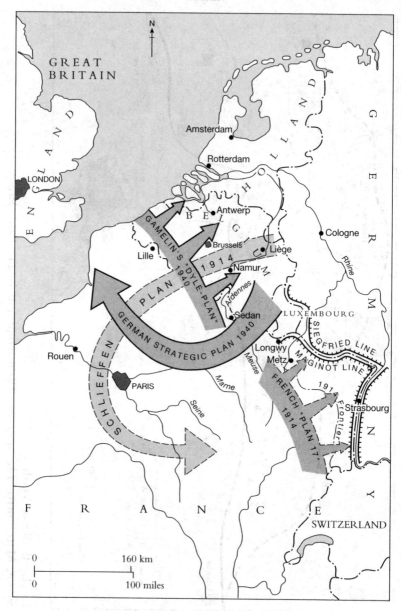

2. French and German strategies in 1914 and 1940
Source: Alistair Horne, *To Lose a Battle* (Penguin, 1973)

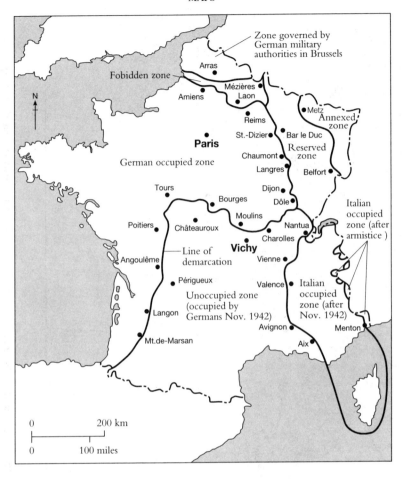

3. Zones of occupied France
Source: Robert Gildea, *France since 1945* (Oxford University Press, 1995)

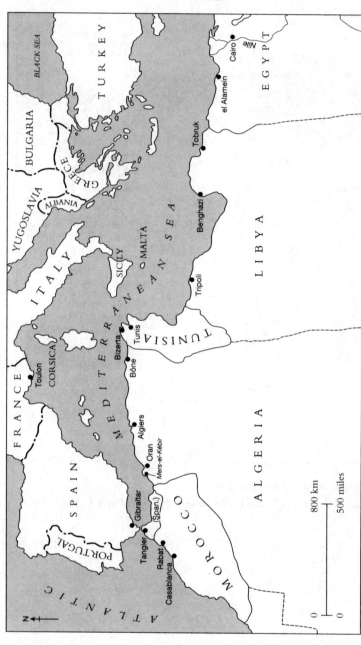

4. North Africa, 1942
Source: Geoffrey Warner, *Pierre Laval and the Eclipse of France* (Eyre and Spottiswood, 1968)

INDEX